CINEMAS OF
THE MIND

A CRITICAL HISTORY OF FILM THEORY

EDITED BY NICOLAS TREDELL

CRITICAL HISTORIES SERIES

CONSULTANT EDITOR: NICOLAS TREDELL

ICON BOOKS UK TOTEM BOOKS USA

CINEMAS OF THE MIND

A CRITICAL HISTORY OF FILM THEORY

Published in the UK in 2002
by Icon Books Ltd., Grange Road,
Duxford, Cambridge CB2 4QF
E-mail: info@iconbooks.co.uk
www.iconbooks.co.uk

Published in the USA in 2002
by Totem Books
Inquiries to: Icon Books Ltd.,
Grange Road, Duxford,
Cambridge CB2 4QF, UK

Sold in the UK, Europe, South Africa
and Asia by Faber and Faber Ltd.,
3 Queen Square, London WC1N 3AU
or their agents

Distributed to the trade in the USA by
National Book Network Inc.,
4720 Boston Way, Lanham,
Maryland 20706

Distributed in the UK, Europe,
South Africa and Asia by
Macmillan Distribution Ltd.,
Houndmills, Basingstoke RG21 6XS

Distributed in Canada by
Penguin Books Canada,
10 Alcorn Avenue, Suite 300,
Toronto, Ontario M4V 3B2

Published in Australia in 2002
by Allen & Unwin Pty. Ltd.,
PO Box 8500, 83 Alexander Street,
Crows Nest, NSW 2065

ISBN 1 84046 354 6

Front cover foreground image: *Psycho* (Kobal Collection)

CRITICAL HISTORIES series
Consultant editor: Nicolas Tredell
Originating editor: Duncan Heath

Typesetting: Wayzgoose

Printed and bound in the UK by
Biddles Ltd., Guildford and King's Lynn

Contents

NOTE

In the extracts included in this Critical History, two ellipses indicate the omission of a paragraph break and/or part of a paragraph.

Editorial insertions in extracts are enclosed in square brackets.

When a film, book title or director's name is given for the first time in an extract, the date of release, or first publication, or of birth and/or death, has been inserted where this is not already given in the original. Forenames have also sometimes been inserted in extracts for clarity. The wording of the extracts has sometimes been changed slightly to facilitate these insertions.

Birth/death dates for actors and actresses, authors and other figures are given only when such dates seem especially relevant to the discussion.

Where alternative titles for films are provided, they are prefaced by the abbreviation 'aka' = also known as.

Where references to books and journals are given in notes by the authors of extracts, these references have been standardised to accord with the style of the editor's notes. In some extracts, the spacing between sections and the format of section headings has been altered to accord with the overall format of this Critical History.

Introduction

One of the founding images of Western philosophy has also provided film theory with a key metaphor for the cinema. In Book 7 of *The Republic*, Plato projects a kind of moving picture of the relationship of human beings to reality. We are chained in a cave, watching the shadows that are cast against a wall by a fire. We may take the shadows for substance; but the reality of which they are phantoms lies beyond our vision. This image seems to anticipate and correspond to key aspects of the classic cinematic experience: sitting in the dark with others, with a light throwing shadows on a screen. While cinema viewing today, in the age of the video and DVD player, can and often does take other forms, the reference back to this kind of cinematic experience remains. How often do we see, on film or TV, an image of spectators in a cinema?[1] How often do people try to recreate, at their domestic hearth, an experience akin to that of being in a cinema – the lights turned down, the images unrolling on a home screen that is now expanding to cinematic proportions? The classic experience of cinema continues to fascinate; and this is not only, as certain psychoanalytic film theories argue, the dubious, perhaps perverse fascination of voyeurism. It is also a *philosophical* fascination that makes us ask: what is going on here? What is its relationship to our wider life in the world? Is it, perhaps, a microcosm of that life, the modern version of Plato's cave? It is these questions, and others like them, that have led film theorists to create cinemas of the mind: philosophical models of the nature and operations of film.

By now, at the start of the twenty-first century, a large number of models, of varying degrees of sophistication, have accumulated. This Critical History selects those that continue to seem vitally interesting, not only because of their importance in terms of the history of film theory, but also because of the insights and challenges they continue to offer. The introduction to a recent selection of contemporary film theory assures us that classical film theory – the theory of Rudolf Arnheim, Sergei Eisenstein, Béla Balázs, André Bazin, Siegfried Kracauer – was in the grip of the 'naturalist fallacy' that assumed a relatively unproblematic relationship between film and reality, and that such theory has now been superseded.[2] This is to assume that the development of film theory is like the development of scientific theory, in which an accumulation of anomalies finally forces a paradigm shift that renders an earlier theory obsolete – the idea that the sun goes around the earth, to take the most notable example. But the development of film theory is more like the development of philosophy: paradigm shifts – decisive changes in the protocols of argument and evidence and the stated topics of interest – may occur, but they do not render earlier theories obsolete, or of merely historical interest; Plato has not been superseded by Locke, nor even by Derrida, though a temporary and rather unphilosophical euphoria made some *fin-de-siècle* writers of the twentieth century think otherwise as far as Derrida was concerned.[3] No more has classical film theory been superseded by psychoanalytic or semiotic theory; nor has cognitive film theory simply replaced the psychoanalytic film theory to which it emerged as a challenger in the late 1980s and the 1990s. To say this is not to endorse an easy postmodernist eclecticism, in which all theories are equal (even if some, like postmodernism itself, are more equal than others). All film theories – and any other kinds of theory – must be scrutinised for their coherence and for their correspondence to relevant data. But in order to perform such scrutinies effectively, all theories must be given their due and not set within a quasi-scientific narrative in which some can be summarily dismissed as obsolete. This Critical History is designed to contribute to the important task of giving key film theories of the past hundred years their due, and of opening them up for scrutiny in the twenty-first century.

The History begins by looking at 'theory before theory' – at those seeds of theory, sometimes widely scattered, sometimes more concentrated, that emerged in the early days of cinema, especially in France, where critics and film-makers were trying to understand this strange, fascinating new medium of shadows and silence, existing in an ambiguous space between reality and illusion. From there, it moves into selections from what has now become the canon of classical film theory: Münsterberg, Arnheim, Balázs, Eisenstein; all of these are concerned, in their distinctive ways, to argue for film as a formative, artistic medium that shapes reality for aesthetic and sometimes also political ends. The History then turns, in the second chapter, to two further canonical figures – André Bazin and Siegfried Kracauer – who are more concerned, again in their distinctive ways, with film's relationship to reality. In the third and fourth chapters, attention shifts from specific theorists to selections from journals that, in their most creative periods, strongly influenced the directions of film theory – the French journal *Cahiers du Cinéma* in the 1950s and the British journal *Screen* in the 1970s. Chapter three, on *Cahiers*, looks at the development of *auteur* theory, in which the director is seen as a kind of author who stamps a recognisable style on his work, and includes contributions from a number of critics who would become known as film directors themselves – Jacques Rivette, Claude Chabrol, Eric Rohmer – and a further contribution, on the issue of the *auteur*, from Bazin. Chapter four, on *Screen*, features work by its driving intellectual forces in the 1970s, Stephen Heath and Colin MacCabe, and by Laura Mulvey, whose essay 'Visual Pleasure and Narrative Cinema' was to provoke an extraordinary volume of comment and dissent. Mulvey decisively put gender on the agenda of film theory: chapter five of this Critical History looks at key responses to Mulvey – from Mulvey herself, rethinking some aspects of her essay; from Steve Neale, revising Mulvey's ideas in terms of an analysis of the representation of masculinity in film; and from Jackie Stacey, opening up the issues of the positive images of women in Hollywood cinema. The chapter concludes with an extract from an essay that takes much more fundamental issue with Mulvey; its author is Noël Carroll, one of the leading exponents of the kind of film theory that, as already mentioned, was to mount a strong challenge to psychoanalytic film theory in the later 1980s and in the 1990s: cognitive film theory. The final chapter examines a powerful example of cognitive film theory in the 1990s by the Danish writer Torben Grodal, considers Oliver Bartlet's provocative account of the challenges that African cinemas pose to film critics and theorists, looks at Gregory Currie's substantial 'manifesto' for film theory, and concludes with an affirmation of the importance, in the age of digital culture, of seeking a comprehensive film theory based on an endeavour to understand the relationship of cinema to reality.

While this History aims to give the theories it considers their due, and while it does not assume that any strong theory can be easily superseded, it does not claim to be neutral. It takes the view that the key problem of film theory remains the problem illustrated by the image of Plato's cave: the relation of representation to reality. That problem takes us into all the other questions of cinema – art, *auteur*ism, genre, gender, representation, signification, cognition. To set the problem aside – as happens in some simplified versions of formalist, semiotic and post-structuralist theory★ – is to enervate film theory, to take away the philosophical

★See 'Glossary of Cinematic and Critical Terms' on pp. 259–69.

challenge that can produce intellectual results Formalist and semiotic theories have been immensely stimulating and remain of great value; but unless they engage with the problem of reality, they will remain limited. Such engagement is all the more important at the start of the twenty-first century, which is experiencing a massive shift from analogue to digital culture – from a culture based on the idea that images derive from, or point to, their likenesses in reality to a culture informed by the notion that images can be manipulated and even generated independently of any real-world referents. In this context, it might be tempting to abandon the idea of reality altogether; but such a dereliction would be philosophically and ethically inane.[4]

As this book is a History of theory, it necessarily engages with abstractions, but it often moves from the abstract to the concrete – that is, from general ideas about film to the analysis of specific films and genres. It is not quite the case that one of the tests of the validity of a theory is the quality of the interpretations of specific films that it can produce; a dubious theory may result in high-quality interpretations – much still depends on the critical perspicacity of the theorist. But while the quality of interpretations of specific films may not constitute a true test of theory, a theory is certainly enriched by any insightful interpretations that may be associated with it. This History provides a range of enriching interpretations.

It is hoped that the readers of this book will reconsider the films it discusses, and will also enjoy the activity of theorising itself, a pleasure equal, in its way, to that of watching a movie. Engaged in film theory, we sit in Plato's cave, watching the shadows: we experience and acknowledge their fascination, but we also try to understand what the shadows are, how they compel us, and what their relationship to reality is – a no less fascinating pursuit, which also brings revelations.

CHAPTER ONE

Forming an Art: Münsterberg, Arnheim, Balázs, Eisenstein

The first quarter of the twentieth century saw revolutionary changes in the traditional arts – the painting of Picasso, the music of Stravinsky, the poetry of T. S. Eliot, the fiction of James Joyce – and it also witnessed the emergence and rapid development of a possible new art that proved both fascinating and controversial. From its first flickers, film raised questions that would later become the topics of explicit theory. What was the nature of film? What was its relation to reality? Was it an art or a form of mechanical reproduction?

In 1907, the French film-maker Georges Méliès (1861–1938) provided a classification of 'four broad categories of cinematographic views' which could also be seen as successive stages in the development of cinema as a medium. First, there were 'natural views', cinematographic reproductions of 'scenes from ordinary life', 'animated documentary photographs'. But these were only the basis of the cinema as an art form. The second category comprised 'scientific views',[1] although Méliès acknowledged that, strictly speaking, these could be placed in the first category of 'natural views': anatomical studies of human and animal movement, surgical operations, craft and manufacturing processes, the use of a microscope to record the workings of very small creatures – a use of the cinema that was to seem significant to Béla Balázs (1884–1949), as this chapter will show later. The third category consisted of 'composed subjects or scenic genres' '[a]ll subjects, of any sort, in which action is readied as it is in the theater and performed by the actors in front of the camera'.[2] In relation to this category, Méliès makes an interesting point that looks towards the idea that cinema, as an art form, is characterised by its capacity to represent the products of the imagination rather than to reproduce reality. The cinematographic realm is boundless because it is suitable for, and seizes upon, all subjects that the imagination can provide

– and 'the subjects conceived by the imagination are infinitely varied and inexhaustible'. Film exhibitors call the fourth category 'transformation views', but Méliès – himself the creator of these kinds of views, as in his film of a train going to the moon – sees the term 'fantastic views' as more accurate, since such views do not always involve metamorphoses or transformations.[3] Méliès claims that, of his four categories, this last is the most extensive, because:

■ it encompasses everything from natural views (documentary [non-preparée] or contrived [truquée] although shot outdoors) to the most imposing theatrical performances. It includes all the illusions that can be produced by prestidigitation, optics, photographic tricks, set design and theatrical machinery, the play of light, dissolves ..., and the entire arsenal of fantastic, magical compositions that turn the most intrepid into madmen.[4] □

Méliès thus implicitly endorses an idea of cinema as primarily characterised by its ability to produce representations of fantasy – in contrast to a later thinker like Kracauer, who regards fantasy as somewhat suspect.

The critic, essayist, poet and novelist Rémy de Gourmont (1858–1915) is interested not so much in categorising different kinds of film as in the general effect of cinema on its audiences, and he broaches what was to become a concern of cognitive film theorists in the later 1980s and in the 1990s – the way in which film arouses emotion. In 'Épilogues: Cinématograph', first published in *Mercure de France* on 1 September 1907, he observes: 'Such is the power of the illusion that a series of photographs projected on the screen can stimulate our passions just as reality can.'[5] By describing film as 'a series of photographs', Gourmont also implicitly raises the issue of the relationship of film to still photography, which was to remain, right up to the post-war work of André Bazin and Siegfried Kracauer, a significant way of thinking about film.

But it was the relation of film to theatre rather than to photography that interested other early twentieth-century critics. Writing in *Le Temps* on 22 November 1908, the drama critic Adolphe Brisson (1860–1925) suggests that at least some stage dramatists will be 'curious to experiment with a new form of theater, and, if possible, to codify its aesthetic':[6]

■ What is a cinematographic play? What should it become? What are its essential features as well as the rules to which it must adapt? What are its conditions, its limits? How can these be made clear? Let's see.[7] □

Brisson's own 'codification' is premised, of course, on silent cinema:

- First, whatever speech alone is able to express – thought, abstract ideas, intense passion – is excluded. We are in the world of the concrete. The actors must perform and they must perform clearly; their movements must be unified, coherent, according to the laws of cause and effect. In some way, their movements must be refined, freed of all superfluity, and reduced to the essential.

  Now, this work of refinement is a work of art. Ever since Nature was simplified by human effort, there has been style. The actor who poses for the cinema and tries to do exactly what is expected of him *stylizes* the actions of the character he must embody by means of a sober balance of gestures and proper facial expressions.

  In the theater, the details of dialogue and the varieties of intonation, to a degree, take the place of an exactness of gesture. Here, gesture is unadorned and obliged to be true. It cannot be otherwise without producing an intolerable sense of unease …

  But can this form of art, from which the word has been excluded, be confused with pantomime? … [Ellipsis in original] Not at all. Pantomime has a language or grammar of immutable signs whose sense never varies. One of them means 'avarice', another 'pride', another 'c[o]quettishness', and so on. The cinema abstains from using this alphabet. Its province is life itself.

  To observe, select, fix, and stylize living figures and momentary phenomena – that is the task it has set for itself. It aspires not only to reproduce current affairs but to animate the past, to reconstruct the great events of History, through the performance of the actor and the evocation of atmosphere and milieu.[8] □

It is interesting to observe two potentially contradictory directions in Brisson's remarks that will find echoes in the later development of film theory. On the one hand, there is the sense that the province of cinema is 'life itself' and that it can 'reproduce current affairs' – it is a reflection of reality. On the other hand, there is the idea that cinema observes, selects, fixes and stylises – it shapes and alters reality.

Ricciotto Canudo (1877–1923), an Italian writer living in Paris in the early twentieth century, provided a more extensive exploration of the aesthetics of cinema than those of Méliès, Gourmont or Brisson. Canudo pursued the issue of the relationship between film and theatre further than Brisson, and into different areas. 'The Birth of a Sixth Art', first published in *Les Entretiens Idéalistes* on 25 October 1911, sees cinema as an emerging art that will take its place alongside the five existing arts that Canudo identifies: music, poetry, painting, sculpture and architecture.[9] (His later writings on film adopt the more common idea of cinema as the 'seventh art', in addition to the six existing arts of architecture, music, poetry, painting, sculpture and dance.[10]) In 'The Birth of a Sixth Art', Canudo finds in cinema 'a superb conciliation of Rhythms of Space (the Plastic Arts) and the Rhythms of Time (Music and Poetry)'. Until now, the theatre 'best realized such a conciliation, but in an ephemeral manner because the plastic characteristics of the theater are identified with those of the actors, and consequently are always different'. A more precise term for the new art would be '*a Painting and a Sculpture developing in Time*, as in music and poetry, which realize themselves by transforming air into rhythm for the duration of their execution'.[11] Canudo identifies two aspects of the significant elements of which film is composed:

■ [These are] the *symbolic* and the *real*, both absolutely modern; that is to say only possible in our era, composed of certain essential elements of modern spirit and energy.

The *symbolic aspect* is that of velocity. Velocity possesses the potential for a great series of combinations, of interlocking activities, combining to create a spectacle that is a series of visions and images tied together in a vibrant agglomeration, similar to a living organism. This spectacle is produced exactly by the excess of movement to be found in film, those mysterious reels impressed by life itself. The reels of the engraved celluloid unroll in front of and within the beam of light so rapidly that the presentation lasts for the shortest possible time. No theater could offer half the changes of set and location provided by the cinematograph with such vertiginous rapidity, even if equipped with the most extraordinarily modern machinery.

Yet more than the motion of images and the speed of representation, what is truly symbolic in relation to velocity are the actions of the characters. We see the most tumultuous, the most inverisimilitudinous [unrealistic] scenes unfolding with a speed that appears impossible in real life ... The cinematograph, moreover, will present to [the spectator] the farthest countries, the most unknown people, the least known of human customs, moving, shaking, throbbing before the spectator transported by the extreme rapidity of the representation. Here is the second symbol of modern life constituted by the cinematograph ... It is the symbolic destruction of distances by the immediate connaissance [knowledge] of the most diverse countries, similar to the real destruction of distances performed for a hundred years now by monsters of steel.[12] □

Here Canudo insightfully argues that film is a symbol of modernity in its speed and its capacity to abolish distance by bringing representations of faraway places before us. Indeed, his formulation of the latter anticipates the 'immediate [knowledge] of the most diverse countries' provided today by TV and the Internet.

Along with the way in which cinema symbolises velocity, there is the real aspect of cinema, 'made up of elements which arouse the interest and wonder of the audience'.

■ It is increasingly evident that present day humanity actively seeks its own show, the most meaningful representation of its self ... Suddenly the cinematograph has become popular ... and has imposed itself in a peculiar way as a new kind of theater, a scientific theater built with precise calculations, a mechanical mode of expression. Restless humanity has welcomed it with joy. It is precisely this theater of plastic Art in motion which seems to have brought us the rich promise of the *Festival* which has been longed for unconsciously, the ultimate evolution of the ancient *Festival* taking place in the temples, the theaters, the fairgrounds of each generation.[13] The thesis of a plastic Art in motion has recreated the *Festival*. It has created it scientifically rather than *aesthetically*, and for this reason it is succeeding in this age, although fatally and irresistibly moving towards the attainment of Aesthetics ...[14] □

There is a large aesthetic problem, however:

■ Art has always been essentially a stylization of life into stillness; the better an artist has been able to express the greater number of 'typical' conditions, that is, the synthetic and immutable states of souls and forms, the greater the recognition he has attained. The cinematograph, on the contrary, achieves the greatest mobility in the representation of life. The thought that it might open the unsuspected horizon of a new art different from all pre-existing manifestations cannot fail to appeal to an emancipated mind, free from all traditions and constraints. The ancient painters and engravers of prehistoric caves who reproduced on reindeer bones the contracted movements of a galloping horse, ... the artists who sculpted cavalcades on the Parthenon friezes, also developed the device of stylizing certain aspects of life in clear, incisive movements. But the cinematograph does not merely reproduce one aspect; it represents the whole of life in action, and in such action that, even when the succession of its characteristic events unravel[s] slowly, it is developed with as much speed as possible.

In this way cinematography heightens the basic psychic condition of western life which manifests itself in action ... [It is] *Painting in motion* ... the new *dance of manifestations*.[15] ☐

But is it an art?

■ It is not yet an art, because it lacks the freedom of choice peculiar to plastic *interpretation*, conditioned as it is to being the *copy* of a subject, the condition that prevents photography from becoming an art. In executing the design of a tree on a canvas, the painter expresses without any doubt, unconsciously and in a particular and clear configuration, his global interpretation of the vegetative soul, that is of all the conceptual elements deposited deep in his creative spirit by an examination of all the trees he has seen in his life ... With that particular form he synthesizes corresponding souls and his art, I repeat, will gain in intensity in proportion to the artist's skill in *immobilizing* the essence of things and their universal meanings in a particular and clear configuration. Whoever contented himself with copying the outlines, with imitating the colors of a subject, would be a poor painter; the great artist extends a fragment of his cosmic soul in the representation of a plastic form.

Arts are the greater the less they *imitate* and the more they *evoke* by means of a synthesis. A photographer, on the other hand, does not have the faculty of choice and elaboration fundamental to Aesthetics; he can only put together the forms he wishes to reproduce, which he really is not reproducing, limiting himself to cutting out images with the aid of the luminous mechanism of a lens and a chemical composition. The cinematograph, therefore, cannot today be an art. But for several reasons, the cinematographic theater is the first abode of the new art – an art which we can just barely conceive. Can this abode become a 'temple' for aesthetics?

A desire for an aesthetic organization drives entrepreneurs

towards certain kinds of research. In an age lacking in imagination, such as ours, when an excess of documentation is everywhere, weakening artistic creativity, and patience games are triumphing over expressions of creative talent, the cinematograph offers the paroxysm of the spectacle: objective life represented in a wholly exterior manner, on the one hand with rapid miming, on the other with documentaries. The great fables of the past are retold, mimed by ad hoc actors chosen from the most important stars. What is shown above all is the appearance rather than the essence of contemporary life, from sardine fishing in the Mediterranean to the marvel of flying steel and the indomitable human courage of the races at Dieppe or the aviation week at Rheims.

But the entertainment makers are already experimenting with other things. It is their aim that this new mimetic representation of 'total life' take ever deeper root ... ... [T]he cinematographic theater *is the first new theater*, the first authentic and fundamental theater of our time. When it becomes truly aesthetic, complemented with a worthy musical score played by a good orchestra, even if only representing life, real life, momentarily fixed by the photographic lens, we shall be able to feel then our first *sacred* emotion, we shall have a glimpse of the spirits, moving towards a vision of the temple, where Theater and Museum will once more be restored for a new religious communion of the spectacle and Aesthetics ... ...

It is desire for a new *Festival*, for a new joyous *unanimity*, realized at a show, in a place where together, all men can forget in greater or lesser measure, their isolated individuality. This forgetting, soul of any religion and spirit of any aesthetic, will one day be superbly triumphant. And the Theater, which still holds the vague promise of something never dreamt of in previous ages: *the creation of a sixth art, the plastic Art in motion*, having already achieved the rudimentary form of the modern pantomime.[16] □

Canudo, then, has the highest hopes for the development of film as an art. As a plastic art in motion, it will effect a revival of theatre and bring about a new sense of human community. If his vision seems utopian today, it stands as a kind of tribute to the imaginative possibilities opened up by the cinema; and the utopian aspiration, the idea that cinema has a progressive or redemptive social function, will recur, in different forms, in later theorists, notably Eisenstein and Kracauer. But the approach represented by Canudo, and by Brisson before him – of seeing film as, effectively, a development of theatre – would be strongly opposed by another line of argument that aimed to distinguish between film and theatre. To pursue this, it is helpful to move from France to the USA, and to the work of Hugo Münsterberg (1863–1916), a German psychologist who had emigrated to America in 1897 to take up a post at Harvard and who was to publish, in 1916, the first sustained work of film theory: *The Film: A Psychological Study: The Silent Photoplay in 1916.*

In this book, Münsterberg aims to establish the distinctiveness of film (or what he calls 'the photoplay') as a separate art form, and in particular to dissociate it from the stage play – an aim that would be taken up by Béla Balázs, in his account of the differences between film and 'photographed theatre' that appears later in this chapter. As Münsterberg puts it – the italics are his own:

■ *The art of the photoplay has developed so many new features of its own, features which have not even any similarity to the technique of the stage, that the question arises: is it not really a new art which long since left behind the mere film reproduction of the theater and which ought to be acknowledged in its own esthetic independence?*[17] □

Münsterberg attacks the notion that film is merely an inferior reproduction of the elements of a stage play; whereas a photograph of a painting may be seen as an inferior substitute for that painting, and a gramophone record may be seen as an inferior substitute for the live performance that it partly preserves, a film exists in its own right and has the potential, at least, to be art of a distinctive kind:

■ … [T]he chromo[lithograph] print and the graphophone [*sic.* An early instrument for recording and reproducing sound] and the plaster cast are indeed nothing but inexpensive substitutes for art with many essential artistic elements left out, and therefore ultimately unsatisfactory to a truly artistic taste … [T]he relation of the photoplay to the theater is a completely different one … [Moving pictures] *are not and ought never to be imitations of the theater. They can never give the esthetic values of the theater; but no more can the theater give the esthetic values of the photoplay.* With the rise of the moving pictures has come an entirely new independent art which must develop its own life conditions … *The drama and the photoplay are two coordinated arts, each perfectly valuable in itself.*[18] □

In his study, Münsterberg first seeks to establish the distinctiveness of film in terms of its relation to human psychology. He contends that the techniques that are possible in film, but impossible (or at least much more difficult) on the stage, match key subjective operations of the human mind: memory, imagination, attention, emotion, and unifying perception. The memory can produce images of the past; film can produce flashbacks. The imagination can produce objects or situations or processes that could not exist in the actual world, or that might exist in the future; film can do the same. The attention focuses on one object to the exclusion or marginalisation of other objects; the film does this through the close-up. Emotion can suffuse our subjective perceptions; film can represent this suffusion by means of camera movements that, for example, plunge a landscape into turmoil. Perception can unite the apparently disparate; film can also bring them together. Human consciousness can move between a range of interests and concerns while retaining a sense of unity; film can move between different places, times and plots while weaving them together. In each case, film remoulds the objective world so that it accords with the subjective movements of the mind.

■ One general principle seem[s] to control the whole mental mechanism of the spectator, or rather the relation between the mental mechanism and the pictures on the screen … [I]n every case the objective world of outer events had been shaped and molded until it became adjusted to the subjective movements of the mind. The mind develops memory ideas and imaginative ideas; in the moving pictures they become reality. The mind concentrates itself on a special detail in its act of attention; and in the close-up of the moving pictures this inner state is objectified. The mind is filled with emotions; and by means of the camera the whole scenery echoes them. Even in the most objective factor of the mind, the perception, we find this peculiar oscillation. We perceive the movement; and yet we perceive it as something which has not its independent character as an outer world process, because our mind has built it up from single pictures rapidly following one another. We perceive things in their plastic depth; and yet again the depth is not that of the outer world. We are aware of its unreality and of the pictorial flatness of the impressions.[19] □

Münsterberg draws on a particular idea of what art is. In his definition, art is not imitation; it takes elements from life but recombines and transforms them in a separate sphere:

■ Wherever we examine without prejudice the mental effects of true works of art in literature or music, in painting or sculpture, in decorative arts or architecture, we find that the central esthetic value is directly opposed to the spirit of imitation. A work of art may and must start from something which awakens in us the interests of reality and which contains traits of reality, and to that extent it cannot avoid some imitation. But *it becomes art just in so far as it overcomes reality, stops imitating and leaves the imitated reality behind it.* It is artistic just in so far as it does not imitate reality but changes the world, selects from it special features for new purposes, remodels the world and is through this truly creative. To imitate the world is a mechanical process; to transform the world so that it becomes a thing of beauty is the purpose of art. The highest art may be furthest removed from reality.[20] □

For Münsterberg, art arouses real interests and emotions but also, within a given art-work, satisfies them fully, producing an ultimate effect of unity and harmony.

■ *The work of art shows us the things and events perfectly complete in themselves, freed from all connections which lead beyond their own limits, that is, in perfect isolation.*[21] □

In Münsterberg's view, sound, in the sense of spoken dialogue or sound effects, would compromise the 'perfect isolation' of the film as a distinctive art form. Only music is acceptable because it 'does not tell a part of the plot and does not replace the picture as words would do, but simply reënforces the emotional setting'.[22] Münsterberg is aware of attempts, so far unsuccessful, to produce talking pictures by synchronising 'the kinematoscope with the phonograph', but contends that 'the real difficulty' is not 'technical' but 'esthetic and internal'. Audible dialogue would perturb the 'visual purity'[23] of the film: 'the conservation of the spoken word [in the film] is as disturbing as color would be on the clothing of a marble statue'[24] (an ironic comparison insofar as Greek statues, the archetypes of the colourless statue in Western culture, were originally brightly coloured). Similarly, sound effects – hoofbeats, rain, hail and thunder, guns firing, locomotives whistling, ships' bells clanging, dogs barking, Charlie Chaplin tumbling downstairs – are 'intrusions from another sphere' that 'have no right to existence in a work of art which is composed of pictures'.[25] Münsterberg predicts that the 'photoplay of the day after tomorrow will surely be freed from all elements which are not really pictures'.[26] It is the kind of prediction that shows just how wrong a prophet can be; and Münsterberg's premise of the purity and persistence of silent film clearly limits his theory. But the ghost of the aesthetic superiority of the silent film, the fascination of that moment of silence before the fall into sound, has continued to haunt cinema.

Given Münsterberg's uneasiness at the idea of coloured marble statues in the quotation above, it is perhaps not surprising that he is also uneasy about colour film. He believes that the technological capacity to produce adequate colour film is more imminent than the capacity to produce talking pictures – 'the perfect solution of the technical problem may be expected in the near future'[27] – but he feels that colour impairs the unreality and separateness of the film, and thus detracts from the realisation of 'that inner freedom, that victory of the mind over nature, which remains the ideal of the photoplay'.[28]

Münsterberg creates a kind of template for the film theories that will follow him in the 1920s and 30s. Characteristically, such theories will aim to identify the features of film that make it a distinctive medium and permit it to claim the status of art; they will be interested in the relationship between the formal features of film and its psychological effects; and they will be suspicious of sound and colour on the grounds that they will compromise the artistic integrity of silent black-and-white film. In *Film* (1933), the German film theorist Rudolf Arnheim (born 1904) is, like Münsterberg, concerned to establish that the film is, at least potentially, art rather than nature. His stated aim in the book is 'to help ... those who still prefer the printed word to the moving picture, to understand film art'. He points to the newness of film as an art, even if it is now a little older than it was for Münsterberg – 'twenty-five' rather than fifteen years old – and stresses its 'marvellous potentialities ... as an artistic medium'.[29] While Münsterberg, and Balázs after him, sets out primarily to distinguish film from theatre, Arnheim aims to distinguish it from mechanical reproduction in general. His account of the genesis of film sees it as developing out of what was initially conceived merely as a form of mechanical reproduction:

■ [T]he art of film was derived in the first instance from a desire to record mechanically real events. The camera was therefore primarily considered purely as a recording machine in front of which were grouped suitably the various objects to be recorded, that is, to be photographed. It was not until film began to become an art that the

intcrest was moved from the material to the formal. What had hitherto been merely the urge to record certain actual events, now became
the aim to represent objects by special means exclusive to film. These
means obtrude themselves, show themselves to be appropriate, to do
more than simply reproduce the required object; they make it more
telling, emphasise it, show up special features, make it particularly
vivid, particularly decorative, etc., etc. The attention is no longer
riveted to the actual object, but is directed gradually to the picture
which is to be made of it and to the important peculiarities of form
which the picture may have even though they are not contained in the
object itself. Art only begins where mechanical reproduction leaves
off, where the conditions of reproduction serve in some way to mould
the object. And the spectator shows himself to be lacking in proper
aesthetic appreciation when he is satisfied to see the picture as purely
objective – to be content with recognizing that this is the picture of
an engine, that of a couple of lovers, and this again a waiter in a tem-
per. He must now be prepared to turn his attention to the form and
to be able to judge how the engine, the lovers, the waiter, are
depicted.[30] □

How far this account of film's origin and development is historically
accurate is open to question; it may be that 'artistic' or at least formal
considerations entered into the 'desire to record mechanically real
events' from the beginning. But this questionable history serves to reinforce a key theoretical distinction for Arnheim between film as the
mechanical reproduction of reality and film as art; and this distinction
could apply even if his historical sketch were untrue.

For Arnheim, film as art involves an understanding and appreciation
of formal qualities that are specific to film. In particular, he locates these
formal qualities in a peculiar property of film's effect upon the viewer;
and, like Münsterberg, Arnheim draws upon the experimental psychology of the time for his analysis: 'The effect of film is neither that of an
absolutely two-dimensional picture nor absolutely three-dimensional,
but something between the two. Film pictures are at once plane and
solid.'[31] Such dimensional ambiguity has the further effect that 'we can
feel objects and events on the screen as simultaneously living and imaginary, as real objects and as simple light-effects on the plane of projection'.[32] This clearly differs from the view that film encourages passive
reception of an illusory world – rather, in Arnheim's terms, the spatial
and ontological ambiguity of film can make us feel its artificiality. The

capacity of film to appear 'simultaneously plane and solid'[33] increases its aesthetic possibilities:

■ Every good film shot is satisfying in a purely formal sense as a linear composition. The lines are harmoniously disposed with reference to each other as well as to the margins of the screen. The distribution of light and shade in the shot is dexterous either by being evenly balanced or – according to the mood of the scene – by laying purely graphical stresses, such as massing all the shadows in one corner of the shot. It is only because the spatial effect is so slight that the spectator's attention is drawn to the two-dimensional pattern of lines and shadow masses. These, however, are actually the components of three-dimensional bodies and only become elements in the shot through being projected on to a plane surface … The same lack of depth – with the same advantage to dramatic effect – is found in painting. A picture whose space illusion is very strong is correspondingly difficult to evaluate for its formal qualities. This deficiency in naturalness is not a cause to regret from an aesthetic standpoint; indeed, on the contrary, it makes it possible to achieve artistic results. It is one of the most important formal qualities of film that every object that is reproduced appears simultaneously in two entirely different sets of conditions with absolutely different functions. And still the object always remains the same object.[34] □

As Arnheim's comparison with painting in the above extract shows, his aesthetic of film relates to a more general aesthetic position – that the formal qualities of an art become apparent when it distances itself to some extent from the production of an illusion of reality. In film, he implies, this distance is produced by the way in which the moving images hover between two and three dimensions. He senses, however, a technological threat to this way of producing distance – the attempt to develop stereoscopic film that provides a distinct three-dimensional experience and does away with the spatial ambiguity that is so crucial to Arnheim's aesthetic. He discusses this in a passage that adds a further element to his aesthetic of film – that its images, as well as being formally pleasing in their composition, should also have symbolic connotations:

■ [H]ow important to the artist is the lack of depth in a shot and how it eliminates the normal mental adjustment to perspectival alteration in size – thereby giving the power to show objects large or small, increasing and decreasing, according to the mood of the scene. Moreover, it permits of objects that lie *behind* one another appearing as though they were *upon* one another. Thus the spectator is obliged to seek some internal (symbolic) connection between the various objects that are coupled in this manner – in other words, to regard the pictorial incisions and superimpositions as intentional and fraught with meaning. Attention will also have to be drawn to the decorativeness of the flat effect within the frame of the shot.

If all this has been realised, the efforts of technicians to achieve plastic film, that is, film with a good stereoscopic effect, will be watched with mixed feelings. In a film which gives the complete illusion of space the perspectival alterations in size have scarcely more effect than they have in real life. Their efficacy as an artistic device will be practically negligible. The plane effect of course also becomes almost as slight, and the manner in which one object appears behind another in space will be so obvious that the optical as well as any inherent symbolic connections will hardly make themselves felt at all. Technicians are not artists. They do not therefore direct their efforts towards providing the artist with a more effective medium, but towards increasing the naturalness of film pictures. It vexes the technician that film is so lacking in stereoscopic quality. His ideal is exactly to imitate real life. It provokes him that film should be lacking in colours and sounds; and so he devotes his attention to colour photography and [sound] film. The general inartistic public feels much the same. An audience demands the greatest possible likeness to nature in its cinema and it therefore prefers plastic film to flat, coloured to black-and-white, talkie to silent. Every step which brings film closer to nature creates a sensation. Each new sensation means full houses. Hence the avid interest of the film industry in new discoveries.[35] □

This passage is an example of the challenge that the idea and actuality of stereoscopic film provokes to Arnheim's aesthetic.[36] It is significant that he sees the desire for stereoscopic film as driven by three forces that are all regarded as enemies to film as art: 'the technician', the 'general inartistic public' and 'the film industry'. In Arnheim's study, the sense that film as art is under threat from these forces is in tension with his notion that film, at least of the non-stereoscopic kind, almost automatically achieves the distance from illusion that is, for him, crucial to art. This latter notion troubles his distinction between mere mechanical reproduction and art, between the technician and the artist, since it seems that the formal qualities that characterise film as an art rather than as a means of mechanical reproduction are inherent in its particular means of mechanical reproduction. In an especially eloquent passage, Arnheim acknowledges this, claiming that 'unlimited possibilities are contained in the essential elements of photography itself', that the techniques of mechanical reproduction allow a freedom that makes art possible:[37]

■ The film artist chooses a particular scene that he wishes to photograph; within this scene he can leave out objects, cover them up, make them prominent, without in any way taking liberties with nature. He can increase or decrease the size of details, can make small objects larger than big ones, and *vice versa*.

He can put beside, behind, among one another, things that are absolutely separate in space and time. He can pick out what is important, however small and inconspicuous it may be, and thus let the part represent the whole. He can lay down what is upright, and set upright what is recumbent, can move what is quiescent, and arrest what is moving. He can eliminate at will sensations and emotions, and thereby bring others into higher relief, ingeniously making them take the place of those that are missing. He can let the dumb speak and thereby interpret the sphere of sound.

He shows the world not only as it appears objectively but also subjectively. He creates new realities, in which things are duplicated, turns their movements and actions backwards, distorts them, retards or accelerates them. He calls into existence magical kingdoms where the force of gravity disappears, and mysterious powers move inanimate objects and make whole things that are broken. He brings into being mystical bridges between events and objects that have never had any connection in reality. He intervenes in the structure of nature to make quivering, disintegrate ghosts of concrete bodies and spaces. He arrests the progress of the world and of things, and changes them to stone. He breathes life into stone and bids it move. Of chaotic and illimitable space he creates pictures beautiful in form and of profound significance, as subjective and rich in technical possibilities as painting.[38] □

The enormous possibilities of cinema that Arnheim so richly evokes in this passage and that resound throughout his book are, however, limited, in his view, by the nature of film as a mass art, driven by the need to make money from an ill-educated audience. His vision of the potential of cinema and his concern about its mass influence were shared by a third major theorist who emerged in the early days of film: Béla Balázs.

Balázs was a man of many parts: as well as being, like Münsterberg and Arnheim, a pioneering film theorist, he was also the librettist of the composer Béla Bartók and an author of children's books. A Hungarian, he wrote, in German, two early books on film: *Der Sichtbare Mensch* (*The Visible Man*, 1924) and *Der Geist des Films* (*The Spirit of Film*, 1930). The book that made his ideas available to an Anglophone audience, however, did not appear until 1952: *Theory of the Film* (*Character and Growth of a New Art*). This is a hybrid book; while certain parts of it were clearly written after the Second World War, much of it refers to an earlier era – the era, in fact, in which Münsterberg, Arnheim and Eisenstein were developing their theories – and Balázs incorporates into the book substantial passages from his two earlier works.[39] J. Dudley Andrew's claim that *Theory of the Film* 'organizes both [Balázs's] early and later essays into a systematic whole'[40] is hardly accurate:[41] but the book can nonetheless be seen as a partly consistent summary of Balázs's theoretical work,[42] and it remains of considerable interest.

In *Theory of the Film*, Balázs begins by advocating the theory of film as 'the most important field for present-day art theory', given that cinema is the 'potentially greatest instrument of mass influence ever devised in the whole course of human cultural history'.[43] He goes on:

■ No one would deny to-day that the art of the motion picture is *the* popular art of our century – unfortunately not in the sense that it is the product of the popular spirit but the other way round, in the sense that the mentality of the people, and particularly of the urban population, is to a great extent the product of this art, an art that is at the same time a vast industry. Thus the question of educating the public to a better, more critical appreciation of the films is a question of the mental health of the nations.[44] □

Balázs's advocacy of film theory thus rests on a familiar concern of critics at this time (one that has already been seen in Arnheim) – that film must be understood because its popularity, its capacity to reach a 'mass' audience, makes it potentially dangerous. He perceives signs, in the late 1940s, that film is starting to be studied more seriously, but still finds it absent from the curricula of schools and universities, a situation that he sees as lamentable in view of the number of people who watch films as contrasted with the minorities who like literary works or the traditional fine arts. 'Millions hear about the aesthetics of literature and painting who will never make use of such knowledge because they read no books and look at no pictures.' Instead, they should be taught 'to appreciate film art'.[45] But it is not only a question of educating the masses; Balázs also proposes a redefinition of the cultured 'man', in which a knowledge and understanding of film is an essential requirement:

■ [W]hat is needed is not specialized knowledge [of film]: it is a general level of culture. No one who had not the faintest conception of literature or music would be considered well-educated. A man who had never heard of Beethoven or Michelangelo would be out of place among people of culture. But if he has not the faintest idea of the rudiments of film art and had never heard of [the Danish film star] Asta Nielsen (1882–1972) or [the American director] David Wark Griffith (1875–1948), he might still pass for a well-educated, cultured person, even on the highest level. The most important art of our time is that about which one need know nothing whatever. And yet it is an urgent need that we should cultivate enough discrimination to influence the art which shapes the popular taste in the highest degree.[46] □

In Balázs's view, then, a knowledge and understanding of film is vital to improving its aesthetic quality. The collective and commercial nature of film-making means that it is impossible for a lone cinematic genius working in isolation to advance his or her art, as a writer, painter or composer might do. To improve the quality of films, it is necessary to form a public taste that will demand higher quality cinema from the film industry:

■ The film as a product of a large-scale industry costs too much and is too complicated a collective creative process for any individual genius to create a masterpiece in defiance of the tastes or prejudices of his day. And this applies not only to the capitalist film industry which envisages immediate cash returns. Even a socialized film production cannot make films for the public of some coming century. A certain degree of success – in other words, appreciation – is an inexorable material postulate for the birth of any film. The situation is paradox[ical]: in the sphere of film art the public must be available before the film, the making of which is rendered possible only by an appreciation ensured in advance, on which the producers of the film can count. What is required is not a passive appreciation which enjoys what is already available, but an inspiring, encouraging, *creative* appreciation; we need theoretical understanding and a sort of aesthetics which does not draw conclusion[s] from already existing works of art but demands and expects such works of art on the basis of theoretical forecasts.[47] □

Film theory will thus be 'an initiating theory pointing into the future and drawing charts of unknown oceans for some future Columbus. It will be an inspiring theory that will fire the imagination of future seekers for new worlds and creators of new arts.' At the start of the twenty-first century, the notion of 'theory as a new Columbus'[48] has dubious connotations of imperial appropriation and oppression, but in a mid-twentieth-century context, the idea that theory had a key role to play in fostering creativity was a challenging one – especially, as Herbert Marshall's introduction to Balázs's book points out, in an English culture suspicious or contemptuous of theory.[49] Balázs goes on to contend that the 'fact that the art of the film is not yet fully developed offers an unprecedented opportunity for aestheticists to study the laws governing the evolution of an art in the making'.[50]

Balázs's formulation of his theory of film proceeds partly by way of a history of the medium. Film emerged, he suggests, 'at the time when other intellectual products were also beginning to be produced on a large industrial scale', when 'the giant publishing houses, the great theatrical concerns and concert agencies, the newspaper trusts and wholesale picture-dealing were born. The wholesale industrialization of art and literature did not start with the film, but the film arrived when this trend was just gathering momentum.'[51] Film was a means of mechanical reproduction that was 'immediately used for the large-scale exploitation of dramatic art':

- The cinematographic camera made it possible to substitute a machine-made – one might say 'industrial' – production for the actual flesh-and-blood 'hand-made' performance of the stage. It was turned into a commodity capable of being reproduced in unlimited quantities, and distributed at low cost.[52] □

In this account, the first widespread use of film was to provide 'photographic theatre' – though it might also, as Balázs observes, be used to provide images of some actual, non-fictional event. In the early years, 'cinematography was merely a fairground sideshow, a moving picture of some sensational event or a means to the mass reproduction of stage performances. It was not an autonomous art ruled by its own laws.'[53] To become such an autonomous art, it had to differentiate itself from 'photographed theatre' and develop 'a totally different form-language'.[54] In an important discussion, Balázs defines the 'form-language' of film by a comparison with what he regards as the formal principles of theatre:

■ The basic formal principle of the theatre is that the spectator sees the enacted scene as a whole in space, always seeing the whole of the space. Sometimes the stage presents only one corner of a larger hall, but that corner is always totally visible all through the scene in question, and everything that happens in it is seen within one and the same frame.

The second basic formal principle of the theatre is that the spectator always sees the stage from a fixed unchanging distance.[55] True, the photographed theatre already began to photograph different scenes from different distances, but within one and the same scene the distance was never changed.

The third basic formal principle of the theatre is that the spectator's angle of vision does not change. The photographed theatre did change the perspective sometimes from scene to scene, but within one and the same scene the perspective never changed, any more than the distance.

These three basic formal principles of the stage are of course interconnected, they form the groundwork of dramatic style and means of expression. In this connection it makes no difference whether we see the scenes on the living stage or in photographic reproduction; nor does it matter whether the scenes presented are such as could not be shown on the stage at all, but only in the open air and by means of photographic technique.

It was these three basic principles of theatrical art that were discarded by the art of the film – it begins where the three principles no longer apply and are supplanted by new methods. These are:

1. Varying distance between spectator and scene within one and the same scene; hence varying dimensions of scenes that can be accommodated within the frame and composition of a picture.

2. Division of the integral picture of the scene into sections, or 'shots'.

3. Changing the angle, perspective and focus of 'shots' within one and the same scene.

4. Montage, that is the assembly of 'shots' in a certain order in which not only whole scene follows whole scene (however short) but pictures of smallest details are given, so that the whole scene is composed of a mosaic of frames aligned as it were in chronological sequence.[56] □

It is these four formal principles that characterise film as a distinctive new art form. Balázs's definition of film is not only formalist, however; it also incorporates a theory of changes that come about in the spectator, 'the subjective faculties which, created through a dialectical interaction, enable us to see and appreciate the newly-emerging beautiful things'. Indeed, Balázs affirms that the purpose of his book is 'to investigate and outline that sphere of the development of human sensibility which developed in mutual interaction with the evolution of the art of the film'.[57] There are two key aspects of this development: 'we have learnt ... to integrate single disjointed pictures into a coherent scene, without even becoming conscious of the complicated psychological process involved'; and we have also acquired the ability to interpret 'picture metaphors and picture symbols'[58] that convey situations and emotions indirectly. This is one example that he gives of the latter faculty:

■ A man is sitting in a dark room in gloomy meditation. The spectator knows from the previous scene that a woman is in the next room. We see a close-up of the man's face. Suddenly a light falls on it from one side. The man raises his head and looks towards the light with an expression of hopeful expectation. Then the light fades from his face and with it the expression of hope. He lowers his head in disappointment. Complete darkness falls slowly. It is the last shot of a tragic scene. No more is needed. What happened here? Every picture-goer knows and understands this language now. What happened was that the door of the next room opened for a moment, the woman came to the threshold of the lighted room, hesitated, but turned back and closed the door for ever. Even this 'for ever' could be felt in the slow and complete darkening of the picture. Precisely the fact that no more was shown stimulated our imagination and induced the right mood in us. Therein lay its subtlety.[59] □

In his analysis of the acquired skills of the film audience, Balázs departs from those cultural critics who contend that cinema-goers are merely passive consumers of an easily digestible product. His argument implies that the viewing of film requires sophisticated acts of interpretation that construct coherence out of disjointedness and grasp the implied, indirect meanings of metaphors and symbols. Even if these acts are unconscious, their complexity remains.

Balázs's account of the phenomenon of 'identification' might seem to bring him closer to the critics who regard the viewing of film as passive consumption, since it could appear that 'identification', as he describes it, involves a loss of critical distance (and here it should be compared with other accounts, such as that of Laura Mulvey from a psycho-analytical–feminist perspective in chapters four and five of this Critical History). But Balázs does not look askance at this process; he sees it, rather, as an effect that demonstrates the artistic newness of film. This is his summary of 'identification':

■ In the cinema the camera carries the spectator into the film picture itself. We are seeing everything from the inside as it were and are surrounded by the characters of the film. They need not tell us what they feel, for we see what they see and see it as they see it.

Although we sit in our seats for which we have paid, we do not see Romeo and Juliet from there. We look up to Juliet's balcony with Romeo's eyes and look down on Romeo's with Juliet's. Our eye and with it our consciousness is identified with the characters in the film, we look at the world out of their eyes and have no angle of vision of our own. We walk amid crowds, ride, fly or fall with the hero and if one character looks into the other's eyes, he looks into our eyes from the screen, for our eyes are in the camera and become identical with the gaze of the characters. They see with our eyes. Herein lies the psychological act of 'identification'.

Nothing like this 'identification' has ever occurred as the effect of any other system of art and it is here that the film manifests its absolute artistic novelty.[60] □

The loss of distance that is an element of 'identification' can be related to another aspect of Balázs's theory of the effect of film. It is not only that film creates the complex interpretative competence that is necessary if film itself is to be understood; film also results in an enhanced perception of reality. Loss of distance is a key aspect of this enhancement, as is evident from Balázs's elaboration of the combined effects of the first and second formal principles of film that he has identified: the variation of distance, particularly insofar as it permits the 'close-up'; and the division of scenes into shots:

- One of the specific characteristics of the art of the film is that not only can we see, in the isolated 'shots' of a scene, the very atoms of life and their innermost secrets revealed at close quarters, but we can do so without any of the intimate secrecy being lost, as always happens in the exposure of a stage performance or of a painting. The new theme which the new means of expression of film art revealed was not a hurricane at sea or the eruption of a volcano: it was perhaps a solitary tear slowly welling up in the corner of a human eye.[61] □

Balázs is particularly fascinated by the close-up. In the silent film, without the distractions of sound, this technique has the effect of renewing and enhancing our perception of the processes of life, as he suggests in an almost poetic, slightly purple passage:

- The first new world discovered by the film camera in the days of the silent film was the world of very small things visible only from very short distances, the hidden life of little things. By this the camera showed us not only hitherto unknown objects and events: the adventures of beetles in a wilderness of blades of grass, the tragedies of day-old chicks in a corner of the poultry-run, the erotic battles of flowers and the poetry of miniature landscapes. It brought us not only new themes. By means of the close-up the camera in the days of the silent film revealed also the hidden mainsprings of a life which we had thought we already knew so well. Blurred outlines are mostly the result of our insensitive short-sightedness and superficiality. We skim over the teeming substance of life. The camera has uncovered that cell-life of the vital [t]issues[62] in which all great events are ultimately conceived; for the greatest landslide is only the aggregate of the movements of single particles. A multitude of close-ups can show us the very instant in which the general is transformed into the particular. The close-up has not only widened our vision of life, it has also deepened it. In the days of the silent film it not only revealed new things, but showed us the meaning of the old.[63] □

The close-up thus functions as a means of what the Russian Formalist critics called '*ostranenie*' or 'defamiliarisation', in which art strips the scales of familiarity from the eyes to make us look at the world afresh. It reanimates what Balázs calls 'visual life':[64]

- The close-up can show us a quality in a gesture of the hand we never noticed before when we saw that hand stroke or strike something, a quality which is often more expressive than any play of the features. The close-up shows you your shadow on the wall with which you have lived all your life and which you scarcely knew; it shows the speechless face and fate of the dumb objects that live with you in your room and whose fate is bound up with your own. Before this you looked at your life as a concert-goer ignorant of music listens to an orchestra playing a symphony. All he hears is the leading melody, all the rest is blurred into a general murmur. Only those can really understand and enjoy the music who can hear the contrapuntal architecture of each part in the score. This is how we see life: only its leading melody meets the eye. But a good film with its close-ups reveals the most hidden parts in our polyphonous life, and teaches us to see the intricate visual details of life as one reads an orchestral score.[65] □

Balázs's image of the symphony, however, suggests a problem with his theory of film at this point; for while the technique of the close-up may be specific to film (though it surely has static precedents in painting, for example in the representations of the minutiae of woodland flora in 'The Fairy Feller's Master-Stroke' (1855–64), by the Victorian artist Richard Dadd (1817–86)), the effect of the close-up, as he posits it, could arguably be found in other arts or genres – in fiction or poetry, say. Indeed, the Russian Formalist critics, who developed an idea of defamiliarisation that links up with Balázs's film theory, focused on fiction and poetry, on literature. The capacity to represent minute detail and process is not peculiar to film.

A further issue is raised by the examples that Balázs gives in the above quotation. The gesture of the hand, the shadow on the wall, the dumb objects that live with you in your room – all of these, foregrounded and defamiliarised by the close-up, could have an alienating, even alarming quality, an effect akin to that evoked by Freud in his essay on 'The Uncanny' (1919);[66] the original German title, 'Die Unheimlich' – the unhomely – has particular relevance to 'the dumb objects that live with you in your room'. It could also be related to Sartre's 'nausea',[67] an overwhelming awareness of the contingent quiddity of things. Balázs goes on to propose, however, that the close-up, far from being alienating in such ways, possesses a 'lyrical charm':[68]

- The close-up may sometimes give the impression of a mere natural-ist preoccupation with detail. But good close-ups radiate a tender human attitude in the contemplation of hidden things, a delicate sol-icitude, a gentle bending over the intimacies of life-in-the-miniature, a warm sensibility. Good close-ups are lyrical; it is the heart, not the eye, that has perceived them.[69] □

In this passage, the emphasis shifts from 'defamiliarisation', from a stress on the shock of the new or at least of new ways of freshly perceiving the old, to the notion of a much more Romantic, benign intimacy with things. Balázs then makes a further shift to consider the ways in which the close-up signifies psychological reality or functions as a symbolic anticipation of future narrative developments:

- Close-ups are often dramatic revelations of what is really happening under the surface of appearances. You may see a medium shot of someone sitting and conducting a conversation with icy calm. The close-up will show trembling fingers nervously fumbling a small object – sign of an internal storm. Among pictures of a comfortable house breathing a sunny security, we suddenly see the evil grin of a vicious head on the carved mantelpiece or the menacing grimace of a door opening into darkness. Like the *leitmotif* of impending fate in an opera, the shadow of some impending disaster falls across the cheerful scene.[70] □

As with the earlier simile of the symphony, the comparison to opera highlights a problem in Balázs's formulation. While the close-up may be specific to film, the use of symbolism to signify psychological turmoil or forthcoming disaster can be found across a range of arts, in music, opera, literature and painting. Furthermore, it can be seen that Balázs here departs once more from the idea of defamiliarisation that he approached in his earlier discussions of the effects of the close-up. He now gives examples of symbolism that depend for their effects on their familiarity: the audience knows what these signs and symbols are supposed to sig-nify, and interprets them accordingly. This is not a world of things and processes that resist us and escape our interpretation; it is a humanised, humanist world, as Balázs makes clear:

■ When the film close-up strips the veil of our imperceptiveness and insensitivity from the hidden little things and shows us the face of objects, it still shows us man, for what makes objects expressive are the human expressions projected on to them. The objects only reflect our own selves ... When we see the face of things, we do what the ancients did in creating *gods* in man's image and breathing a human soul into them. The close-ups of the film are the creative instruments of this mighty visual anthropomorphism.[71] □

Balázs goes on to elaborate the connection between this anthropomorphic emphasis and the close-up. He draws a distinction between a close-up that isolates a part of an object and a close-up of a human face. The audience that sees a close-up of a hand will usually connect it with a body, even if that body is not visible on the screen; it will assume that the hand exists in space. Without this connection to a larger whole in a spatial dimension, 'the isolated hand would lose its meaning, its expression'. But the 'facial expression on a face is complete and comprehensible in itself'. The face isolated by the close-up 'takes us out of space, our consciousness of space is cut out and we find ourselves in another dimension: that of physiognomy'.[72] While the single features 'appear in space', 'the significance of their relation to one another is not a phenomenon pertaining to space; no more are the emotions, thoughts and ideas which are manifested in the facial expressions we see. They are picture-like and yet they seem outside space; such is the psychological effect of facial expression.'[73]

The close-up of the human face makes possible the 'silent soliloquy',[74] in which the face speaks, whether the character is alone or with others, mute or in conversation: 'the close-up can lift a character out of the heart of the greatest crowd and show how solitary it is in reality and what it feels in this crowded solitude', and the 'film, especially the sound film, can separate the words of a character talking to others from the mute play of features by means of which, in the middle of such a conversation[,] we are made to overhear a mute soliloquy and realize the difference between this soliloquy and the audible conversation'.[75] Film, through the close-up, can make possible 'the "polyphonic" play of features ... the appearance on the same face of contradictory expressions' so that 'a variety of feelings, passions and thoughts are synthesized in the play of the features as an adequate expression of the multiplicity of the human soul'.[76] This reveals to the audience 'a strange new dimension', 'a new world' – 'the world of microphysiognomy which could not otherwise be seen with the naked eye or in everyday life'.[77] It can take us even further:

- [T]he camera can get so close to the face that it can show 'micro-physiognomic' details even of this detail of the body and then we find that there are certain regions of the body which are scarcely or not at all under voluntary control and the expression of which is neither deliberate nor conscious and may often betray emotions that contradict the general expression appearing on the rest of the face.[78] □

Balázs thus sees the close-up as the royal road to the unconscious. In what seems to be an implicit repudiation of Freud's view that slips of the tongue can enable us to hear the emergence of the unconscious into everyday life, Balázs affirms that 'the speech of an adult and sober human being ... has no involuntary and unconscious elements'.[79] But the unconscious can manifest itself in the facial details accessible through the movie camera, and every film spectator can learn the 'art of reading faces'. It was the silent film that taught the masses this 'very useful' skill.[80]

As well as the capacity for varying distance, which, for Balázs, yields particularly significant results in the case of the close-up, the art of film is also characterised by its capacity to change 'set-up' and camera angle. It is through its capacity to change set-ups and angles that film can express different moods. Changing angles and set-ups is crucial to 'the most specific effect of film art' – identification:

- The camera looks at the other characters and their surroundings out of the eyes of one of the characters. It can look about it out of the eyes of a different character every instant. By means of such set-ups we see the scene of action from the inside, with the eyes of the *dramatis personae* and know how they feel in it. The abyss into which the hero is falling opens at *our* feet and the heights which he must climb rear themselves into the sky before *our* faces. If the landscape in the film changes, we feel as if we had moved away. Thus the constantly changing set-ups give the spectator the feeling that he himself is moving ...[81] □

Balázs further explores the relationship between changing set-up and identification, drawing on his notion, already cited above, of the 'visual anthropomorphism' of film, and using the humanist metaphor of the facc, or 'physiognomy', of objccts and appcaranccs: '[o]ur anthropo-morphous world-vision makes us see a human physiognomy in every phenomenon'.[82] His concern here is also with the relationship between the 'objective' and the 'subjective' in film:

■ The physiognomy of every object in a film picture is a composite of two physiognomies – one is that of the object, its very own, which is quite independent of the spectator – and another physiognomy, determined by the viewpoint of the spectator and the perspective of the picture. In the shot the two merge into so close a unity that only a very practised eye is capable of distinguishing these two compon-ents in the picture itself. The cameraman may pursue several aims in choosing his angle. He may wish to stress the real objective face of the object shown; in that case he will search for the outlines which express this character of the object most adequately – or he may be more concerned with showing the state of mind of the spectator, in which case he will, if he wants to convey the impressions of a fright-ened man, present the object at a distorting angle, lending the object a terrifying aspect; or if he wants to show us the world as seen by a happy man, give us a picture of the object from the most favourable, flattering angle. By such means is achieved the emotional identifica-tion of the spectator with the characters in the film, and not only with their position in space but with their state of mind as well. Set-up and angle can make things hateful, lovable, terrifying, or ridiculous at will.

Angle and set-up lend the pictures in a film pathos or charm, cold objectivity or fantastic romantic qualities. The art of angle and set-up are to the director and cameraman what style is to the narrator and it is here that the personality of the creative artist is the most imme-diately reflected.[83] □

Balázs here links his analysis of the formal principles, techniques and psychological effects of film with a kind of *auteur* theory, in which a film is seen as an expression of an author. He equivocates as to whether the cameraman or the director, or both, are to be seen as the author; but he affirms that the personality of the author comes through in his choice of set-up and camera angle.

Varying distance, angle and set-up create individual shots; but the 'last process in creative film-making is the crowning job of editing' – though Balázs prefers the term 'montage', in the sense of 'assembly', to 'edit-ing'.[84] He justifies its importance in psychological and authorial terms:

■ Montage is the association of ideas rendered visual, it gives the single shots their ultimate meaning ... because the spectator presupposes that in the sequence of pictures that pass before his eyes there is an intentional predetermination and interpretation. This consciousness, this confidence that we are seeing the work of a creative intention and purpose, not a number of pictures thrown and stuck together by chance, is a psychological precondition of film-watching and we always expect, presuppose and search for meaning in every film we see.

This is a basic, irresistible intellectual requirement of the spectator and it operates even if by some reason or other the film seen is really merely a chance collection of pictures stuck together without rhyme or reason. Seeking a meaning is a fundamental function of human consciousness and nothing is more difficult than to accept with complete passivity meaningless, purely accidental phenomena. Our mechanism of idea association and our imagination will always tend to put some meaning into such a meaningless conglomeration, even though perhaps only in play.[85] □

It is interesting to link this psychological model with Balázs's earlier observations on the way in which film changes human sensibility. Balázs's affirmation, in the above extract, that '[s]eeking a meaning is a fundamental function of human consciousness', casts into doubt his earlier assertion that 'new human faculties' have emerged as a result of the birth of film; rather, it could be said that these faculties are not so much new as an example of a general function of human consciousness engaging with a new medium. It is also significant that Balázs again comes close to *auteur* theory by conflating the desire for meaning with the idea of an author, or at least 'a creative intention'. But to 'expect, presuppose and search for meaning' in a film, or in any other phenomenon, does not entail the belief in the existence of an intention or an author: indeed, Balázs's point that '[o]ur mechanism of idea association and our imagination' will read meaning even into 'a meaningless conglomeration' reinforces the point that meaning can emerge without an actual or posited author.

Montage, or editing, can be used to produce a number of important effects. For example, to convey the sense that time has elapsed between two scenes, it can interpolate another scene in another place. In his discussion of this kind of interpolation, Balázs proposes 'a most interesting link between time effect and space effect ... [T]he farther away the site of the inserted scene is from the site of the scenes between which it is inserted, the more time we will feel to have elapsed'. The 'interpolated-scene technique' is 'difficult to avoid' and 'renders it necessary to make several threads of action run parallel to one another'.[86] As well as conveying a sense of time and interweaving several strands of image and narrative, montage also creates associations of ideas, either by suggesting indirectly 'the inner sequence of the spectators' idea-associations' or by 'actually showing the pictures which follow each other in the mind and lead from one thought to the next'. The flashback is an example of the latter approach. This may be used in a relatively simple way, in which the transition from fictional present to fictional past is strongly marked, but in which the representation of the past itself takes a straightforward narrative form; on the other hand, it may aim to reproduce the psychological process of remembering the past: Balázs gives an example from *Fragment of an Empire* (1929), a film made by the Soviet director Friedrich Ermler (1898–1967):

■ The hero is a soldier who has lost his memory in the [F]irst [W]orld [W]ar, and with it his knowledge of himself. The film showed the train of ideas which restored his memory, his knowledge of himself and of the world. The spectator was made to follow a train of ideas of the sort psycho-analysis might have brought to light in a similar case. But no words could express such a train of ideas as adequately as pictures, because the rational, conceptual nature of words bars them from conveying the irrational correlation of such inner pictures. Further, the speed at which the pictures follow each other in the film can reproduce the original speed of this process of idea-association. The written or spoken word is always much slower than the inner rhythm of idea-association.

Ermler's soldier sees a sewing-machine and hears it rattle. The rattle suddenly quickens and grows louder. Now it is the rattling of a machine-gun. Strange tatters of visions, a mosaic of bits and pieces surge up, one bringing up the other by force of some formal or tonal similarity. Nevertheless the string of associations runs in a definite direction. A rubble of war memories – wheels of a gun … sewing-machine needle … bayonet … convulsively gripping hands … The sequence irresistibly carries along the soldier's unconsciousness and drives him nearer to the breaking-point, to that spectacle of horror which made him lose memory and consciousness, in order that he may find himself again and continue his interrupted existence.[87] □

As well as working in this way, montage can also work 'poetically', to produce a 'non-rational correlation of shapes and images'.[88] For this to be successful, however, the images that work poetically and metaphorically must be 'organic part[s] of the film story that [are] raised to symbolic significance'; otherwise they will merely be allegories that appear to be thrust into the film to make a point, like the intercutting in *New Year's Eve* (1923; aka *Sylvester*), a film by the German director Lupu Pick (1886–1931), between 'shots of a stormy sea' and 'urban scenes',[89] even though the story has nothing to do with the sea. Similarly, 'intellectual montage' – a term that will be explored in relation to Eisenstein later in this chapter – may use the sequences in a film as 'a sort of hieroglyphic writing', a 'rebus' or 'picture puzzle',[90] in a way that empties the pictures themselves of meaning and sensuous content, rather than letting the intellectual meanings grow out of pictures that are meaningful and sensuously powerful in themselves. Balázs's emphasis on the organic and his preference for symbol over allegory exemplify the application to film of Romantic and Modernist aesthetics which argued that general and intellectual meaning should grow out of sensuous particularity.

Balázs also discusses fades – 'the darkening of the scene by a slow stopping down of the iris diaphragm'[91] – and dissolves, in which one shot dissolves into another. His term for these, 'photo-technical effects', might make them sound mechanical; but while they are mechanical in one sense – they are effects of the mechanism of the camera – they also provide the director who employs them with important means of self-expression: with fades and dissolves, 'we are no longer facing only objective reproductions of things – here the narrator, the author, the film-maker himself is speaking to us'.[92] Fades and dissolves are the signs of the *auteur*.

Moreover, the dissolve is an element of film language that calls forth a particular response in the viewer:

■ The dissolve between two shots means a deeper connection between them. It is an accepted convention, expression, turn of speech in the language of the film, that if two pictures slowly dissolve into each other, the two are bound together by a deep, dramaturgically important, connection which may not be of a nature capable of being expressed by a series of shots depicting actual objects. The technique of the dissolve permits the placing of lyrical and intellectual emphasis where required in a film.[93] □

Balázs has identified a range of elements that comprise the formal language of film: varying distance, especially the close-up; division of the picture into integral scenes or 'shots'; changing set-up, angle, perspective and focus; montage; fades and dissolves. He has also provided a theory of audience psychology in terms of 'identification'. But he has not discussed sound, and when he comes to do so, he recalls his observations of twenty years before, in the book *Der Geist des Films*. In that book, he argued that, while the coming of sound endangered the 'whole rich culture of the silent film'[94] and prevented its further artistic development, sound film could itself develop into an art if it could achieve a kind of acoustic equivalent of the silent film. As Balázs puts it in an impassioned passage in *Theory of the Film* reprinted from his earlier study:

■ [I]f the sound film will merely speak, make music and imitate sounds as the theatre has already done for some thousands of years, then even at the peak of its technical perfection it will remain nothing but a copying device. But in art only that counts for a discovery which discovers, reveals something hitherto hidden from our eyes – or ears.[95]

The silent film, when it became an art, discovered for us an unknown visual world. It showed us the face of things, the mimicry of nature and the microdramatics of physiognomy. In the sequence of shots produced by editing a hitherto hidden interrelation of figures and movements was revealed to us and the linking of pictures evoked new powerful trains of association. ... ...

It is the business of the sound film to reveal for us our acoustic environment, the acoustic landscape in which we live, the speech of things and the intimate whisperings of nature; all that has speech beyond human speech, and speaks to us with the vast conversational powers of life and incessantly influences and directs our thoughts and emotions, from the muttering of the sea to the din of a great city, from the roar of machinery to the gentle patter of autumn rain on a window-pane. The meaning of a floor-board creaking in a deserted room, a bullet whistling past our ear, the death-watch beetle ticking in old furniture and the forest spring tinkling over the stones. Sensitive lyrical poets always could hear these significant sounds of life and describe them in words. It is for the sound film to let them speak to us more directly from the screen ... ... The sounds of our day-to-day life we hitherto perceived merely as a confused noise, as a formless mass of din, rather as an unmusical person may listen to a symphony ... The sound film will teach us to analyse even chaotic noise with our ear and read the score of life's symphony ... The vocation of the sound film is to redeem us from the chaos of shapeless noise by accepting it as expression, as significance, as meaning.[96] □

The vocation of sound in film, as of sight in film, is to enhance our perception of reality in order that we may see life as art. But in Balázs's view, the vocation of the sound film has not been fulfilled. 'The art of the silent film is dead, but its place was taken by the mere technique of the sound film which in twenty years has not risen and evolved into an art. On the whole the film has reverted again to a speaking photographed theatre.' He allows that there are exceptions, 'signs that the independent acoustic manifestation of the sound film is not dead yet and that this abortive great possibility of human culture ... is still seeking its own forms of expression'.[97] But the overall verdict is negative.

Balázs's rejection of most sound film because it seemed to refuse to conform to the prescription he had written twenty years before shows the extent to which his theory remains locked in the past. Rather than proposing a theory that could account for the actuality of sound film as it had developed, he rejects the reality because it does not accord with his theory. The issue of sound also came to preoccupy Sergei Mikhailovich Eisenstein (1898–1948), who aimed to incorporate it into his complex and developing theory of what he saw as the crucial component of film: montage. Eisenstein occupies a unique place in the history of film theory. He completed only six films: *Strike* (1924); *Potemkin* (1925); *October* (1928); *Old and New* (1929); *Alexander Nevsky* (1938); and *Ivan the Terrible* (1945–6). But these films have had a huge, rich and continuing impact upon cinema throughout the world. No director of his stature has been so prolific in theorising about film; and his writings on cinema are fascinating not only because of their vigour and inventiveness but also because they show his ideas about film developing in response to his own work as a director, to the films of other directors, and to the turbulent political and social situation of the Soviet Union from 1917; he recalls that in 1922, he was 'one of the most uncompromising champions of LEF, the left front, which wanted a new art that corresponded to the new social relationships'.[98]

Eisenstein's writings on films, comprising essays, articles and lectures, are not systematic or consistent, though it is possible to trace recurrent themes and lines of development. He is usually engaged in polemics, which he himself interprets to mean 'literary fighting';[99] his

preferred weapons are the aphorism, the axiom and the dogmatic statement, rather than measured and qualified argument; he contradicts himself and digresses, though not with a Walt Whitman-like insouciance that
shrugs its shoulders at or even celebrates such lapses – 'Do I contradict
myself?/Very well then I contradict myself';[100] he wants to be consistent
and systematic. But, perhaps because of these features, his writings constantly give a sense of an enormously energetic mind tearing into the
problems and challenges of film theory and of practical film-making in a
range of complex and challenging cultural and political contexts – the
Soviet Union, the USA, Western Europe. His writing demonstrates a
wide, eclectic and voracious cultural appetite, drawing on reading in four
languages and incorporating an impressive and insightful knowledge of
literature, painting and music. To read Eisenstein's work is not only to
learn an enormous amount about the theory and practice of film; it is
also to learn more about Leonardo da Vinci, about John Milton, about
Charles Dickens, about Claude Debussy, about Kazusika Hokusai,
about Japanese Kabuki theatre. His appropriation of these sources may
be open to question in a range of respects; but it is intellectually and culturally enlivening. For all his dogmatism and his continuing commitment
to a Soviet Union that became more and more murderously repressive,
his writing does not give a sense of monolithic confinement; he does not
mention the Russian critic Mikhail Bakhtin (1895–1975), whose views
would hardly have been widely disseminated at the time, even within the
Soviet Union, but his writings might be seen, in Bakhtinian terms, as
'heteroglossic', releasing a play of voices not in some comfortable version
of carnival but in a vigorous tourney in which dogmatic statements joust
lustily and in which any party may be unhorsed by an affirmation like:
'Art admits *all* methods except those that fail to achieve their end.'[101]

In contrast to Hugo Münsterberg, Eisenstein is not so concerned, in
his early writings, to differentiate theatre from cinema; working both as
a theatre and film director himself in this period, he is interested in what
the two media have in common; at the same time, he is aware of the
distinctiveness of film. In an essay of 1924, 'The Montage of Film
Attractions', he affirms that cinema and theatre share 'a common (identical) *basic* material – the *audience*', and 'a common purpose – *influencing
this audience in the desired direction* through a series of calculated pressures
on its psyche'.[102] Cinema and theatre have different methods, but 'they
have one basic device in common: the montage of attractions'.[103] He
offers this definition of 'an attraction':

■ An attraction ... is in our understanding any demonstrable fact (an action, an object, a phenomenon, a conscious combination, and so on) that is known and proven to exercise a definite effect on the attention and emotions of the audience and that, combined with others, possesses the characteristic of concentrating the audience's emotions in any direction dictated by the production's purpose. From this point of view a film cannot be a simple presentation or demonstration of events: rather it must be a tendentious selection of, and comparison between, events, free from narrowly plot-related plans and moulding the audience in accordance with its purpose ...
... I should call cinema 'the art of comparisons' because it shows not facts but conventional (photographic) representations ... For the exposition of even the simplest phenomena cinema needs comparison (by means of consecutive, separate presentation) between the elements which constitute it: montage (in the technical, cinematic sense of the word) is fundamental to cinema, deeply grounded in the conventions of cinema and the corresponding characteristics of perception.
... [A]n effect ... in cinema ... is made up of the juxtaposition and accumulation, in the audience's psyche, of associations that the film's purpose requires, associations that are aroused by the separate elements of the stated (in practical terms, in 'montage fragments') fact, associations that produce, albeit tangentially, a similar (and often stronger) effect only when taken as a whole. Let us take [the representation of a murder on film] as an example: a throat is gripped, eyes bulge, a knife is brandished, the victim closes his eyes, blood is spattered on a wall, the victim falls to the floor, a hand wipes off the knife – each fragment is chosen to 'provoke' associations.
An analogous process occurs in the montage of attractions: it is not in fact phenomena that are compared but chains of associations that are linked to a particular phenomenon in the mind of a particular audience.[104] □

Eisenstein argues that audiences are primarily defined in class terms – a working-class audience will react differently from an audience of ex-cavalry officers to the same set of images – and that there will also be differences within classes, for example between metal workers and textile workers. In this perspective, a sense of the potential audience is clearly crucial to the film-maker who wants to achieve certain effects.
At this stage, Eisenstein's analysis of film takes in three complemen-

tary aspects: the formal qualities of film; its psychological effects; and its political effects. Through the use of the 'montage of attractions', film can produce certain psychological effects that are related to the political situations of the audience. Again in contrast to Münsterberg, Eisenstein's psychology does not invoke memory and imagination; it is based on the idea, most notably exemplified in Pavlov's experiments, that specific stimuli can be arranged so as to produce a specific response.[105] This accords with his affirmation in 1926 that his 'artistic principle ... is: not intuitive creativity but the rational constructive composition of effective elements; the most important thing is that the effect must be calculated and analysed in advance'.[106] In the same year, he attacks Béla Balázs for his use of 'unpleasant' terms such as '[a]rt', 'creativity', 'eternity' and 'greatness'.[107]

In the 1920s and 30s, Eisenstein developed his ideas about montage. A 'Conversation' with Eisenstein in 1929 calls him 'the greatest enthusiast for montage in cinema generally',[108] and Eisenstein's own statements bear out the crucial role of montage in his ideas about film. In 'Beyond the Shot', which also appeared in 1929, he declares: 'Cinema is, first and foremost, montage.'[109] The shot, or frame, is obviously an essential component of montage, but it is nothing in itself: it remains 'neutral in terms of [its] meaning'.[110] As he says in a further 1929 essay, 'The Dramaturgy of Film Form', each piece of montage 'has in itself no reality at all'.[111] These claims may seem questionable, since it could be argued that a shot might have intrinsic interest and quality, just as a photograph may. In a later article, '"Eh!" On the Purity of Film Language' (1934), Eisenstein acknowledges this but argues that the better the shot, the worse the picture:

■ In films you do encounter individual good shots but in these circumstances the independent pictorial qualities of the shot and its value stand in mutual contradiction. As they are not linked by montage thought and composition, they become mere playthings and an end in themselves. The better the shots, the closer the film comes to being a disjointed collection of beautiful phrases, a shop window of unrelated objects or an album of postage stamps with views.[112] □

The 'value' of the individual shot, its transformation from a 'neutral' to a meaningful state, is achieved only when 'it is joined with another piece, when it suddenly acquires and conveys a sharper and quite different meaning than that planned for it at the time of filming'.[113]

For Eisenstein, the juxtaposition that creates meaning is charac terised by the collision and conflict between two adjacent but independent shots that 'gives rise to an idea'.[114] This kind of juxtaposition enacts the process by which ideas are arrived at: 'montage form as structure is a reconstruction of the laws of the thought process', although 'this by no means implies that the *thought process as a montage form* always necessarily has to have a train of thought as its subject'.[115] In other words, montage is not necessarily *about* a train of thought; whatever topic montage tackles, it *works in the same way as* a train of thought. Montage in film exemplifies and activates a universal mechanism of the human mind, which Eisenstein summarises in the essay 'Montage 1938':

■ [A]*ny two sequences, when juxtaposed, inevitably combine into another concept which arises from that juxtaposition as something qualitatively new* … … This is by no means a purely cinematic phenomenon, but one which inevitably accompanies the juxtaposition of two events, two facts, two objects. We are almost automatically prone to draw a quite specific, conventional conclusion – a generalisation, in fact – whenever certain discrete objects are placed side by side before us.[116] □

The fundamental general definition of montage, then, is that it is juxtaposition that gives rise to an idea. But within this general definition, there are different categories or methods of montage. In a key essay of 1929, 'The Fourth Dimension in Cinema', Eisenstein proposes that there are five categories of montage of increasing sophistication:

1. Metric
2. Rhythmic
3. Tonal
4. Overtonal
5. Intellectual

Metric montage in film is rather like metre in poetry; it provides a formula for the combination of units. 'The basic criterion is the *absolute length* of the shots. The shots are joined together according to their lengths in a formula-scheme. This is realised in the repetition of these formulas.' The 'primitive form of the method' can be found in the films of Lev Kuleshov (1899–1970), in his 'montages in three:four time, march-time and waltz-time (3:4, 2:4, 1:4, etc.)'. Tension can be 'achieved by the effect of mechanical acceleration through repeated shortening of the lengths of shots while preserving the formula of the relationship between these lengths ("double", "triple", "quadruple", etc.)'.[117] The audience should not be conscious of the metre, but it is 'an indisputable precondition for the organisation of our feeling'. The 'clarity' of the metre 'joins the "pulse-beat" of the film and the "pulse-beat" of the audience "in unison"'.[118] The metre should not, however, become too complex, or this unison, and the physiological and emotional effect of the 'beat', will be lost.

The second category or method of montage, rhythmic montage, does not adhere to a strict metric scheme. Whereas in metric montage the content of the shot is wholly subordinated to the length of the shot within a metrical scheme, in rhythmic montage the content within the shot helps to determine its length. 'Abstract scholastic determination of the lengths is replaced by a flexibility in the correlation between *actual* lengths ... ... Here the actual length does not coincide with the mathematical length allotted to it in accordance with the metric formula. Here the practical length of a shot is defined as the derivative of the specific quality of the shot and of the "theoretical" length allocated to it according to the scheme.'[119] Whereas formal tension in metric montage is achieved by shortening the length of shots but retaining the same metrical formula, formal tension in rhythmic montage is achieved by shortening the shots in ways that may contradict the metre: Eisenstein gives an example from the famous 'Odessa Steps' sequence of his *Potemkin*:

■ There the 'drum-beat' of the soldiers' feet descending the steps destroys all metrical conventions. It occurs outside the intervals prescribed by the metre and each time it appears in a different shot resolution. The final build-up of tension is produced by *switching* from the rhythm of the soldiers' tread as they descend the steps to another, new form of movement – the next stage in the intensification of the same *action* – the pram rolling down the steps.

Here the pram works in relation to the feet as a direct staged accelerator.

The 'descent' of the feet becomes the 'rolling down' of the pram.[120] □

The 'next stage after rhythmic montage' is tonal montage. In this method, shots are assembled according to their degrees of luminosity ('light tonality') and sharpness ('graphic tonality') to produce particular emotional effects. Eisenstein is concerned to rebut any implication that this form of montage is 'impressionistic', less precise and measurable than metric montage:

- ■ If we give a conventional emotional designation of 'more gloomy' to a shot that is to be predominantly resolved by lighting, this can be successfully replaced by a mathematical coefficient for a simple degree of illumination (a case of 'light tonality').

  In another instance, where we designate the shot as a 'sharp sound', it is extremely easy to apply this designation to the over-whelming number of acutely angled elements of the shot that prevail over the rounded elements (a case of 'graphic tonality').[121] □

Tonal montage, then, works through variations of light and of the sharpness of forms in the shot that can be precisely calibrated.

The fourth category or method that Eisenstein defines is overtonal montage. Overtonal montage breaks away from what he calls the 'montage by *dominants*', in which shots are combined according to their predominant 'sign'. In an anticipation of the post-structuralist emphasis on the instability of the sign, Eisenstein argues that the 'dominant' of a shot is not 'independent, absolute and invariably stable' but 'variable and profoundly relative'.[122] The shot is 'always ... an ambiguous hieroglyph', and 'can be read only in context ... only *in combination with* a separate reading or a small sign or reading indicator placed alongside it'.[123] Even a series of shots will not necessarily fix the meaning of the 'dominant' of each shot. He gives an example of this in 'The Fourth Dimension in Cinema':

- ■ 1. A grey-haired old man,
  2. a grey-haired old woman,
  3. a white horse,
  4. a snow-covered roof.[124] □

The 'dominant' of each of these shots and of the series that they comprise could be, Eisenstein suggests, 'old age' or 'whiteness'; but it is not clear which of these is the 'dominant', and the series 'might continue for a very long time before we finally c[a]me upon the signpost shot that immediately "christens" the whole series with a particular "sign"'.[125]

In 'orthodox montage', it is advisable to place an 'indicator' as near as possible to the beginning of a series of shots to reduce this ambiguity; in silent film, this indicator might even be an intertitle. But overtonal montage does not aim to reduce but to exploit the ambiguity of the shot. Eisenstein cites his own unfinished film *The General Line* as an example of a kind of montage that differed 'from orthodox montage by individual dominants':

■ The 'aristocracy' of unambiguous dominants was replaced by the method of 'democratic' equal rights for all the stimulants, viewed together as a complex.

The point is that the dominant (with all due obeisance to its relativity) is far from being the only stimulant in the shot, even if it is the most powerful. For example, the 'sex appeal' of the American heroine-beauty is accompanied by various stimulants: texture – like the material of her dress; light – the character of the lighting; race and nation (positive: the 'all-American type' or negative: the 'coloniser-oppressor' for a Negro or Chinese audience); social class, etc.

In a word a whole complex of secondary stimulants always accompanies the *central* stimulant (like the sexual one in our example).[126] □

If Eisenstein's references to the ambiguity of the sign sound as if he were anticipating post-structuralism, his use of the term 'stimulants' here links him once more with a Pavlovian stimulus-response psychology grounded in physiology. The idea that the shot comprises a number of stimulants that cannot be fully subordinated to a 'dominant' is the basis, Eisenstein argues, of overtonal montage, which *The General Line* exemplifies:

■ This montage is not constructed on the *individual dominant* but takes the sum of *stimuli* of all the stimulants as the dominant.

That distinctive *complex within the shot* that arises from the collisions and combinations of the individual stimulants inherent within it, ... stimulants that vary according to their 'external nature' but are bound together in an iron unity through their reflex physiological essence.

Physiological, in so far as the 'psychic' in perception is merely the physiological process of a *higher nervous activity*.

In this way the physiological sum total of the resonance of the shot *as a whole*, as a complex unity of all its component stimulants, is taken to be the general sign of the shot.

This is the particular 'feeling' of the shot that the shot as a whole produces.

... ... The basic sign of the shot can be taken to be the final sum total of its effect on the cortex of the brain as a whole, irrespective of the ways in which the accumulating stimulants have come together.

The *sum totals* thus achieved can be put together in any conflicting combination, thereby opening up quite new possibilities for montage resolutions.[127] □

These first four categories of montage emerge by a dialectical progression in which conflicts result in new syntheses at progressively higher levels: 'the transition from the metric to the rhythmic method arose from the emergence of conflict between the length of the shot and movement within the shot ... ... [t]he transition to tonal montage resulted from the conflict between the rhythmic and tonal principles of the shot ... overtonal montage resulted from the conflict between the tonal principle of the shot (the dominant) and the overtonal'.[128] The fifth category of montage will emerge from the dialectical conflict between physiological overtones and intellectual overtones. The new and higher synthesis that should result is intellectual montage; and intellectual montage is an adumbration of 'an unheard-of form of cinema':[129] intellectual cinema.

Intellectual cinema is not, for Eisenstein, abstract in a pure or arid way. Within his physiologically-based model of the human being, the processes of abstract thought echo the processes of the instincts, senses and emotions, but they do so 'in the centres of higher nervous activity'.[130] Thus intellectual cinema will synthesise the instincts, senses, emotions and intellect, and heal the breach between logic and image and mind and body, as he says in 'Perspectives' (1929):

■ Only *intellectual* cinema will be able to put an end to the conflict between the 'language of logic' and the 'language of images'. On the basis of the language of the cinema dialectic.

An intellectual cinema of unprecedented form and social functionalism. A cinema of extreme cognition and extreme sensuality that has mastered the entire arsenal of affective [emotional] optical, acoustical and biomechanical stimulants.[131] □

In his 1930 essay 'The Principles of the New Russian Cinema', Eisenstein develops his idea of the way in which intellectual cinema aims to make the abstract concrete, and stresses the importance of this task:

■ [This is] the greatest task of our art: filming abstract ideas through an image, making them in some way concrete. We have done this, not by translating an idea through some kind of anecdote or story, but by finding directly in an image or in a combination of images the means of provoking emotional reactions that are predicted and calculated in advance ... ... It is a matter of producing a series of images that is composed in such a way that it provokes an affective movement which in turn triggers a series of ideas. From image to emotion, from emotion to thesis ... cinema is the only concrete art that is at the same time dynamic and can release the operations of the thought process ... [T]his task of intellectual stimulation can be accomplished through cinema. This will also be the historic artistic achievement of our time because we are suffering from a terrible dualism between thought (pure philosophical speculation) and feeling (emotion).[132] □

It is interesting to see here the similarities between Eisenstein's ideas in the passage above from 1930, and those expressed in 1919 and 1921 by the poet and critic T. S. Eliot (1888–1965) – a figure whose influence on twentieth-century literature rivals that of Eisenstein on cinema. Eisenstein's 'terrible dualism' is akin to Eliot's idea of the 'dissociation of sensibility', the split between thought and feeling that, in Eliot's view, occurred in the seventeenth century and 'from which we have never recovered';[133] while Eisenstein's notion of 'a series of images that is composed in such a way that it provokes an affective movement which in turns triggers a series of ideas' resembles to some extent Eliot's idea of the 'objective correlative' which provides, in Eliot's view, the 'only way of expressing emotion in the form of art'. An 'objective correlative' is 'a set of objects, a situation, a chain of events which shall be the formula of that *particular* emotion; such that when the external facts, which must terminate in sensory experience, are given, the emotion is immediately evoked'.[134] Significantly, however, Eliot's definition incorporates the senses and emotions but leaves out thought – the thought that, for Eisenstein, leads to political action; and the respective responses of Eisenstein and Eliot to the problem of the 'terrible dualism' or 'dissociated sensibility' are, of course, very different. In the sphere of the arts, it is poetry for Eliot, film for Eisenstein; in the social and political sphere, it is religion for Eliot, revolution for Eisenstein.[135]

If 'intellectual cinema' in the fullest sense remained out of reach for Eisenstein, it stood as an image of his desire for wholeness – and the idea of the 'whole' remained crucial for him. For all his dismissal of the Romantic aesthetic vocabulary of Balázs, and despite the hints of post-structuralism that might be discerned in his notions of the ambiguity of the sign and the instability of the 'dominant', he did not endorse or celebrate formal fragmentation or semantic and semiotic uncertainty. He had identified different methods of montage, but a key question remained: how might these different methods, employed within the same film, fuse into a unity? The answer could lie in the idea of 'polyphonic montage', which he discusses in the essay 'Vertical Montage' (1940):

■ [In polyphonic montage] sequence after sequence is not simply linked by a single factor – movement, lighting, stages of the plot, etc. [It is a kind of montage] in which the *simultaneous movement* of a number of motifs advances through a succession of sequences, each motif having its own rate of compositional progression, while being at the same time inseparable from the overall compositional progression as a whole.[136] □

Eisenstein gives an example of 'polyphonic montage' from the 'procession sequence' in *Old and New*:

■ In that episode we see a whole skein of separate motifs which unfold simultaneously yet independently right through the sequence of frames, of which the following are some examples:

1. *The motif of 'heat'*, progressing, growing all the time, from sequence to sequence.
2. *The motif of successive close-ups*, increasing in purely graphic intensity.
3. *The motif of the mounting intoxication of religious fanaticism*, i.e. the *histrionic content* of the close-ups.
4. *The motif of female 'voices'* – the faces of the peasant women singing and carrying icons.
5. *The motif of male 'voices'* – the faces of the peasant men singing and carrying icons.
6. *The motif of a rising tempo* of movement by the people 'diving' under the icons. This counter-flow of people passing through the procession from the opposite direction imparted movement to the chief contrasting theme, a movement which, in the shots themselves and by way of montage intercutting, becomes enmeshed with the primary theme, i.e., the theme of people carrying the icons, crosses and religious banners.
7. *The general theme of 'grovelling'*, which unites both streams of people in a common progression of sequences 'from the sky to the dust',

i.e. from the crosses and the tops of the banner-staffs in the sky to the people prostrate in the dust and ashes as they senselessly beat their foreheads against the dry earth.

This theme was actually adumbrated in a separate, prior sequence, which gave as it were the keynote of what follows: the sweeping panoramic shot of the bell-tower, from the cross at the top, gleaming bright in the sky, down to the door of the church whence the procession is starting out, etc., etc.

The overall procession of the montage advanced uninterrupted, weaving all these diverse themes and motifs into a single, cumulative movement. Furthermore, apart from the *general direction* of that movement as a whole, each montage sequence also took strict account of all the vagaries of movement *within each separate motif*.[137] □

While Eisenstein's example here demonstrates 'polyphonic montage' in a montage *sequence* – that is, in a part rather than in the whole of a film – the notion of 'polyphonic montage' could easily be applied to a film as a whole: a film could be characterised as a polyphonic montage in which a range of montage methods were woven together into a unity, 'a *single organic* whole':[138]

■ [P]olyphonic structure basically works by creating an *overall perception of a sequence as a whole*. It forms, as it were, the 'physiognomy' of a sequence [or of a finished film], summarising all its separate elements into a *general perception of the sequence* [or film].[139] □

The term 'polyphony' is borrowed from music, and implicitly invokes another issue for a theory of montage – that of the relationship between visual montage and sound. Indeed, the idea of 'polyphonic montage' occurs in the course of one of Eisenstein's discussions of the relationship between visual image and sound image, which will be further explored later in this chapter. But many of Eisenstein's ideas about montage were developed in the era of silent film, and some of his most memorable montage effects depend on soundless cinema. A famous sequence from *Potemkin* has '[t]hree short shots: a stone lion asleep; a stone lion with open eyes; a rampant stone lion'. As Roger Scruton points out, this is 'one of Eisenstein's most striking visual metaphors. A stone lion rises to its feet and roars.' But this 'amazing image' is 'impossible ... outside the limitations of the silent screen'.[140] Eisenstein seemed determined, however, to welcome sound and to see it as a potential enrichment of montage.

In 1928, the USA produced the first talking picture, *The Jazz Singer*. Although sound films were not yet technically possible in the Soviet Union, a 'Statement on Sound' was published that welcomed the new development, though with reservations; its authors were named as Eisenstein, his fellow director Vsevolod Pudovkin (1893–1953) and his co-scenarist on *October*, Grigori Alexandrov (1903–84), who would start to direct films himself in 1930. The 'Statement' affirmed the centrality of montage: '[t]he confirmation of montage as the principal means of influence has become the indisputable axiom upon which world cinema culture rests'. In view of this, the 'significant features' for 'the further development of cinema … appear to be those that strengthen and broaden the montage methods of influencing the audience'. By this criterion, colour and stereoscopic cinema were insignificant compared with 'the great significance of *sound*'. Sound is, however, 'a double-edged invention' and its initial use will probably lie 'in the field of the *satisfaction of simple curiosity*' and the 'commercial exploitation of the most saleable goods', that is, of '*talking pictures* – those in which the sound is recorded in a natural manner, synchronising exactly with the movement on the screen and creating a certain "illusion" of people talking, objects making a noise, etc.'.[141] At first this will do no harm to the development of film as an art; but if it persists it will threaten what is, for Eisenstein, the very core of cinema – montage:

- Sound used in this way will destroy the culture of montage, because every mere *addition* of sound to montage fragments increases their inertia as such and their independent significance; this is undoubtedly detrimental to montage which operates above all not with fragments but through the *juxtaposition* of fragments.

  Only the contrapuntal use of sound vis-à-vis the visual fragment of montage will open up new possibilities for the development and perfection of montage.

  The first experiments in sound must aim at a sharp discord with the visual images. Only such a 'hammer and tongs' approach will produce the necessary sensation that will result consequently in the creation of a new *orchestral counterpoint* of visual and sound images … …

  Every day the problems of theme and plot grow more complex; attempts to solve them by methods of purely 'visual' montage either lead to insoluble problems or involve the director in fantastic montage constructions, provoking a fear of abstruseness and reactionary decadence.

  Sound, treated as a new element of montage (as an independent variable combined with the visual image), cannot fail to provide new and enormously powerful means of expressing and resolving the most complex problems, which have been depressing us with their insurmountability using the imperfect methods of a cinema operating only in visual images.

The *contrapuntal method* of structuring a sound film not only does not weaken *the international nature of cinema* but gives to its meaning unparalleled strength and cultural heights.[142] □

'Counterpoint' is a musical term that means a 'melody added as an accompaniment to a given melody' (*OED*); Eisenstein uses the term metaphorically, to refer to a relationship between sound and visual image. The sense of an analogy between sound as an element in film and musical composition survived into Eisenstein's later writings on the topic, for example in his discussion of 'polyphonic montage'. He did not himself develop the musical analogy of a 'discord' between sound and the visual image, though such a disjunction did recur as an *avant-garde*, 'art film' technique, for example in the work of the French film director Jean-Luc Godard (born 1930).[143]

Eisenstein's resistance to the most obvious use of sound – for 'talking pictures' – was again evident in his observations in 1932 on his abortive project for a film adaptation of Theodore Dreiser's novel *An American Tragedy* (1925), for which he and Ivor Montagu wrote a script. Here, Eisenstein's analogy is not musical but literary, which perhaps befits a discussion of the adaptation of a novel – though it is the modernist methods of James Joyce, not the naturalist technique of Dreiser himself, that provide a positive example. '[T]he raw material of sound film', Eisenstein affirms, 'is not *dialogue*': '*The true material of sound film is, of course, monologue.*'[144] Eisenstein claimed that 'the concept of "inner monologue" in cinema' was 'an idea [he had] been carrying around for six years before the advent of sound made its practical realisation possible'. He was well aware of literary experiments in inner monologue – he had met Joyce in Paris and knew *Ulysses* (1922), which he particularly commended for 'the immortal "inner monologues"' of Leopold Bloom. But despite Joyce's 'exceptionally brillian[t]' resolution of the problem of conveying inner monologue in *Ulysses*, 'the cruel framework of literature's limitations' remained. The 'inner monologue' 'can of course find its full expression only in cinema', and only in sound cinema, because 'only the sound film is capable of reconstructing all the phases and all the specifics of a train of thought'.[145]

Focusing on the projected film of *An American Tragedy*, Eisenstein offers a fascinating general account of the 'montage lists' developed to convey Clyde Barrow's 'inner monologue' when he takes his pregnant girlfriend out in a boat and finds his plan to murder her wavering as 'the conflict between pity and aversion for the girl, between his characterless indecision and his greedy desire to escape to glittering material comforts, reaches its apogee':[146]

■ What wonderful sketches those montage lists were!

Like thought itself they sometimes proceeded through visual images, with sound, synchronised or non-synchronised ...

sometimes like sounds, formless or formed as representational sound images ...

now suddenly in the coinage of intellectually formed words, as 'intellectual' and dispassionate as words that are spoken, with a blank screen, a rushing imageless visuality ... [Ellipses in original]

now in passionate disjointed speech, nothing but nouns or nothing but verbs; then through interjections, with the zigzags of aimless figures, hurrying along in synchronisation with them.

Now visual images racing past in complete silence,

now joined by a polyphony of sounds,

now by a polyphony of images.

Then both together.

Then interpolated into the external course of action, then interpolating elements of the external action into themselves.

As if on their faces were represented the inner play, the conflict of doubts, of explosions of passion, of voice, of reason, in 'slow motion' or 'speeded up', marking the different rhythms of the one and the other and jointly contrasting with the almost complete absence of external action: the fever of inner debates as opposed to the stony mask of the face.[147] □

But Paramount Studios rejected the script produced by Eisenstein and Montagu. The task of directing the film adaptation of *An American Tragedy* was assigned to Josef von Sternberg (1894–1969) who, to Eisenstein's disappointment, threw the idea of the 'inner monologue' overboard. So the attempt to effect what Eisenstein saw as a '180[-degree] advance in sound film culture'[148] in the USA was thwarted. But Eisenstein's observations on sound film and on the possibilities of the 'inner monologue' remain of considerable interest.

In the same essay in which he developed the notion of 'polyphonic montage' considered earlier in this chapter, Eisenstein elaborated a view of sound – by which he seems mainly to mean music – as one element in 'audiovisual montage', which he calls 'the *very highest stage* of montage'.[149] He affirms that:

■ [T]here is no difference in principle between purely visual montage and montage that embraces different areas of sensory perception, in particular the visual image and the auditory image, for the purpose of creating a single, generalising audiovisual image.[150] □

He sees the kind of 'polyphonic montage' that he has discussed in relation to the silent film as exemplifying the sort of montage that could incorporate sound, and he coins a new term for this kind of montage: 'vertical montage'. The term alludes to an orchestral score:

■ There are a certain number of staves on the page, each stave being allotted to the part for one particular instrument. Each part develops in a forward movement along the horizontal. No less important and decisive a factor, however, is the vertical: the musical interaction between the various elements of the orchestra in every given bar. Thus the advancing movement of the *vertical*, which permeates the entire orchestra and moves horizontally, creates the complex harmonic movement of the orchestra as a whole.[151] □

'Vertical montage' thus becomes a metaphor for a form of montage that can incorporate visual and auditory images into a harmonious whole. Eisenstein goes on to define four modes of audiovisual combination – metric, melodic, rhythmic and tonal – that relate, to some extent, to the modes of purely visual montage that he identified in 'The Fourth Dimension in Cinema' (1929). He also explores the possibility of incorporating colour into montage in a 'chromophonic' concordance.[152]

By this point in Eisenstein's development, however – it is 1940 – there is a sense that his theory is growing increasingly scholastic, generating definitions and sub-divisions that have lost touch with filmic reality – or perhaps simply with reality *tout court*. One might speculate on the relationship of this to the brutal repression in the Soviet Union as the 1930s advanced; but whatever its causes, it marks a limit to Eisenstein's film theory, although his comments on his own films, and on work in other, more traditional artistic forms such as poetry, remain of great interest at this stage. The film theorists to be considered in the next chapter, André Bazin and Siegfried Kracauer, are very different from each other, but they share a common aim that is contrary to that of Eisenstein: to think about film in ways that explore its links to reality.

CHAPTER TWO

Touching the Real: Bazin and Kracauer

Like Sergei Eisenstein, André Bazin (1918–58) was a prolific and enormously influential theorist of cinema whose contributions to film theory were first made in the course of topical essays and articles rather than in theoretical treatises. Although not a film-maker himself, Bazin was a friend and father-figure to a number of young critics who found a platform in the journal that he co-founded in 1951, *Cahiers du Cinéma*, and who went on to become key directors of the French New Wave in film: Claude Chabrol, Jean-Luc Godard, Jacques Rivette, Eric Rohmer, François Truffaut. The next chapter of this History will consider the contribution of *Cahiers* to film theory in the 1950s; this chapter focuses first on the work of Bazin himself, and his attempt to outline 'the ontological foundations of the art of cinema', or, 'in less philosophical terms, cinema as an art of reality'.[1] Ontology is the study of the nature of being, and Bazin's concern is: how does film relate to the nature of being, and what is the being of a film? The two-volume series of his selected essays and articles, *What is Cinema?* (1958, 1959), begins with an essay called 'The Ontology of the Photographic Image' (originally published 1945) and locates photography in a much longer history and psychology of the plastic arts. It is worth exploring this here in order to grasp Bazin's idea of cinema more fully.

Bazin posits a fundamental psychological need of human beings: to defend themselves against time. He suggests that the plastic arts emerged as a form of magic intended to provide this defence; his example is the ancient Egyptian mummy: 'To preserve, artificially, his bodily appearance is to snatch it from the flow of time, to stow it away neatly, so to speak, in the hold of life.'[2] The mummy was the first kind of Egyptian statue. As art and civilisation evolved, the plastic arts and magic parted company – 'Louis XIV did not have himself embalmed. He was content to survive in his portrait by Le Brun'[3] – but the need for a defence against time, and the use of art for this purpose, remained, though translated into more rational terms: 'No one believes any longer in the ontological identity of model and image, but all are agreed that the image helps us to remember the subject and to preserve him from a second spiritual death.' In a more sophisticated development, it was no longer a question of the survival of a particular individual through an artistic representation, but 'of a larger concept, the creation of an ideal world in the likeness of the real, with its own temporal destiny'[4] – in other words, not subject to the ravages of time.

Prior to the fifteenth century, however, painting in general had maintained a balance between realism and symbolism. But the invention of perspective allowed the artist to create a stronger impression of reality by producing an illusion of three-dimensional space. From that point, Western painting was 'torn between two ambitions: one, primarily aesthetic, namely the expression of spiritual reality wherein the symbol transcended its model; the other, purely psychological, namely the duplication of the world outside'.[5] Little by little, this need of illusion spread across the plastic arts.

The debate about realism in art is based on this 'confusion between the aesthetic and the psychological; between true realism, the need that is to give significant expression to the world both concretely and [in] its essence, and the pseudorealism of a deception aimed at fooling the eye (or for that matter the mind)'. It is the invention, first of photography, then of cinema, that frees the plastic arts from their obsession with producing likenesses. 'Painting was forced ... to offer us illusion and this illusion was reckoned sufficient unto art. Photography and the cinema on the other hand are discoveries that satisfy, once and for all and in its very essence, our obsession with realism.'[6] They do so because they eliminate the subjective trace that inevitably lingers in a painting, and the consequent suspicion that this trace casts on the veracity of a painting, no matter how realistic it may seem. A photograph, however, is objective:

■ Originality in photography as distinct from originality in painting lies in the essentially objective character of photography ... For the first time, between the originating object and its reproduction there intervenes only the instrumentality of a nonliving agent. For the first time an image of the world is formed automatically, without the creative intervention of man. The personality of the photographer enters into the proceedings only in his selection of the object to be photographed and by way of the purpose he has in mind. Although the final result may reflect something of his personality, this does not play the same role as is played by that of the painter. All the arts are based on the presence of man, only photography derives an advantage from his absence. Photography affects us like a phenomenon in nature, like a flower or a snowflake whose vegetable or earthly origins are an inseparable part of their beauty.

This production by automatic means has radically affected our psychology of the image. The objective nature of photography confers on it a quality of credibility absent from all other picture-making. In spite of any objections our critical spirit may offer, we are forced to accept as real the existence of the object reproduced, actually *re*-presented, set before us, that is to say, in time and space. Photography enjoys a certain advantage in virtue of this transference of reality from the thing to its reproduction.

A very faithful drawing may actually tell us more about the model but despite the promptings of our critical intelligence it will never have the irrational power of the photograph to bear away our faith.[7] □

Thus still photography is the culmination of a process that began with the mummy of ancient Egypt. More effectively than the mummy, the photograph embalms the fleeting phenomena of time. But, like the mummy, it remains limited by stasis: it fixes an appearance but it cannot make that appearance move. This is where cinema takes over:

■ [C]inema is objectivity in time. The film is no longer content to preserve the object, enshrouded as it were in an instant, as the bodies of insects are preserved intact, out of the distant past, in amber. The film delivers baroque art from its convulsive catalepsy. Now, for the first time, the image of things is likewise the image of their duration, change mummified as it were.[8] □

Cinema thus shares the defining ontological quality of photography – its essential objectivity – and extends it into the temporal dimension. Film is more, however, than animated photography: it is also a language; and in 'The Evolution of the Language of Cinema' (1950–5), Bazin aims to define this language. He once again takes a historical approach, though this time he stays within a specific period of the development of cinema:

■ I will distinguish, in the cinema between 1920 and 1940, between two broad and opposing trends: those directors who put their faith in the image and those who put their faith in reality. By 'image' I here mean, very broadly speaking, everything that the representation on the screen adds to the object there represented. This is a complex inheritance but it can be reduced essentially to two categories: those that relate to the plastics of the image and those that relate to the resources of montage, which, after all, is simply the ordering of images in time.

Under the heading 'plastics' must be included the style of the sets, of the make-up, and, up to a point, even of the performance, to which we naturally add the lighting and, finally, the framing of the shot which gives us its composition. As regards montage, derived initially as we all know from the masterpieces of Griffith, we have the statement of Malraux in his *Esquisse d'une psychologie du cinéma* [*Outline of a psychology of cinema*] (1946)[9] that it was montage that gave birth to film as an art, setting it apart from mere animated photography, in short, creating a language.

The use of montage can be 'invisible' and this was generally the case in the prewar classics of the American screen. Scenes were broken down just for one purpose, namely, to analyze an episode according to the material or dramatic logic of the scene. It is this logic which conceals the fact of the analysis, the mind of the spectator quite naturally accepting the viewpoints of the director which are justified by the geography of the action or the shifting emphasis of dramatic interest.

But the neutral quality of this 'invisible' editing fails to make use of the full potential of montage. On the other hand these potentialities are clearly evident from the three processes generally known as parallel montage, accelerated montage, montage by attraction. In creating parallel montage, Griffith succeeded in conveying a sense of the simultaneity of two actions taking place at a geographical distance by means of alternating shots from each. In *La Roue* (*The Wheel*, 1922) Abel Gance (1889–1981) created the illusion of the steadily increasing speed of a locomotive without actually using any images of speed (indeed the wheel could have been turning on one spot) simply by a multiplicity of shots of ever-decreasing length.

Finally there is 'montage by attraction', the creation of S.M. Eisenstein [see pp. 45–6 of this Critical History], and not so easily described as the others, but which may be roughly defined as the reenforcing of the meaning of one image by association with another image not necessarily part of the same episode – for example the fireworks display in *The General Line* following the image of the bull. In this extreme form, montage by attraction was rarely used even by its creator but one may consider as very near to it in principle the more commonly used ellipsis, comparison, or metaphor, examples of which are the throwing of stockings onto a chair at the foot of a bed, or the milk overflowing in the *Quai des orfèvres* (1947) of Henri-Georges Clouzot (1907–77). There are of course a variety of possible combinations of these three processes.

Whatever these may be, one can say that they share that trait in common which constitutes the very definition of montage, namely, the creation of a sense of meaning not proper to the images themselves but derived exclusively from their juxtaposition. The well-known experiment of Kuleshov with the shot of Mozhukhin in which a smile was seen to change its significance according to the image that preceded it, sums up perfectly the properties of montage.

Montage as used by Kuleshov, Eisenstein, or Gance did not give us the event; it alluded to it. Undoubtedly they derived at least the greater part of the constituent elements from the reality they were describing but the final significance of the film was found to reside in the ordering of these elements much more than in their objective content.

The matter under recital, whatever the realism of the individual image, is born essentially from these relationships – Mozhukhin plus dead child equal pity – that is to say an abstract result, none of the concrete elements of which are to be found in the premises; maiden plus appletrees in bloom equal hope. The combinations are infinite. But the only thing they have in common is the fact that they suggest an idea by means of a metaphor or by an association of ideas. Thus between the scenario properly so-called, the ultimate object of the recital, and the image pure and simple, there is a relay station, a sort of aesthetic 'transformer'. The meaning is not in the image, it is in the shadow of the image projected by montage on to the field of consciousness of the spectator.

Let us sum up. Through the contents of the image and the resources of montage, the cinema has at its disposal a whole arsenal of means whereby to impose its interpretation of an event on the spectator. By the end of the silent film [era] we can consider this arsenal to have been full. On the one side the Soviet cinema carried to its ultimate consequences the theory and practice of montage while the German school did every kind of violence to the plastics of the image by way of sets and lighting. Other cinemas count too besides the

Russian and German, but whether in France or Sweden or the United States, it does not appear that the language of cinema was at a loss for ways of saying what it wanted to say.

If the art of cinema consists in everything that plastics and montage can add to a given reality, the silent film was an art on its own. Sound could only play at best a subordinate and supplementary role: a counterpoint to the visual image. But this possible enhancement – at best only a minor one – is likely not to weigh much in comparison with the additional bargain-rate reality introduced at the same time by sound.

Thus far we have put forward the view that expressionism of montage and image constitute the essence of cinema. And it is precisely on this generally accepted notion that directors from silent days, such as Erich von Stroheim (1885–1957), F[riedrich] W[ilhelm] Murnau (1888–1931) and Robert Flaherty (1884–1951), have by implication cast a doubt. In their films, montage plays no part, unless it be the negative one of inevitable elimination where reality superabounds. The camera cannot see everything at once but it makes sure not to lose any part of what it chooses to see. What matters to Flaherty, confronted with Nanook hunting the seal [in *Nanook of the North* (1921)], is the relation between Nanook and the animal; the actual length of the waiting period. Montage could suggest the time involved. Flaherty however confines himself to showing the actual waiting period; the length of the hunt is the very substance of the image, its true object. Thus in the film this episode requires one set-up. Will anyone deny that it is thereby much more moving than a montage by attraction?

Murnau is interested not so much in time as in the reality of dramatic space. Montage plays no more of a decisive part in *Nosferatu* (1921) than in *Sunrise* (1927). One might be inclined to think that the plastics of his image are impressionistic. But this would be a superficial view. The composition of his image is in no sense pictorial. It adds nothing to the reality, it does not deform it, it forces it to reveal its structural depth, to bring out the preexisting relations which become constitutive of the drama. For example, in *Tabu* (1931), the arrival of a ship from left screen gives an immediate sense of destiny at work so that Murnau has no need to cheat in any way on the uncompromising realism of a film whose settings are completely natural.

But it is most of all Stroheim who rejects photographic expressionism and the tricks of montage. In his films reality lays itself bare like a suspect confessing under the relentless examination of the commissioner of police. He has one simple rule for direction. Take a close look at the world, keep on doing so, and in the end it will lay bare for you all its cruelty and its ugliness. One could easily imagine as a matter of fact a film by Stroheim composed of a single shot as long-lasting and as close-up as you like. These three directors do not exhaust the possibilities. We would undoubtedly find[,] scattered among the works of [other directors,] elements of nonexpressionistic cinema in which montage plays no part – even including Griffith. But these examples suffice to reveal, at the very heart of the silent film, a cinematographic art the very opposite of that which has been identified as '*cinema par excellence*', a language the semantic and syntactical unit of which is in no sense the Shot; in which the image is evaluated not according to what it adds to reality but what it reveals of it. In the latter art the silence of the screen was a drawback, that is to say, it deprived reality of one of its elements. Stroheim's *Greed* (1924), like the *Jeanne d'Arc* (*Joan of Arc*, 1928) of Carl-Theodor Dreyer (1889–1968), is already virtually a talking film. The moment that you cease to maintain that montage and the plastic composition of the image are the very essence of the language of cinema, sound is no longer the aesthetic crevasse dividing two radically different aspects of the seventh art [that is, the art of the cinema – see p. 16 of this Critical History]. The cinema that is believed to have died of the soundtrack is in no sense '*the* cinema'. The real dividing line is elsewhere. It was operative in the past and continues to be through thirty-five years of the history of the language of the film.[10] □

It can be seen here that Bazin takes issue with the theorists of the last chapter who felt that sound threatened or had indeed harmed an art of the silent film that was characterised primarily by montage. He goes on to provide a positive evaluation of Hollywood cinema, implicitly challenging the view that such cinema is corrupted by commercialism and the need to appeal to a mass audience:

■ From 1930 to 1940 there seems to have grown up in the world, originating largely in the United States, a common form of cinematic language. It was the triumph in Hollywood, during that time, of five or six major kinds of film that gave it its overwhelming superiority: (1) American comedy (*Mr Smith Goes to Washington* (1939)); (2) The burlesque film (The Marx Brothers); (3) The dance and vaudeville film (Fred Astaire and Ginger Rogers and the Ziegfeld Follies); (4) The crime and gangster film (*Scarface* (1932), *I Am a Fugitive from a Chain Gang* (1932), *The Informer* (1935)); (5) Psychological and social dramas (*Back Street* (1932), *Jezebel* (1938)); (6) Horror or fantasy films (*Dr. Jekyll and Mr. Hyde* (1931), *The Invisible Man* (1933), *Frankenstein* (1931)); (7) The western (*Stagecoach* (1939)). During that time the French cinema undoubtedly ranked next. Its superiority was gradually manifested by way of a trend towards what might be roughly called stark somber realism, or poetic reason, in which four names stand out: Jacques Feyder (1885–1948, born Jacques Frédérix), Jean Renoir (1894–1979), Marcel Carné (1909–96), and Julien Duvivier (1896–1967) ... American and French production sufficiently clearly indicate that the sound film, prior to World War II, had reached a well-balanced stage of maturity.

First as to content. Major varieties with clearly defined rules capable of pleasing a worldwide public, as well as a cultured elite, provided it was not inherently hostile to the cinema.

Secondly as to form: well-defined styles of photography and editing perfectly adapted to their subject-matter; a complete harmony of image and sound. In seeing again today such films as *Jezebel* by William Wyler (1902–81), *Stagecoach* by John Ford (1895–1973, born Sean Aloysius O'Feeney), or *Le Jour se lève* (*Daybreak*, 1939) by Marcel Carné, one has the feeling that in them an art has found its perfect balance, its ideal form of expression, and reciprocally one admires them for dramatic and moral themes to which the cinema, while it may not have created them, has given a grandeur, an artistic effectiveness, that they would not otherwise have had. In short, here are all the characteristics of the ripeness of a classical art.[11] □

Bazin moves on to consider the evolution of cinematic cutting since the emergence of the sound film, to develop his attack on montage, and to identify the use of deep focus – in which all the elements of a shot are in sharp focus, thus giving a sense of depth – as 'a dialectical step forward',[12] indeed a 'revolution' in the language of cinema:[13]

■ In 1938 there was an almost universal standard pattern of editing. If, somewhat conventionally, we call the kind of silent films based on the plastics of the image and the artifices of montage, 'expressionist' or 'symbolistic', we can describe the new form of storytelling [as] 'analytic' and 'dramatic'. Let us suppose, by way of reviewing one of the elements of the experiment of Kuleshov, that we have a table covered with food and a hungry tramp. One can imagine that in 1936 it would have been edited as follows:

1. Full shot of the actor and the table.
2. Camera moves forward into a close-up of a face expressing a mixture of amazement and longing.
3. Series of close-ups of food.
4. Back to full shot of person who starts slowly towards the camera.
5. Camera pulls slowly back to a three-quarter shot of the actor seizing a chicken wing.

Whatever variants one could think of for this scene, they would all have certain points in common:

1. The verisimilitude of space in which the position of the actor is always determined, even when a close-up eliminates the décor.
2. The purpose and the effects of the cutting are exclusively dramatic or psychological.

In other words, if the scene were played on a stage and seen from a seat in the orchestra, it would have the same meaning, the episode would continue to exist objectively. The changes of point of view provided by the camera would add nothing. They would present the reality a little more forcefully, first by allowing a better view and then by putting the emphasis where it belongs.

It is true that the stage director like the film director has at his disposal a margin within which he is free to vary the interpretation of the action but it is only a margin and allows for no modification of the inner logic of the event. Now, by way of contrast, let us take the montage of the stone lions in *Potemkin* [see p. 55 above]. By skilful juxtaposition a group of sculptured lions [is] made to look like a single lion getting to its feet, a symbol of the aroused masses. This clever device would be unthinkable in any film after 1932. As late as 1936 Fritz Lang (1890–1976), in *Fury*, followed a series of shots of women dancing the can-can with shots of clucking chickens in a farmyard. This relic of associative montage came as a shock even at the time, and today seems entirely out of keeping with the rest of the film. However decisive the art of Marcel Carné, for example, in our estimate of the respective values of *Quai des Brumes* (1938; aka *Port of Shadows* in USA) or of *Le Jour se lève* his editing remains on the level of the reality he is analyzing. There is only one proper way of looking at it. That is why we are witnessing the almost complete disappearance of optical effects such as superimpositions, and even, especially in the United States, of the close-up, the too violent impact of which make the audience conscious of the cutting. In the typical American comedy the director returns as often as he can to a shot of the characters from the knees up, which is said to be best suited to catch the spontaneous attention of the viewer – the natural point of balance of his mental adjustment.

Actually this use of montage originated with the silent movies. This is more or less the part it plays in Griffith's films, for example in *Broken Blossoms* (1919), because with *Intolerance* (1916) he had already introduced that synthetic concept of montage which the Soviet cinema was to carry to its ultimate conclusion and which is to be found again, although less exclusively, at the end of the silent era. It is understandable, as a matter of fact, that the sound image, far less flexible than the visual image, would carry montage in the direction of realism, increasingly eliminating both plastic impressionism and the symbolic relation between images.

Thus around 1938 films were edited, almost without exception, according to the same principle. The story was unfolded in a series of set-ups numbering as a rule about 600. The characteristic procedure was by shot-reverse-shot, that is to say, in a dialogue scene, the camera followed the order of the text, alternating the character shown with each speech.

It was this fashion of editing, so admirably suitable for the best films made between 1930 and 1939, that was challenged by the shot in depth introduced by Orson Welles (1915–85) and William Wyler. *Citizen Kane* (1941) can never be too highly praised. Thanks to the depth of field, whole scenes are covered in one take, the camera remaining motionless. Dramatic effects for which we had formerly relied on montage were created out of the movements of the actors within a fixed framework. Of course Welles did not invent the in-depth shot any more than Griffith invented the close-up. All the pioneers used it and for a very good reason. Soft focus only appeared with the montage. It was not only a technical must consequent upon the use of images in juxtaposition, it was a logical consequence of montage, its plastic equivalent. If at a given moment in the action the director, as in the scene imagined above, goes to a close-up of a bowl of fruit, it follows naturally that he also isolates it in space through the

focusing of the lens. The soft focus of the background confirms therefore the effect of montage, that is to say, while it is of the essence of
the storytelling, it is only an accessory of the style of the photography.
Jean Renoir had already clearly understood this, as we see from a
statement of his made in 1938 just after he had made *La Bête
Humaine* (1938; aka *The Human Beast, Judas Was a Woman*) and *La
Grande Illusion* (1937) and just prior to *La Règle du Jeu* (1939; aka
The Rules of the Game): 'The more I learn about my trade the more I
incline to direction in depth relative to the screen. The better it works,
the less I use the kind of set-up that shows two actors facing the
camera, like two well-behaved subjects posing for a still portrait'.[14]
The truth of the matter is, that if you are looking for the precursor of
Orson Welles, it is not Louis Lumière (1864–1948) or Ferdinand
Zecca (1864–1947), but rather Jean Renoir. In his films, the search
after composition in depth is, in effect, a partial replacement of montage by frequent panning shots and entrances. It is based on a respect
for the continuity of dramatic space and, of course, [for] its duration.[15]

To anybody with eyes in his head, it is quite evident that the
sequence of shots used by Welles in *The Magnificent Ambersons* (1942)
is in no sense the purely passive recording of an action shot within the
same framing. On the contrary, his refusal to break up the action, to
analyze the dramatic field in time, is a positive action the results of
which are far superior to anything that could be achieved by the
classical 'cut'.

All you need to do is compare two frame shots in depth, one from
1910, the other from a film by Wyler or Welles, to understand just by
looking at the image, even apart from the context of the film, how different their functions are. The framing in the 1910 film is intended,
to all intents and purposes, as a substitute for the missing fourth wall
of the theatrical stage, or[,] at least in exterior shots, for the best van-
tage point to view the action, whereas in the second case the setting,
the lighting, and the camera angles give an entirely different reading.
Between them, director and cameraman have converted the screen
into a dramatic checkerboard, planned down to the last detail. The
clearest if not the most original examples of this are to be found in
The Little Foxes (1941) where the *mise-en-scène* takes on the severity
of a working drawing [*mise-en-scène* literally means 'putting in the
scene'. As David A. Cook points out, it includes 'the action, lighting,
décor, and other elements within the shot itself, as opposed to the
effects created by cutting. Realists [such as Bazin] generally prefer the

process of *mise-en-scène* to the more manipulative techniques of montage.'[16]]. Welles's pictures are more difficult to analyze because of his fondness for the over-baroque. Objects and characters are related in such a fashion that it is impossible for the spectator to miss the significance of the scene. To get the same results by way of montage would have necessitated a detailed succession of shots.

What we are saying then is that the sequence of shots 'in depth' of the contemporary director does not exclude the use of montage – how could he [exclude it], without reverting to a primitive babbling – he makes it an integral part of his 'plastic'. The storytelling of Welles and Wyler is no less explicit than John Ford's but theirs has the advantage over his that it does not sacrifice the specific effects that can be derived from unity of image in space and time. Whether an episode is analyzed bit by bit or presented in its physical entirety cannot surely remain a matter of indifference, at least in a work with some pretensions to style. It would obviously be absurd to deny that montage has added considerably to the progress of film language, but this has happened at the cost of other values, no less definitely cinematic.

This is why depth of field is not just a stock in trade of the cameraman like the use of a series of filters or of such-and-such a style of lighting, it is a capital gain in the field of direction – a dialectical step forward in the history of film language.

Nor is it just a formal step forward. Well used, shooting in depth is not just a more economical, a simpler, and at the same time a more subtle way of getting the most out of a scene. In addition to affecting the structure of film language, it also affects the relationships of the minds of the spectators to the image, and in consequence it influences the interpretation of the spectacle.

It would lie outside the scope of this article to analyze the psychological modalities of these relations, as also their aesthetic consequences, but it might be enough here to note, in general terms:

1. That depth of focus brings the spectator into a relation with the image closer to that which he enjoys with reality. Therefore it is correct to say that, independently of the contents of the image, its structure is more realistic.

2. That it implies, consequently, both a more active mental attitude on the part of the spectator and a more positive contribution on his part to the action in progress. While analytical montage only calls for him to follow his guide, to let his attention follow along

smoothly with that of the director who will choose what he should see, here he is called upon to exercise at least a minimum of personal choice. It is from his attention and his will that the meaning of the image in part derives.

3. From the two preceding propositions, which belong to the realm of psychology, there follows a third which may be described as metaphysical. In analyzing reality, montage presupposes of its very nature the unity of meaning of the dramatic event. Some other form of analysis is undoubtedly possible but then it would be another film. In short, montage by its very nature rules out ambiguity of expression. Kuleshov's experiment proves this [ad] absurdum [to the point of absurdity] in giving on each occasion a precise meaning to the expression on a face, the ambiguity of which alone makes the three successively exclusive expressions possible.

On the other hand, depth of focus reintroduced ambiguity into the structure of the image if not of necessity – Wyler's films are never ambiguous – at least as a possibility. Hence it is no exaggeration to say that *Citizen Kane* is unthinkable shot in any other way but in depth. The uncertainty in which we find ourselves as to the spiritual key or the interpretation we should put on the film is built into the very design of the image.

It is not that Welles denies himself any recourse whatsoever to the expressionistic procedures of montage, but just that their use from time to time in between sequences of shots in depth gives them a new meaning. Formerly montage was the very stuff of cinema, the texture of the scenario. In *Citizen Kane* a series of superimpositions is contrasted with a scene presented in a single take, constituting another and deliberately abstract mode of storytelling. Accelerated montage played tricks with time and space while that of Welles, on the other hand, is not trying to deceive us; it offers us a contrast, condensing time, and hence is the equivalent for example of the French imperfect [a verbal form expressing a continuous but incomplete past action, for example 'he was watching a film', or repeated past actions, for example 'he used to watch films'] or the English frequentative tense [a verbal form expressing frequent repetition or intensity of action, for instance 'chatter', 'dribble' and 'twinkle' (*OED*)]. Like accelerated montage and montage of attractions these superimpositions, which the talking film had not used for ten years, rediscovered a possible use related to temporal realism in a film without montage.

If we have dwelt at some length on Orson Welles it is because the date of his appearance in the filmic firmament (1941) marks more or less the beginning of a new period and also because his case is the most spectacular and, by virtue of his very excesses, the most significant.

Yet *Citizen Kane* is part of a general movement, of a vast stirring of the geological bed of cinema, confirming that everywhere up to a point there had been a revolution in the language of the screen ... ... [T]he decade from 1940 to 1950 marks a decisive step forward in the development of the language of the film. If we have appeared since 1930 to have lost sight of the trend of the silent film as illustrated particularly by Stroheim, F.W. Murnau, Robert Flaherty, and Dreyer, it is for a purpose. It is not that this trend seems to us to have been halted by the talking film. On the contrary, we believe that it represented the richest vein of the so-called silent film[,] precisely because it was not aesthetically tied to montage, but was indeed the only tendency that looked to the realism of sound as a natural development. On the other hand it is a fact that the talking film between 1930 and 1940 owes it virtually nothing save for the glorious and retrospectively prophetic exception of Jean Renoir. He alone in his searchings as a director prior to *La Règle du Jeu* forced himself to look back beyond the resources provided by montage and so uncovered the secret of a film form that would permit everything to be said without chopping the world up into little fragments, that would reveal the hidden meanings in people and things without disturbing the unity natural to them.

It is not a question of thereby belittling the films of 1930 to 1940, a criticism that would not stand up in the face of the number of masterpieces, it is simply an attempt to establish the notion of a dialectic[al] progress, the highest expression of which was found in the films of the 1940[s]. Undoubtedly, the talkie sounded the knell of a certain aesthetic of the language of film, but only wherever it had turned its back on its vocation in the service of realism. The sound film nevertheless did preserve the essentials of montage, namely discontinuous description and the dramatic analysis of action. What it turned its back on was metaphor and symbol in exchange for the illusion of objective presentation. The expressionism of montage has virtually disappeared but the relative realism of the kind of cutting that flourished around 1937 implied a congenital limitation which escaped us so long as it was perfectly suited to its subject matter. Thus American comedy reached its peak within the framework of a form of editing in which the realism of the time played no part. Dependent on logic for its effects, like vaudeville and plays on words, entirely conventional in its moral and sociological content, American comedy had everything to gain, in strict line-by-line progression, from the rhythmic resources of classical editing.

Undoubtedly it is primarily with the Stroheim–Murnau trend – almost totally eclipsed from 1930 to 1940 – that the cinema has more or less consciously linked up once more over the last ten years. But it has no intention of limiting itself simply to keeping this trend alive. It draws from it the secret of the regeneration of realism in storytelling and thus of becoming capable once more of bringing together real time, in which things exist, along with the duration of the action, for which classical editing had insidiously substituted mental and abstract time. On the other hand, so far from wiping out once and for all the conquests of montage, this reborn realism gives them a body of reference and a meaning. It is only an increased realism of the image that can support the abstraction of montage. The stylistic repertory of a director such as Alfred Hitchcock (1899–1980), for example, ranged from the power inherent in the basic document as such, to superimpositions, to large close-ups. But the close-ups of Alfred Hitchcock are not the same as those of Cecil B. de Mille (1881–1959) in *The Cheat* (1915). They are just one type of figure, among others, of [Hitchcock's] style. In other words, in the silent days, montage evoked what the director wanted to say; in the editing of 1938, it described it. Today we can say that at last the director writes in film. The image – its plastic composition and the way it is set in time, because it is founded on a much higher degree of realism – has at its disposal more means of manipulating reality and of modifying it from within. The film-maker is no longer the competitor of the painter and the playwright, he is, at last, the equal of the novelist.[17] ☐

Bazin thus puts forward an idea of the film-maker as almost literally an *auteur*, an author, the equivalent of the novelist – though, as the next chapter will show, he had his reservations about the *auteur* theory with which his journal *Cahiers du Cinéma* would become closely associated in the 1950s. In his perspective, the enhanced creative status of the director is due to the development in 1940s cinema of a greater realism, especially through the use of deep focus, which brings the spectator into a relationship with the image more like his relationship with reality, provokes him to use his attention and will to draw meaning from the image, opens up the potential of the image for ambiguity, and allows the director more flexibility. For Bazin, realism – a realism located first of all in the still photograph and released into motion by the cinema of the deep-focus shot – is not constricting but enabling.

Like Bazin, the German film theorist Siegfried Kracauer (1889–1966) also bases his argument for realism in film on an ontology of the still photograph. Kracauer, a prolific cultural journalist for the *Frankfurter Zeitung* in the 1920s and 30s, had to leave Germany in 1933 and settled in the USA, producing, in 1947, a classic history of German film, *From Caligari to Hitler*. In 1960, his *Theory of Film* appeared, a massive synthesis of the ideas about cinema that he had been developing since the 1920s. Stressing the power that photography has to convey material reality, *Theory of Film* offers, by Kracauer's own account, 'a *material* aesthetics, not a formal one':[18]

■ My book ... rests upon the assumption that film is essentially an extension of photography and therefore shares with this medium a marked affinity for the visible world around us. Films come into their own when they record and reveal physical reality.[19] □

Kracauer suggests that there is a particular sort of physical reality that film alone can render:

■ [Physical reality] includes many phenomena which would hardly be perceived were it not for the motion picture camera's ability to catch them on the wing. And since any medium is partial to the things it is uniquely equipped to render, the cinema is conceivably animated by a desire to picture transient material life, life at its most ephemeral. Street crowds, involuntary gestures, and other fleeting impressions are its very meat. Significantly, the contemporaries of Lumière praise his films – the first ever to be made – for showing 'the ripple of the leaves stirred by the wind.'[20] □

For Kracauer, it is cinema's capacity to capture physical reality that is the foundation of its artistic credentials. He affirms that 'films may claim aesthetic validity if they build from their basic properties; like photographs, that is, they must record and reveal physical reality'.[21] But he perceives a problem with such a claim: the widely-held view that films attain to the level of art to the extent to which they escape the constraints of physical reality, the extent to which they 'organize the raw material to which they resort into some self-sufficient composition instead of accepting it as an element in its own right'. Such a view means that 'artistic qualities must be attributed precisely to films which neglect the medium's recording obligations in an attempt to rival achievements in the fields of the fine arts, the theater, or literature', and 'tends to obscure the aesthetic value of films which are really true to the medium'.[22] The concept of art as the organisation of reality into self-sufficient compositions 'does not, and cannot, cover truly "cinematic" films – films, that is, which incorporate aspects of physical reality with a view to making us experience them. And yet it is they, not the films reminiscent of traditional art works, which are valid aesthetically. If film is an art at all, it certainly should not be confused with the established arts ... [E]ven the most creative film maker is much less independent of nature in the raw than the painter or poet; [the film-maker's] creativity manifests itself in letting nature in and penetrating it.'[23]

The function of film is to let nature in and penetrate it. If this dependence on nature is constricting in one way, preventing the film from escaping into the self-sufficient autonomy of the traditional work of art, in another sense it opens an enormous prospect: the 'hunting ground of the motion picture camera is in principle unlimited; it is the external world expanding in all directions'. Despite this potential, however, there are 'certain subjects within that world which may be termed "cinematic" because they seem to exert a peculiar attraction on the medium. It is as if the medium were predestined (and eager) to exhibit them.'[24]

Kracauer divides these 'cinematic subjects' into two categories: recording functions and revealing functions. The recording functions of film encompass movement and inanimate objects. Only film can record all kinds of movements, and there are three kinds of movement that are especially cinematic: the chase, a 'complex of interrelated movements' that 'is motion at its extreme, one might almost say, motion as such';[25] dancing, not the staged sort, but of the sort that seems to emerge from, or move into, the flow of real-life events; and what Kracauer calls 'nascent motion',[26] in which movement is contrasted with motionlessness, for example by suddenly freezing the frame and then restarting it.

The other recording function of film is its capacity to focus on inanimate objects and make them bearers of significance. 'In using its freedom to bring the inanimate to the fore and make it a carrier of action, film only protests its peculiar requirement to explore all of physical existence, human or nonhuman.'[27] The inanimate can almost become an actor in the drama:

■ From the malicious escalators, the unruly Murphy beds, and the mad automobiles in silent comedy to the cruiser Potemkin, the oil derrick in *Louisiana Story* (1948) and the dilapidated kitchen in *Umberto D* (1952), a long procession of unforgettable objects has passed across the screen – objects which stand out as protagonists and all but overshadow the rest of the cast [A 'Murphy bed' is a name given to various types of folding bed developed from an original design by the American manufacturer William Lawrence Murphy (1876–1959).] ... Or remember the powerful presence of environmental influences in *The Grapes of Wrath* (1940); the part played by nocturnal Coney Island in *Little Fugitive* (1953); the interaction between the marshland and the guerrilla fighters in the last episode of *Paisà* (1946).[28] □

The two recording functions of cinema, then, are the rendering of movement and of the inanimate. The revealing functions of cinema are three in number: 'things normally unseen'; 'phenomena overwhelming consciousness'; and 'special modes of reality'. Things normally unseen – the 'many material phenomena which elude observation under normal circumstances'[29] – fall into three groups. The first group encompasses both the very small, that cannot be seen by the naked eye, and the very large; in cinema, the close-up makes the very small visually accessible to the audience, and a combination of shots of varying distances can convey the very big: vast vistas of landscape and cityscape, and also that new and disturbing large-scale phenomenon that emerged in the nineteenth century – the mass, the agglomeration of people, that the traditional arts cannot take in. The new medium of photography can 'portray crowds as the accidental agglomerations they are', but 'only film, the fulfilment of photography in a sense, [is] equal to the task of capturing them in motion'.[30]

Kracauer's second group of 'things normally unseen' consists of the transient. Firstly, these are fleeting impressions like the shadow of a cloud or a leaf borne off by the wind, which are visible to the naked eye but which film is particularly able to capture. 'The motion picture camera seems to be partial to the least permanent components of our environment.' Secondly, there are those processes so fleeting that neither the naked eye nor the movie camera could capture them without the aid of two cinematic techniques: 'accelerated-motion, which condenses extremely slow and, hence, unobservable developments, such as the growth of plants, and slow-motion, which expands movements too fast to be registered',[31] like racing legs. Kracauer sees slow-motion shots as the equivalent in time to close-ups; 'they are, so to speak, temporal close-ups achieving in time what the close-up proper is achieving in space'.[32]

The third and final group of 'things normally unseen' posited by Kracauer are those concealed by the blind spots of the mind produced by habit and prejudice. This third group can itself be further subdivided into three: unconventional complexes, refuse, and the familiar. The term 'complex' is used by Kracauer in a visual sense, to denote the relationships between the parts of a visual perception, and the figure–ground relationship:

■ Imagine a man in a room: accustomed as we are to vizualize the human figure as a whole, it would take us an enormous effort to perceive instead of the whole man a pictorial unit consisting, say, of his right shoulder and arm, fragments of furniture and a section of the wall. But this is exactly what photography and, more powerfully, film may make us see. The motion picture camera has a way of disintegrating familiar objects and bringing to the fore – often just in moving about – previously invisible interrelationships between parts of them. These newly arising complexes lurk behind the things known and cut across their easily identifiable contexts. *Jazz Dance* (1954), for instance, abounds with shots of ensembles built from human torsos, clothes, scattered legs and what not – shapes which are almost anonymous. In rendering physical existence, film tends to reveal configurations of semi-abstract phenomena.[33] □

As well as revealing unconventional complexes, film can also reveal refuse: 'Most people turn their backs on garbage cans, the dirt underfoot, the waste they leave behind. Films have no such inhibitions; on the contrary, what we ordinarily prefer to ignore proves attractive to them precisely because of this common neglect.'[34]

The third subdivision of things that are concealed by the blind spots of the mind are familiar things, things that we take for granted. 'Intimate faces, streets we walk day by day, the house we live in – all these things are part of us like our skin, and because we know them by heart we do not know them with the eye.' Kracauer does not use the Russian Formalist term 'defamiliarisation', which was discussed in relation to Balázs in chapter one of this Critical History (see pp. 34–5); but his view of the way in which films 'alienate our environment in exposing it'[35] is very close to defamiliarisation. Unusual camera angles play a significant role in making the familiar strange. Such alienation can also operate retrospectively, making the audience aware of the oddness of an environment they once took for granted:

- The confrontation with objects which are familiar to us for having been part and parcel of our early life is particularly stirring. Hence the peculiar, often traumatic effect of films resuscitating that period. It need not be the period of our own childhood, for in the child real experiences mingle indiscriminately with imagined ones based on picture books and grandmother tales. Such retrospects as *The Golden Twenties*, *50 Years Before Your Eyes*, and *Paris 1900* – documentaries of 1950 assembled from authentic newsreels, contemporary feature films, and photographs – explore patterns of custom and fashion which we once accepted unquestioningly. Now that they resume life on the screen, the spectator cannot help laughing at the ridiculous hats, overstuffed rooms, and obtrusive gestures impressed upon him by the veracious camera. As he laughs at them, however, he is bound to realize, shudderingly, that he has been spirited away into the lumber room of his private self. He himself has dwelt, without knowing it, in those interiors; he himself has blindly adopted conventions which now seem naïve or cramped to him. In a flash the camera exposes the paraphernalia of our former existence, stripping them of the significance which originally transfigured them so that they changed from things in their own right into invisible conduits.[36] □

Reinforcing his view that film is fundamentally concerned with the capture of physical reality, Kracauer draws a contrast between paintings and film images. The latter can strip the significance from 'the paraphernalia of our former existence' because of 'their emphatic concern with raw material not yet consumed':

- The thrill of these old films is that they bring us face to face with the inchoate [unformed], cocoon-like world whence we come – all the objects, or rather sediments of objects, that were our companions in a pupa state. The most familiar, that which continues to condition our involuntary reactions and spontaneous impulses, is thus made to appear as the most alien.[37] □

Things normally unseen, encompassing the big and the small, the transient, and those unconventional visual complexes, refuse items and familiar things to which we are normally blind, form one category of the revealing function of film. The second category is 'phenomena over-whelming consciousness' such as '[e]lemental catastrophes, the atrocities of war, acts of violence and terror, sexual debauchery, and death', all of which 'call forth excitements and agonies bound to thwart detached observation'. All are 'manifestations of crude nature, human or other-wise', that 'fall into the area of physical reality' and thus belong among the cinematic subjects; moreover, '[o]nly the camera is able to represent them without distortion'. Indeed, film 'has always shown a predilection for events of this type'.[38]

This might seem to confirm a common criticism of cinema: that it panders to the desire for cheap sensation. While Kracauer does not deny that the cinema provides the kind of sensational spectacles that, in his view, people have always craved – in the gladiatorial combats of ancient Rome, for example – he contends that 'the cinema does not simply imitate and continue [such spectacles] but adds something new and momen-tous: it insists on making visible what is commonly drowned in inner agitation ... ... [t]he cinema ... aims at transforming the agitated witness into a conscious observer. Nothing could be more legitimate than its lack of inhibitions in picturing spectacles which upset the mind.'[39] Cinematic sensation is not numbing; on the contrary, it makes us more aware of the forces of reality and the drives of human and inanimate nature.

The third category of the revealing function of film is what Kracauer calls 'special modes of reality', that is, 'physical reality as it appears to individuals in extreme states of mind'. Such states of mind may be pro-duced by 'phenomena overwhelming consciousness', by 'mental distur-bances', or by 'any other external or internal causes'. Film reveals such 'special modes of reality' by presenting the images that a person or per-sons in an extreme state of mind will form of a particular physical event or phenomenon: such images 'are distorted from the viewpoint of a detached observer' and 'differ from each other according to the varying states of mind in which they originate'.[40] Kracauer gives an example from Eisenstein of film's capacity to reveal a special mode of reality – the presentation of reality distorted by an extreme state of mind:

■ In [an episode from] his *October* ... Eisenstein composes a physical universe reflecting exultation ... At the beginning of the October Revolution, worker delegates succeed in bringing a contingent of Cossacks over to their side ... the two groups boisterously fraternize in a state of euphoria. The ensuing dance scene is represented in the form of an accelerated montage sequence which pictures the world as experienced by the overjoyed. In their great joy, dancers and onlookers who constantly mingle cannot help perceiving incoherent pieces of their immediate environment in motion. It is a whirling agglomerate of fragments that surrounds them. And Eisenstein captures this jumble to perfection by having follow each other – in a succession which becomes ever faster with the growing ecstasy – shots of Cossack boots executing the *krakoviak* [a whirling, stamping folk dance, the name of which derives from Kracow (Cracow), a city and region in southern Poland], worker legs dancing through a puddle, clapping hands, and faces inordinately broadened by laughter.[41] ☐

For Kracauer, then, film can record and reveal reality in a range of important ways, and it is only in doing so – in 'concentrating on actual physical existence'[42] – that it conforms to the cinematic approach.

Kracauer identifies four affinities shared by photography and film, and each of the four is an aspect of the relationship to physical reality of the two media. Both film and photography have the 'ability to reproduce, indiscriminately, all kinds of visible data', but film 'gravitates towards unstaged reality'; 'the artificiality of stagy settings or compositions runs counter to the medium's declared preference for nature in the raw'.[43] Staging is not wholly ruled out, however; it is 'aesthetically legitimate to the extent that it evokes the illusion of actuality'. In other words, staging is artistically acceptable to the extent that it conceals its staginess. But while 'anything stagy is uncinematic if it passes over the basic properties of the medium',[44] there are at least two categories in which 'the uncinematic effect of staginess is mitigated'. One category comprises 'all the films which, from *The Cabinet of Dr Caligari* (1919) to the Japanese *Gate of Hell* (1953), are palpably patterned on paintings'.[45] While these have a clearly artificial, 'stagy' quality, they exhibit that interplay between stillness and movement that links them with one of the subjects of the recording functions of cinema that Kracauer has earlier identified: 'nascent motion' (see p. 77 above). In films patterned on paintings, the stasis of painting turns into movement, but the painted image, like the freeze-frame, remains as a memory and possibility, creating a sense of motion and stillness side-by-side.

The second case in which staginess may be mitigated is when the 'technical execution [of a film] testifies to a sense of the medium'.[46] Kracauer gives Laurence Olivier's *Hamlet* (1948) as an example: in that film, the continually moving camera shows a sense of the cinema medium despite the staginess of the sets, although this creates a disjunction between the cinematic and 'stagy' aspects of the production.

A second affinity that film and still photography share is for the fortuitous, for what happens by chance. Accident replaces destiny: this contingency is the basis of slapstick film comedy. The close relationship that chance has with film and photography is especially evident in their predilection for public spaces where unexpected patterns and events can always arise:

■ The affinity of film for haphazard contingencies is most strikingly demonstrated by its unwavering susceptibility to the 'street' – a term designed to cover not only the street, particularly the city street, in the literal sense, but also its various extensions, such as railway stations, dance and assembly halls, bars, hotel lobbies, airports, etc. If the medium's descent from, and kinship with, photography needed additional confirmation, this very specific preference, common to both of them, would supply it … [T]he street … is … a region where the accidental prevails over the providential, and happenings in the nature of unexpected incidents are all but the rule.[47] □

To the fortuitous and the unstaged, Kracauer adds a third affinity of film and photography – for endlessness. In principle, there is no point at which the still or movie camera's coverage need terminate: 'it is as if [film] were animated by the chimerical desire to establish the continuum of physical existence'.[48] Of course this desire is chimerical, that is, it can never be realised practically. It is thus necessary for a film-maker to employ technical devices like the fade-in, the fade-out and the lap-dissolve 'to mark the necessary breaks in the representation of the continuum and/or smoothly to connect different sections of it'.[49]

Kracauer identifies five 'routes of passage' through the continuum of physical existence. The first route of passage is that films may appear to 'cover vast expanses of physical reality', as in travelogues or feature films that involve travel and give the audience the sense of being transported to distant places; films can also suggest such expanses – demonstrate the 'solidarity of the universe' – 'by showing phenomena in different places successively in a time sequence', as in chases, 'or by creating the impression that these phenomena offer themselves to view at one and the same moment'. In the latter case, editing can enable the audience 'to witness widely scattered events [as if they were taking place] simultaneously so that [it] gets the feeling of being omnipresent'.[50]

A second route of passage that a film may take through the continuum of physical reality is to 'follow the chain of causes and effects responsible for some event'.[51] Such an emphasis on cause-and-effect may seem to contradict the predilection of film for the fortuitous that Kracauer has earlier discussed; he maintains, however, that the two go well together: the fortuitous can function as a cause and assume its place in the chain. He gives an example:

■ D.W. Griffith insists on detailing, in his last-minute-rescue episodes, all the factors which obstruct or facilitate the rescuers' heroic enterprise. Collisions and interventions, trains missed or jumped, horses on highways and legs negotiating [ice] floes – everything that contributes, in one sense or another, toward the final result is exposed to scrutiny.[52] □

As well as following the unfolding of the cause-and-effect chain in a forward direction, films may also seek to reconstruct it retrospectively, starting from the final result and trying to represent what led up to it, as in *Citizen Kane* or *Rashomon* (1950). Neither *Kane* nor *Rashomon* produces a definitive chain of cause-and-effect that accounts for the result with which it begins; both films provide a number of possible versions of such a chain, but none is conclusive. In this way, Kracauer suggests, they try to 'impress upon us the inexhaustibility of the causal continuum'. They suggest 'causal endlessness', as the first route of passage suggested 'geographical ... endlessness'.[53]

There is a third route of passage that a film can follow through the continuum of physical existence: it can 'caress one single object long enough to make us imagine its unlimited aspects'.[54] Kracauer gives an example from the film *The Titan: The Story of Michelangelo* (1939; American release, 1950), directed by Curt Oertel (1890–1960):

■ Under constantly changing light conditions the camera repeatedly pans or travels at close range over the limbs and the torso of some statue, deriving from the identical original an abundance of two-dimensional patterns. No matter to what extent these patterns still bear on the statue they explore, they are cinematic in as much as they tend to immerse us in the infinity of shapes that lie dormant in any given one.[55] □

This route is rarely used, however, as it provides less possibility of dramatic action than the geographical or causal routes.

A film may take a fourth route through the continuum of physical reality by evoking 'the innumerable experiences which an individual is likely to undergo in a single crucial moment of his life'.[56] Like many instances of causal relationships, this route involves material reality but is not confined to it. The example that Kracauer gives is one that has already been cited in chapter one of this Critical History (p. 58) – Eisenstein's 'montage lists' for an interior monologue, in his planned film adaptation of *An American Tragedy*, that would convey the agitation of Clyde Barrow's mind as he gets ready to drown his pregnant girlfriend. Kracauer remarks:

■ The monologue, as Eisenstein outlined it, clearly exceeds the framework of the story, however generous the allowance made for it; it even exceeds Clyde's own being; what it tends to convey instead is the endless series of circumstances and sensations which close in on Clyde at this particular moment ... ... The true material ... is not merely life in the dimension of articulate meanings but life underneath – a texture of impressions and expressions which reaches deep into physical existence.[57] □

It can be seen how Eisenstein's 'montage lists', as reinterpreted by Kracauer, exemplify the latter's fourth pathway through physical reality, a pathway that entails evoking 'the innumerable experiences which an individual is likely to undergo in a single crucial moment of his life'. But it should be observed that Kracauer's example is from notes for a film that was never made, and that he gives no other example of this route of passage. He does not say, however, that it is rarely used, as he does of the third route ('caressing' an object). It would be an interesting exercise to try to think of actual films that would exemplify this fourth route.

The fifth and final track through the continuum of physical reality is by means of the representation of 'an indefinite number of material phenomena – e.g. waves, machine parts, trees, and what not – in such a way that their forms, movements, and light values jell into comprehensible rhythmical patterns'[58] – as in the *avant-garde* work of Germaine Dulac (1882–1942) that aspired to a pure cinema in which films were visual equivalents of musical compositions.

These five routes of passage constitute the ways in which film represents the endlessness of physical reality. To the affinities that film and photography have for endlessness and the unstaged, Kracauer then adds and elaborates on a third affinity: for the indeterminate. 'Natural objects ... are surrounded with a fringe of meanings liable to touch off various moods, emotions, runs of inarticulate thoughts; in other words, they have a theoretically unlimited number of psychological and mental correspondences.' The converse is also the case: it is 'not only ... objects which function as stimuli; psychological events also form nuclei, and of course they on their part have physical correspondences'.[59] Kracauer terms all of these correspondences 'psychophysical correspondences', comprising 'all these more or less fluid interrelations between the physical world and the psychological dimension in the broadest sense of the word – a dimension which borders on that physical universe and is still intimately connected with it'.[60]

The indeterminacy of natural objects – their capacity 'to touch off ... a theoretically unlimited number of psychological and mental correspondences' – poses a problem for the film-maker, at least in terms of Kracauer's ontology of film. On the one hand, the film-maker wants 'to exhibit and penetrate physical reality for its own sake' and thus to retain the multiple meanings of shots, their capacity to release their psychological correspondences; on the other hand, he wants 'to advance the action [of the film] by assigning to each shot a meaning relevant to the plot'. Kracauer acknowledges that these 'two obligations ... seem to be difficult to reconcile',[61] but nonetheless affirms 'a basic editing principle: any film narrative should be edited in such a manner that it does not simply confine itself to implementing the intrigue but also turns away from it toward the objects represented so that they may appear in their suggestive indeterminacy'.[62]

After indeterminacy, which is the fourth affinity shared by film and photography, Kracauer moves to a fifth affinity that only film can have, since still photography cannot convey life in motion. This affinity is for 'the "flow of life"', which Kracauer defines as 'the stream of material situations and happenings with all that they intimate in terms of emotions, values, thoughts'. This might sound rather like the 'stream of consciousness' as defined by the psychologist William James (1842–1910) and applied by literary criticism to some of the work of James Joyce and Virginia Woolf (1882–1941); but Kracauer gives priority in his phrasing to 'material situations' rather than 'consciousness' ('emotions, values, thoughts'), and, in accordance with his ontology of film, he goes on to suggest that 'the flow of life is predominantly a material rather than a mental continuum, even though, by definition, it extends into the mental dimension'.[63]

As the street epitomised the affinity of the film for the fortuitous, so it demonstrates the affinity of film for the flow of life:

■ The street in the extended sense of the word is not only the arena of fleeting impressions and chance encounters but a place where the flow of life is bound to assert itself ... [In] the city street with its ever-moving anonymous crowds[,] the kaleidoscopic sights mingle with unidentified shapes and fragmentary visual complexes and cancel each other out, thereby preventing the onlooker from following up any of the innumerable suggestions they offer. What appears to him are not so much sharp-contoured individuals engaged in this or that definable pursuit as loose throngs of sketchy, completely indeterminate figures. Each has a story, yet the story is not given. Instead an incessant flow of possibilities and near-intangible meanings appears ... life eternally dissolv[es] the patterns which it is about to form.[64] □

The stage may seem at the opposite pole to the street and to the flow of life that it epitomises. Moreover, Kracauer has identified the affinity for the unstaged as the first of the inherent affinities that film and photography share. But, as he acknowledges, 'stage interludes' occur in many kinds of film and are especially evident in the musical. Do these interludes depart from the medium of film? Not necessarily: Kracauer contends that '[s]tage interludes within otherwise realistic films assume a cinematic function to the extent that they throw into relief the flow of life from which they detach themselves'. Although 'the stagy [is] normally against the grain of the medium', it 'assumes a positive aesthetic function if it is made to enhance the unstaged'.[65]

Film's five inherent affinities are for the unstaged, the fortuitous, endlessness, the indeterminate, and the flow of life – all elements of the physical reality in which we are immersed. But what of those films that explore other fields, especially those of history and fantasy? Surely historical dramas betray their 'inevitable staginess' and seal themselves off from 'the space-time continuum of the living' into a finite capsule, and thus fail to respect two of the five fundamental affinities of cinema, for the unstaged and for endlessness?

The historical film may try to mitigate its staginess and finiteness by 'shift[ing] the emphasis from history proper to camera-reality',[66] 'imbuing history with camera-life';[67] it can include episodes which, allowing for differences in costume, 'almost look like camera penetrations of present-day reality (which in part they are ...)'.[68] A relatively recent example would be the battle scenes in Kenneth Branagh's version of Shakespeare's *Henry V* (1989), especially when compared to those in Laurence Olivier's *Henry V* (1944). Olivier's battle scenes, mainly in medium and long shot, are deliberately theatrical and stylised, punctuated by the astounding visual and aural effect of the flight of arrows loosed by the English archers at Agincourt; the scenes in the Branagh film employ close-ups and a graphic realism in their portrayals of combat, violence and death that make the viewer feel almost as if s/he were watching a news broadcast, complete with a slow-motion replay, from the battlefield. The opposite approach to 'imbuing history with cameralife' is to aim to portray 'the modes of being peculiar to some historical era',[69] for instance in Carl Dreyer's *Day of Wrath* (1943), which seeks to create a sense of a comparatively static medieval cosmos through its painterly composition of scenes; it can thus be cinematic insofar as it suggests nascent movement and attains a cinematic effect of authenticity.

What of fantasy? By 'fantasy', Kracauer means 'all predominantly visual experiences, avowedly imagined or believed to be true in fact, which belong to worlds beyond camera-reality proper – the supernatural, visions of any kind, poetic imagery, hallucinations, dreams, etc.'.[70] In contrast to history, fantasy may emerge in the present and mingle with immediate physical reality; but it is still not the same as that physical reality which, according to Kracauer, it is the peculiar property of the cinema to render. In assessing how far screen fantasy is true to the fundamental property of cinema, Kracauer identifies two issues: a 'technical' issue, about whether 'fantasy is established ... in a stagy manner; with the aid of specifically cinematic devices; or in the material of physical reality itself'; and a 'relational' issue, about 'the relations of fantasy to physical reality'[71] within specific films. The interplay of these two aspects determines the degree to which screen fantasies are cinematic or otherwise.

On the 'technical' level, 'stagy' fantasy, constructed by such elements as 'bizarre settings, contrived accessories, unusual make-up', may have two kinds of relationships with physical reality in films. It may claim 'the same aesthetic legitimacy as actuality', and imply that 'nature has no title to preferential treatment';[72] or it may be assigned a lesser role than camera-reality by being treated as a stage interlude or sent up. Given Kracauer's basic premise that film's primary characteristic is its capacity to capture and convey physical reality, it is the latter relationship, which subordinates stagy fantasy to the physical, that is truer to the nature of film as a medium. Fantasy that, on a 'technical' level, is established by cinematic devices – negatives, one-turn-one-picture techniques, multiple exposures, superimpositions, distorting mirrors – can also have two kinds of relationships, one of equality or even implicit superiority, and one of subordination, in which fantasy functions to high-light material life.

The third 'technical' way in which fantasy may be established in film is by implying it through a rendering of physical reality. As an example of this approach, Kracauer quotes a statement made by the director Carl Dreyer, when working on his film *Vampyr* (1932):

- Imagine that we are sitting in an ordinary room. Suddenly we are told that there is a corpse behind the door. In an instant the room we are sitting in is completely altered: everything in it has taken on another look; the light, the atmosphere have changed, though they are physically the same. This is because *we* have changed, and the objects *are* as we conceive them.[73] □

Fantasies of this kind grow more remote from camera-reality the more they move away from the physical world and use images of that world to corroborate fantasy. 'The more they pretend to otherworldliness, the less will their underlying intention be in keeping with their truth to camera-reality.' Films whose plots 'take the existence of the supernatural more or less for granted' suffer in 'cinematic quality' because 'they picture physical data for a purpose reducing the data's significance';[74] Kracauer gives *Vampyr* and *The Fall of the House of Usher* (1928), directed by Jean Epstein (1897–1953), as examples:

- Instead of being free to get immersed in the images of the tree trunks, the mists, and the toads, the spectator must from the outset conceive of them as tokens of the supernatural. The task, imposed upon these realistic images, of making the unreal seem real, gives them actually the appearance of something unreal.[75] □

Kracauer then turns to the function of the actor within cinema. Once again, his key criterion is fidelity to a cinematic medium primarily characterised in terms of its affinity to physical and quotidian reality.

- The film actor's performance ... is true to the [cinematic] medium only if it does not assume the airs of a self-sufficient achievement but impresses us as an incident – one of many possible incidents – of his character's unstaged material existence. Only then is the life he renders truly cinematic[76] ... ... The cinema ... is not exclusively human. Its subject matter is the infinite flux of visible phenomena – those ever-changing patterns of physical existence whose flow may include human manifestations but need not climax in them.

In consequence, the film actor is not necessarily the hub of the narrative, the carrier of all its meanings. Cinematic action is always likely to pass through regions which, should they contain human beings at all, yet involve them only in an accessory, unspecified way.[77] □

Kracauer then turns from the actor to the issue of sound. Given his emphasis on 'camera-reality', the reality conveyed in pictures that move, it is not surprising that he maintains that sound must be subordinate to the visual image:

■ For sound films to be true to the basic aesthetic principle, their significant communications must originate with their pictures[78]... ... All the successful attempts at an integration of the spoken word ... play down dialogue with a view to reinstating the visuals ... ... [T]he [cinematic] medium calls for verbal statements which grow out of the flow of pictorial communications instead of determining their course.[79] □

The 'reality character' of cinema is also crucial to Kracauer's analysis of the film spectator. Film works first of all on the body: 'film images affect primarily the spectator's senses, engaging him physiologically before he is in a position to respond intellectually'. Kracauer enumerates three key aspects of cinema that contribute to its capacity to engage the body and displace the intellect: 'film records physical reality for its own sake'; 'in keeping with its recording obligations, film renders the world in motion'; and 'film not only records physical reality but reveals otherwise hidden provinces of it'.[80] These three key elements of cinema encourage 'organic tensions, nameless excitements' in the spectator, and dislodge the ego from its controlling role: 'the self as the mainspring of thoughts and decisions relinquishes its power of control'.[81] Kracauer comes up with two major comparisons for the spectator whose self has lost control in this way: the first is the 'hypnotized person',[82] in whom the screen has induced a 'trance-like condition'; and the second is the dreamer, perhaps in the 'stage between waking and sleeping which favours hypnagogic fantasies'.[83]

Kracauer develops the comparison between the film spectator and the dreamer by exploring the elements of film that 'may be sufficiently

dream-like to launch the audience into reveries and perhaps even influence their course'. He first discusses the 'manufactured dreams' prof-
fered by popular films: 'To the extent that films are mass entertainment
they are bound to cater for the alleged desires and daydreams of the
public at large.'[84] It is interesting to note that Kracauer slides here from
suggesting that the film spectator may be in a state akin to that on the
edge of sleep in which hypnagogic images occur, to seeing him/her as a
daydreamer. But the daydreams offered by films are based only on
assumptions and inferences about what the film public wants: 'Each
popular film conforms to popular wants; yet in conforming to them it
inevitably does away with their inherent ambiguity ... Through their very
definiteness films thus define the nature of the inarticulate from which
they emerge.'[85] The dreamlike elements of popular films designed to
satisfy supposed mass daydreams do away with ambiguity and thus, in
a sense, constrict cinema's potential to set its spectators dreaming.
Moreover, such films provide daydreams more on the level of 'intrigue'
than of image.

But there is another way in which films can resemble dreams – and
in defining this, Kracauer is able to bring his definition of the film spectator as a dreamer into line with his emphasis on cinema's capacity to
capture physical reality. Film is most dreamlike, he suggests, not when it
presents clearly signalled dream sequences in which reality is distorted,
but when it focuses on physical, everyday reality. He gives the example
of the 'documentary shots of Harlem houses and streets' in *The Quiet
One* (1949), a film by Sidney Meyer (1906–69):[86]

- Women are standing, all but motionless, in house doors, and non-
descript characters are seen loitering about. Along with the dingy
facades, they might as well be products of our imagination, as kindled
by the narrative. To be sure, this is an intended effect, but it is brought
about by a clear-cut recording of stark reality. Perhaps films look
most like dreams when they overwhelm us with the crude and
unnegotiated presence of natural objects – as if the camera had just
now extricated them from the womb of physical existence and as if
the umbilical cord between image and actuality had not yet been sev-
ered. There is something in the abrupt immediacy and shocking
veracity of such pictures that justifies their identification as dream
images.[87] □

Kracauer's determination to assimilate dreamlike elements in film to his fundamental definition of cinema seems strained here. It exemplifies a dubious kind of thinking in which an apparent opposite is turned into a likeness, a potential contradiction into a confirmation.

Kracauer suggests that there are two directions of dreaming. One is 'toward the object':

■ Released from the control of consciousness, the spectator cannot help feeling attracted by the phenomena in front of him. They beckon him to come nearer. They arouse, as Lucien Sève puts it, disquiet rather than certainty in the spectator and thus prompt him to embark on an inquiry into the being of the objects they record, an inquiry which does not aim at explaining them but tries to elucidate their secrets.[88] So he drifts toward and into the objects … … Yet the spectator cannot hope to apprehend, however incompletely, the being of any object that draws him into its orbit unless he meanders, dreamingly, through the maze of its multiple meanings and psychological correspondences. Material existence, as it manifests itself in film, launches the moviegoer into unending pursuits … Does the spectator ever succeed in exhausting the objects he contemplates? There is no end to his wanderings. Sometimes, though, it may seem to him that, after having probed a thousand possibilities, he is listening, with all his senses strained, to a confused murmur. Images begin to sound, and the sounds are again images. When this indeterminate murmur – the murmur of existence – reaches him, he may be nearest to the unattainable goal.[89] □

This direction of dreaming brings the spectator closer to the reality of objects and indeed of existence, in a more generalised sense, in itself. The other direction of dreaming is driven by 'psychological influences':[90]

■ Once the spectator's organized self has surrendered, his subconscious or unconscious experiences, apprehensions and hopes tend to come out and take over. Owing to their indeterminacy, film shots are particularly fit to function as an ignition spark. Any such shot may touch off chain reactions in the moviegoer – a flight of associations which no longer revolve around their original source but arise from his agitated inner environment. This movement leads the spectator away from the given image into subjective reveries; the image itself recedes after it has mobilized his previously repressed fears or induced him to revel in a prospective wish-fulfilment.[91] □

The two directions of dreaming, towards the object and into the mind, may seem opposites but are inseparably interrelated in practice:

■ Trance-like immersion in a shot or a succession of shots may at any moment yield to daydreaming which increasingly disengages itself from the imagery occasioning it. Whenever this happens, the dreaming spectator, who originally concentrated on the psychological correspondences of an image striking his imagination more or less imperceptibly, moves on from them to notions beyond the orbit of that image – notions so remote from what the image itself implies that there would be no meaning in still counting them among its correspondences proper. Conversely, because of his continued exposure to the radiations from the screen, the absentee dreamer can be expected again and again to succumb to the spell of the images he left behind and to persevere in their exploration. He is wavering between self-absorption and self-abandonment.

Together the two intertwined dream processes constitute a veritable stream of consciousness whose contents – cataracts of indistinct fantasies and inchoate thoughts – still bear the imprint of the bodily sensations from which they issue. This stream of consciousness in a measure parallels the 'flow of life', one of the main concerns of the medium. Consequently, films featuring that flow are most likely to initiate both movements of dreaming.[92] □

Kracauer moves on to consider the question of the gratifications that film offers – and, given his basic premise, it is not surprising that he finds the primary gratification that it provides to be in terms of its reality character: 'there is a widespread hunger for "life" and … film is uniquely equipped to satisfy it'.[93] Film is less a substitute for reality than a means of providing the reality that is lacking in 'the real world' itself:

■ [T]he inveterate moviegoer seems to suffer from alienation, from loneliness [but] he does not feel he is being suppressed or rejected by society. Rather, he traces his suffering to an isolation due not only to his lack of sufficient and satisfactory human relationships but to his being out of touch with the breathing world about him, that stream of things and events which, were it flowing through him, would render his existence more exciting and significant. He misses 'life'. And he is attracted by the cinema because it gives him the illusion of vicariously partaking of life in its fullness.[94] □

Cinema vicariously reconnects the isolated film spectator with life, and also gratifies a desire for child-like omnipotence in an increasingly complicated and confusing world:

■ The world has grown so complex, politically and otherwise, that it can no longer be simplified. Any effect seems separated from its manifold possible causes; any attempt at a synthesis, a unifying image, falls short. Hence a widespread feeling of impotence in the face of influences become uncontrollable for eluding definition. No doubt many among us suffer, consciously or not, from being exposed, helplessly, to these influences. So we look for compensations. And film, it appears, is apt to afford temporary relief. In the cinema 'one grasps all of it'.[95] □

From his analysis of the film spectator, Kracauer goes on to consider film types, which he divides into two broad categories: story film and non-story film. He investigates the hypothesis that 'story telling runs counter to the cinematic approach';[96] if this is true, non-story film, which includes most experimental films and all varieties of the film of fact, should come closer to the cinematic approach than story film. But this is not quite the case; Kracauer sums up his conclusions about the two kinds of non-story film in this way:

■ (1) The experimental film gravitates toward achievements which ... shun story telling but do so with little regard for the affinities of the medium. They omit camera-reality. Whether abstract compositions or projections of dream life, they are not so much films as an extension of contemporary painting or of literary designs. They abolish the story principle only to enthrone instead the art principle. Perhaps Art gains by this *coup d'état*. The cinema does not, or, if it does, only by indirection. (2) The film of fact in the form of the film on [visual] art is likewise a problematic hybrid as long as it is patterned on the experimental film. But [films on art] may well acquire a cinematic quality if they assume the character of regular documentaries, with the works of art being embedded in real-life processes. (3) There remains documentary itself, the main genre of the film of fact ... all such documentaries as show concern for the visible world live up to the spirit of the medium. They channel their messages through the given natural material instead of using the visuals merely as a padding. Moreover, relieved from the burden of advancing an intrigue, they are free to explore the continuum of physical existence. The suppression of the story enables the camera to follow, without constraint, a course of its own and record otherwise inaccessible phenomena.[97] □

This might seem to make the documentary the ideal film type, the type that is closest to the fundamental characteristics of the cinematic medium. But there is a drawback: '[c]onfined ... to the rendering of our environment', the documentary 'misses those aspects of potentially visible reality which only personal involvement is apt to summon. Their appearance is inseparable from human drama, as conveyed by an intrigue. The suppression of the story ... not only benefits documentary but puts it at a disadvantage also.' The result is that, '[p]aradoxically, the desire for story telling develops within a genre which repudiates the story as an uncinematic element'. 'On the one hand, the documentary maker eliminates the intrigue so as to be able to open his lens on the world; on the other, he feels urged to re-introduce dramatic action in the very same interest.'[98] Thus the 'demand for the story ... re-emerges within the womb of the non-story film'.[99] Kracauer is led to conclude that the hypothesis that 'story telling runs counter to the cinematic approach'[100] is 'too broad to cover all the relevant cases'.[101] A more qualified and discriminating proposition is that 'there are different types of stories, some of which, in keeping with that hypothesis, resist cinematic treatment, while others do prove responsive to it'.[102]

The theatrical story is the type of story that perhaps most resists cinematic treatment. There are several reasons for this. 'The theatrical story limits the appropriate use of a medium which does not differentiate between humans and inanimate objects[103] ... ... [T]he theatrical play is composed of units which represent a crude abbreviation of camera-life ... in cinematic terms, the theatrical story proceeds by way of "long shots".'[104] From a cinematic perspective, the patterns of meaning that the theatrical story offers 'give the impression of being prearranged because they assert themselves independently of the flow of visuals; instead of seeming to grow out of it ... they ... determine the direction of that flow, if flow it still is'.[105] In contrast to a 'truly cinematic story, the theatrical intrigue is detachable from the medium [of cinema] ... the imagery conveying it illustrates rather than releases its meanings'.[106] In a theatrical film, 'each image, instead of being established as a fragment of reality which may yield multiple meanings, must assume a meaning derived from contexts alien to the medium – contexts which gravitate toward an ideological center'.[107] Kracauer concludes that the 'theatrical story stems from formative aspirations which conflict irrevocably with the realistic tendency. Consequently, all attempts to adjust it to the cinema by extending its range into regions where the camera is at home result at best in some compromise of a sort.'[108]

Film and the novel are closer than film and the stage. '[I]n general, the differences between the formal properties of film and novel are only differences in degrees.'[109] But the crucial differences lie in the worlds that they embrace. Both 'feature the flow or stream of life'; but while life, 'as captured by the camera, is predominantly a material continuum', the 'world of the novel is primarily a mental continuum' that 'often includes components which elude the grasp of the cinema because they have no physical correspondences to speak of ... there is nothing in camera-reality that would refer to them'.[110] Therefore '[a]ny attempt to convert the mental continuum of the novel into camera-life appears to be hopelessly doomed'.[111] Due to this key difference, the novel 'is not a cinematic literary form'.[112] In fact, Kracauer concludes, there 'are no genuinely cinematic literary forms'.[113]

The film may tell a story, but it cannot tell it in the ways that a novel or short story or stage play may, and it is constantly threatened with distraction by the pressure of camera-reality:

■ The true film artist may be imagined as a man who sets out to tell a story but, in shooting it, is so overwhelmed by his innate desire to cover all of physical reality – and also by a feeling that he must cover it in order to tell the story, any story, in cinematic terms – that he ventures ever deeper into the jungle of material phenomena in which he risks becoming irretrievably lost if he does not, by virtue of great efforts, get back to the highways he has left.[114] □

In terms of content, Kracauer suggests that 'the screen attracts certain types of content, while being unresponsive to others'.[115] 'Uncinematic content' is content which cannot primarily be made known except by non-visual means. Two types of uncinematic content are especially clear: conceptual reasoning and the tragic. Conceptual reasoning cannot be properly represented pictorially, while tragedy works to cut out or claim for symbolic purposes all that seems contingent or superfluous. In these respects, tragedy is opposed to 'the camera's ingrained desire for indefinite rambling',[116] and tragedy's 'appropriation or ... elimination of the accidental is most certainly against the grain of the cinema'.[117]

Kracauer then turns to kinds of content – motifs, as he calls them – that are cinematic because 'they are identical with, or grow out of, one or another property of film'.[118] One of these is unique – the flow of life, which is 'the most general of all possible motifs', and which differs from the other cinematic motifs 'in that it is not only a motif' but 'corresponds to a basic affinity of film. In a manner of speaking it is an emanation of the medium itself.'[119] Other examples of cinematic motifs include sleuthing and the David–Goliath theme. Sleuthing entails close scrutiny of the material world, an openness to the accidental, a concern for the cause-and-effect continuum of physical reality, and a chase in one form or another. The David–Goliath theme is an enactment of the triumph of the small and supposedly weak over the large and supposedly strong, and finds its cinematic correlative in the close-up that turns the tiny into the huge.

In a deeply-felt epilogue to his exhaustive study, Kracauer poses what he calls 'the most central [issue] of all: what is the good of film experience?'. Kracauer sees the situation of humankind in the mid-twentieth century as characterised by two main features: the collapse of traditional structures of belief and an increased abstractness that estranges us from concrete reality. Traditional structures of belief cannot be re-established; but, released from their bonds into fragmentation, we can recover concrete reality by means of film:

- Film renders visible what we did not, or perhaps even could not, see before its advent. It effectively assists us in discovering the material world with its psychophysical correspondences. We literally redeem this world from its dormant state, its state of virtual nonexistence, by endeavoring to experience it through the camera. And we are free to experience it because we are fragmentized. The cinema can be defined as a medium particularly equipped to promote the redemption of physical reality. Its imagery permits us, for the first time, to take away with us the objects and occurrences that comprise the flow of material life.[120] □

To perform its redemptive function properly, however, film must resist the siren call of art. In its traditional modes such as painting, literature and the theatre, art does not really represent nature, but transforms it into a component of a supposedly autonomous work that expresses the intentions of its creator: 'the artist would cease to be one if he incorporated life in the raw, as rendered by the camera'.[121] Conversely, the film-maker ceases to be one if he seeks to transform life in the raw into an element of an artistic whole. 'The intrusion of Art into film thwarts the cinema's intrinsic possibilities.' Moreover, it promotes an idea of wholeness that the breakdown of traditional beliefs has rendered untenable. 'Art in film is reactionary because it symbolizes wholeness and thus pretends to the continued existence of beliefs which "cover" physical reality in both senses of the word.'[122] Truly cinematic film rejects this false holism but affirms an underlying continuity in its attention to reality and contingency:

- The small random moments which concern things common to you and me and the rest of mankind ... constitute the dimension of every-day life, this matrix of all other modes of reality. It is a very substantial dimension. If you disregard for a moment articulate beliefs, ideological objectives, special undertakings, and the like, there still remain the sorrows and satisfactions, discords and feasts, wants and pursuits, which mark the ordinary business of living. Products of habit and microscopic interaction, they form a resilient texture which changes slowly and survives wars, epidemics, earthquakes, and revolutions. Films tend to explore this texture of everyday life, whose composition varies according to place, people, and time. So they help us not only to appreciate our given material environment but to extend it in all directions. They virtually make the world our home.[123] □

Film's capacity to explore the texture of everyday life does not mean that it evades the monstrous. On the contrary, it can enable us to encounter it and survive. In ancient Greek legend, Perseus was able to avoid the direct force of the petrifying gaze of the Medusa, and behead her, by looking at her reflection in a shield that the goddess Athena had given him; Kracauer suggests, in a striking image, that the 'film screen is Athena's polished shield':[124]

- The mirror reflections of horror ... beckon the spectator to take them in and thus incorporate into his memory the real face of things too dreadful to be beheld in reality. In experiencing ... the litter of tortured human bodies in the films made of the Nazi concentration camps, we redeem horror from its invisibility behind the veils of panic and imagination. And this experience is liberating in as much as it removes a most powerful taboo. Perhaps Perseus' greatest achievement was not to cut off Medusa's head but to overcome his fears and look at its reflection in the shield. And was it not precisely this feat which permitted him to behead the monster?[125] □

Film thus provides reflections that enable the spectator to grapple with disturbing truths. It can also 'confront visible material reality with our notions of it'[126] in a confirmatory or contradictory way. Confirmatory confrontations tend to be propagandist, deploying reality to reinforce rather than to authenticate an idea – to make the spectator believe rather than see. Contradictory confrontations that challenge our notions of the physical world are much more interesting for Kracauer; they range from the comic scene in a silent film by Charlie Chaplin (1889–1977), *The Immigrant* (1917), in which a ship's passenger apparently being seasick is revealed, by a change of camera angle, to be fishing, to the dark scene in his *Monsieur Verdoux* (1947), in which an idyllic long shot of a landscape turns into a close-up of an imminent murder.

While these moments of reality 'are meaningful in their own right', film spectators 'do not confine [them]selves to absorbing them but feel stimulated to weave what they are telling us into contexts that bear on the whole of [their] existence'.[127] The moments of reality prompt ideological and metaphysical propositions. But films that are true to the cinematic medium do not start with such propositions and then illustrate them by means of images of the material world; rather, 'they set out to explore physical data and, taking their cue from them, work their way up to some problem or belief. The cinema is materialistically minded; it proceeds from "below" to "above" … … Guided by film … we approach, if at all, ideas no longer on highways leading through the void but on paths that wind through the thicket of things.'[128]

Citing Erich Auerbach's claim, in his magisterial study of the representation of reality in Western literature, *Mimesis* (1946), that the goal of 'a common life of mankind on earth … begins to be visible',[129] Kracauer finally suggests that 'the task of rendering visible mankind on its way toward this goal is reserved for the photographic media; they alone are in a position to record the material aspects of common daily life in many places'.[130] It is a large claim; and to exemplify it, Kracauer first selects, not a film, but a photographic exhibition, Edward Steichen's *The Family of Man*. By 1960, this was not the happiest of choices; for the exhibition had already suffered a razor attack from the French literary and cultural critic Roland Barthes, who had argued in an article included in his *Mythologies* (1957) that it exemplified the mystifying processes of bourgeois culture in its elision of the economic, social and cultural differences between the people that it represented.[131] Barthes's essay was a harbinger of the powerful post-structuralist and deconstructionist attack on representation that would gather force in the later 1960s and the 1970s, leaving Kracauer's *Theory of Film*, for all its richness and fascination, looking a little obsolete. At the start of the twenty-first century, it may seem even more obsolete insofar as Kracauer, like Bazin, founds his argument on the reality of the photographic image: such a basis surely dissolves with the shift from chemical to digital photography, in which still and moving images can be manipulated and generated independently of real-life referents.

While the importance of this shift is undeniable – it is part of the more general move from an analogue to a digital culture identified in the Introduction to this Critical History – it should not be exaggerated: the digital cannot wholly float free of the real. But the digital challenge to Kracauer, like the post-structuralist one, lay in the future. Even while he had been preparing *Theory of Film*, however, another theoretical approach had emerged that moved the emphasis from cinema's relationship with reality to its relationship with the *auteur*-directors who, it was claimed, stamped their distinctive styles on the films that they made. The next chapter of this History focuses on the birth of the *auteur* in the pages of *Cahiers du Cinéma*.

CHAPTER THREE

The Birth of the *Auteur*: *Cahiers du Cinéma*

There are certain moments in modern cultural and intellectual history when journals become especially important: the *Spectator* of Addison and Steele in eighteenth-century England, the great magazines of the mid-Victorian era such as the *Cornhill* and the *Fortnightly Review*, *Scrutiny* in 1930s Britain, *Partisan Review* in mid-twentieth-century America. In the history of film theory, *Cahiers du Cinéma* – literally meaning 'Cinema Exercise (or Note) books'[1] – has acquired a legendary importance, not only as a theoretical journal but also, as the previous chapter observed, because it provided the launching pad for critics who were later to become famous film directors of the French New Wave, especially Jean-Luc Godard and François Truffaut. Founded in 1951 by André Bazin and Jacques Doniol-Valcroze (1920–89), *Cahiers* was the midwife, in the 1950s, of the '*politique des auteurs*'; the 'policy of authors' that the American film critic Andrew Sarris dubbed '*auteur* theory'.[2]

As Jim Hillier has pointed out, ideas about the *auteur* did not originate with *Cahiers*; they can be found in earlier magazines such as the *Revue du Cinéma*, the Communist-sponsored *Écran Français*, and the Catholic journal *Esprit*, and also in a near-contemporary of *Cahiers*, the journal *Positif*, founded in 1952.[3] But *Cahiers* gave these ideas their strongest focus. The promotion of the idea of the director as an *auteur* – an artist who, like the author of a novel, stamps his distinctive vision and style on his works – went along with the elevation of Hollywood cinema as a form that demanded to be taken seriously, since its major products could be seen as the work of such *auteurs*. Jacques Rivette (born 1928) sums up these ideas in the title of an article first published in *Cahiers* no. 23 in May 1953, 'The Genius of Howard Hawks' – Hawks, a Hollywood director, is firmly endowed with genius. Like the literary critic F. R. Leavis (1895–1978), Rivette, in his opening paragraph, makes an ostensive appeal

Hawks's genius is *there*, and should be evident to the viewer who accepts the testimony of his own eyes:

- The evidence on the screen is the proof of Hawks's genius: you only have to watch *Monkey Business* (1952 [not to be confused with the Marx Brothers' 1931 film of the same title]) to know that it is a brilliant film. Some people refuse to admit this, however; they refuse to be satisfied by proof. There can't be any other reason why they don't recognize it.[4] □

In André Bazin's criticism of the *auteur* approach, an extract from which appears later in this chapter, this polemical opening is singled out as if it were the core of Rivette's argument (see pp. 126–7 below); but it is important to observe that Rivette moves on to an analysis that does provide reasons for seeing Hawks's work as a coherent whole, even if it does not wholly justify the opening claims for *Monkey Business*. Rivette identifies Hawks's overall theme as 'the intrusion of the inhuman, or the crudest avatar [incarnation] of humanity, into a highly civilized society':[5]

- Hawks's *oeuvre* is equally divided between comedies and dramas – a remarkable ambivalence. More remarkable still is his frequent fusing of the two elements so that each, rather than damaging the other, seems to underscore their reciprocal relation: the one sharpens the other. Comedy is never long absent from his most dramatic plots, and far from compromising the feeling of tragedy, it removes the comfort of fatalistic indulgence and keeps the events in a perilous kind of equilibrium, a stimulating uncertainty which only adds to the strength of the drama. Scarface's secretary [in *Scarface*] speaks comically garbled English, but that doesn't prevent his getting shot; our laughter all the way through *The Big Sleep* (1946) is inextricable from our foreboding of danger; the climax of *Red River* (1948), in which we are no longer sure of our own feelings, wondering whose side to take and whether we should be amused or afraid, sets our every nerve quivering with panic and gives us a dizzy, giddy feeling like that of a tightrope walker whose foot falters without quite slipping, a feeling as unbearable as the ending of a nightmare.

  While it is the comedy which gives Hawks's tragedy its effectiveness, the comedy cannot quite dispel (not the tragedy, let's not spoil our best arguments by going too far) the harsh feeling of an existence in which no action can undo itself from the web of responsibility.

Could we be offered a more bitter view of life than this? I have to confess that I am quite unable to join in the laughter of a packed theatre when I am riveted by the calculated twists of a fable (*Monkey Business*) which sets out – gaily, logically, and with an unholy abandon – to chronicle the fatal stages in the degradation of a superior mind.

It is no accident that similar groups of intellectuals turn up in both *Ball of Fire* (1941) and *The Thing from Another World* (1951) [known as *The Thing* in the USA; *Halliwell's Film and Video Guide 2001* gives the director of this film as 'Christian Nyby (1919–93) (with mysterious help, either Hawks or Orson Welles)'[6]]. But Hawks is not so much concerned with the subjection of the world to the jaded, glacial vision of the scientific mind as he is with retracing the comic misfortunes of the intelligence. Hawks is not concerned with satire or psychology; societies mean no more to him than sentiments do; unlike [such directors as] Frank Capra (1897–1991) and Leo McCarey (1898–1969), he is solely preoccupied with the adventure of the intellect. Whether he opposes the old to the new, the sum of the world's knowledge of the past to one of the degraded forms of modern life (*Ball of Fire*, *A Song is Born* (1948)), or man to beast (*Bringing Up Baby* (1938)), he sticks to the same story – the intrusion of the inhuman, or the crudest avatar of humanity, into a highly civilized society. In *The Thing*, the mask is finally off: in the confined space of the universe, some men of science are at grips with a creature worse than inhuman, a creature *from another world*; and their efforts are directed towards fitting it into the logical framework of human knowledge.

But in *Monkey Business* the enemy has crept into man himself: the subtle poison of the Fountain of Youth, the temptation of infantilism. This we have long known to be one of the less subtle wiles of the Evil One – now in the form of a hound, now in the form of a monkey – when he comes up against a man of rare intelligence. And it is the most unfortunate of illusions which Hawks rather cruelly attacks: the notion that adolescence and childhood are barbarous states from which we are rescued by education. The child is scarcely distinguishable from the savage he imitates in his games: and a most distinguished old man, after he has drunk the precious fluid, takes delight in imitating a chimp. One can find in this a classical conception of man, as a creature whose only path to greatness lies through experience and maturity; at the end of the journey, it is his old age which will be his judge.

Still worse than infantilism, degradation, or decadence, however,

is the fascination these tendencies exert on the same mind which perceives them as evil; the film is not only a story about this fascination,
it offers itself to the spectator as a demonstration of the power of the
fascination. Likewise, anyone who criticizes this tendency must first
submit himself to it. The monkeys, the Indians, the goldfish are no
more than the guise worn by Hawks's obsession with primitivism,
which also finds expression in the savage rhythms of the tom-tom
music, the sweet stupidity of Marilyn Monroe (that monster of femininity whom the costume designer nearly deformed), or the ageing
bacchante Ginger Rogers becomes when she reverts to adolescence
and her wrinkles seem to shrink away [a bacchante is a priest or
votary of Bacchus, god of wine and wildness]. The instinctive euphoria of the characters' actions gives a lyric quality to the ugliness and
foulness, a denseness of expression which heightens everything into
abstraction: the fascination of all this gives *beauty* to the metamorphoses in retrospect. One could apply the word 'expressionistic' to
the artfulness with which Cary Grant twists his gestures into symbols; watching the scene in which he makes himself up as an Indian,
it is impossible not to be reminded of the famous shot in *The Blue
Angel* (1930) in which Emil Jannings stares at *his* distorted face. It is
by no means facile to compare these two similar tales of ruin: we
recall how the themes of damnation and malediction in the German
cinema had imposed the same rigorous progression from the likeable
to the hideous.

From the close-up of the chimpanzee to the moment when the
diaper slips off the baby Cary Grant, the viewer's head swims with the
constant whirl of immodesty and impropriety; and what is this feeling if not a mixture of fear, censure – and fascination? The allure of
the instinctual, the abandonment to primitive earthly forces, evil,
ugliness, stupidity – all of the Devil's attributes are, in these comedies
in which the soul itself is tempted to bestiality, deviously combined
with logic *in extremis*; the sharpest point of the intelligence is turned
back on itself. *I Was a Male War Bride* (1949; originally known as *You
Can't Sleep Here* in the UK) takes as its subject simply the impossi-
bility of finding a place to sleep, and then prolongs it to the extremes
of debasement and demoralization.

Hawks knows better than anyone else that art has to go to
extremes, even the extremes of squalor, because that is the source of
comedy. He is never afraid to use bizarre narrative twists, once he has
established that they are possible. He doesn't try to confound the

spectator's vulgar tendencies; he sates them by taking them a step further. This is also the genius of Molière (1622–73): his mad fits of logic are apt to make the laughter stick in your throat. It is also Murnau's genius – the famous scene with Dame Martha in his excellent *Tartuffe* (1925) and several sequences of *Der letzte Mann* (1924 [the title literally means 'The Last Man', but the film is usually known as 'The Last Laugh' in English]) are still models of Molièresque cinema.

Hawks is a director of intelligence and precision, but he is also a bundle of dark forces and strange fascinations; his is a Teutonic spirit, attracted by bouts of ordered madness which give birth to an infinite chain of consequences. The very fact of their continuity is a manifestation of Fate. His heroes demonstrate this not so much in their feelings as in their actions, which he observes meticulously and with passion. It is *actions* that he films, meditating on the power of appearance alone. We are not concerned with John Wayne's thoughts as he walks toward Montgomery Clift at the end of *Red River*, or Bogart's thoughts as he beats somebody up: our attention is directed solely to the precision of each step – the exact rhythm of the walk – of each blow – and to the gradual collapse of the battered body.

But at the same time, Hawks epitomizes the highest qualities of the American cinema: he is the only American director who knows how to draw a *moral*. His marvellous blend of action and morality is probably the secret of his genius. It is not an idea that is fascinating in a Hawks film, but its effectiveness. A deed holds our attention not so much for its intrinsic beauty as for its effect on the inner works of his universe.

Such art demands a basic honesty, and Hawks's use of time and space bears witness to this – no flashback, no ellipsis; the rule is continuity. No character disappears without us following him, and nothing surprises the hero which doesn't surprise us at the same time. There seems to be a law behind Hawks's action and editing, but it is a *biological* law like that governing any living being: each shot has a functional beauty, like a neck or an ankle. The smooth, orderly succession of shots has a rhythm like the pulsing of blood, and the whole film is like a beautiful body, kept alive by deep, resilient breathing.

This obsession with continuity imposes a feeling of monotony on Hawks's films, the kind often associated with the idea of a journey to be made or a course to be run (*Air Force* (1943), *Red River*), because everything is felt to be connected to everything else, time to space and space to time. So in films which are mostly comic (*To Have and*

Have Not (1945), *The Big Sleep*), the characters are confined to a few settings, and they move around rather helplessly in them. We begin to feel the gravity of each movement they make, and we are unable to escape from their presence. But Hawksian drama is always expressed in spatial terms, and variations in setting are parallel with temporal variations: whether it is the drama of Scarface, whose kingdom shrinks from the city he once ruled to the room in which he is finally trapped, or of the scientists who cannot dare leave their hut for fear of The Thing; of the fliers in *Only Angels Have Wings* (1939), trapped in their station by the fog and managing to escape to the mountains from time to time, just as Bogart (in *To Have and Have Not*) escapes to the sea from the hotel which he prowls impotently, between the cellar and his room; and even when these themes are burlesqued in *Ball of Fire*, with the grammarian moving out of his hermetic library to face the perils of the city, or in *Monkey Business*, in which the characters' jaunts are an indication of their reversion to infancy (*I Was a Male War Bride* plays on the motif of the journey in another way). Always the heroes' movements are along the path of their destiny.

The monotony is only a façade. Beneath it, feelings are slowly ripening, developing step by step towards a violent climax. Hawks uses lassitude as a dramatic device – to convey the exasperation of men who have to restrain themselves for two hours, patiently containing their anger, hatred, or love before our eyes and then suddenly releasing it, like slowly saturated batteries which eventually give off a spark. Their anger is heightened by their habitual *sangfroid*; their calm façade is pregnant with emotion, with the secret trembling of their nerves and of their soul – until the cup overflows. A Hawks film often has the same feeling as the agonizing wait for the fall of a drop of water.

The comedies show another side of this principle of monotony. Forward action is replaced by repetition, like the rhetoric of Raymond Roussel (1877–1933) replacing that of Charles Péguy (1873–1914); the same actions, endlessly recurring, which Hawks builds up with the persistence of a maniac and the patience of a man obsessed, suddenly whirl madly about, as if at the mercy of a capricious maelstrom.

What other man of genius, even if he were more concerned with continuity, could be more passionately concerned with the consequences of men's actions, or with these actions' relationship to each other? The way they influence, repel, or attract one another makes up a unified and coherent world, a Newtonian universe whose ruling principles are the universal law of gravity and a deep conviction of the gravity of existence. Human actions are weighed and measured by a master director preoccupied with man's responsibilities.

The measure of Hawks's films is intelligence, but a *pragmatic* intelligence, applied directly to the physical world, an intelligence which takes its efficacy from the precise viewpoint of a profession or from some form of human activity at grips with the universe and anxious for conquest. Marlowe in *The Big Sleep* practises a profession just as a scientist or a flier does; and when Bogart hires out his boat in *To Have and Have Not*, he hardly looks at the sea: he is more interested in the beauty of his passengers than in the beauty of the waves. Every river is made to be crossed, every herd is made to be fattened and sold at the highest price. And women, however seductive, however much the hero cares for them, must join them in the struggle.

It is impossible adequately to evoke *To Have and Have Not* without immediately recalling the struggle with the fish at the beginning of the film. The universe cannot be conquered without a fight, and fighting is natural to Hawks's heroes: hand-to-hand fighting. What closer grasp of another being could be hoped for than a vigorous struggle like this? So love exists even where there is perpetual opposition; it is a bitter duel whose constant dangers are ignored by men intoxicated with passions (*The Big Sleep, Red River*). Out of the contest comes esteem – that admirable word encompassing knowledge, appreciation and sympathy: the opponent becomes a partner. The hero feels a great sense of disgust if he has to face an enemy who refuses to fight; Marlowe, seized with a sudden bitterness, precipitates events in order to hasten the climax of his case.

Maturity is the hallmark of these reflective men, heroes of an adult, often exclusively masculine world, where tragedy is found in personal relationships; comedy comes from the intrusion and admixture of alien elements, or in mechanical objects which take away their free will – that freedom of decision by which a man can express himself and affirm his existence as a creator does in the act of creation.

I don't want to seem as if I'm praising Hawks for being 'a genius estranged from his time', but it is the obviousness of his modernity which lets me avoid belabouring it. I'd prefer, instead, to point out how, even if he is occasionally drawn to the ridiculous or the absurd, Hawks first of all concentrates on the smell and feel of reality, giving reality an unusual and long-hidden grandeur and nobility; how Hawks gives the modern sensibility a classical conscience. The father of *Red River* and *Only Angels Have Wings* is none other than Pierre Corneille (1606–84); ambiguity and complexity are compatible only with the noblest feelings, which some still consider 'dull', even though it is not these feelings which are soonest exhausted but rather the barbaric, mutable natures of crude souls – that is why modern novels are so boring.

Finally, how could I omit mentioning those wonderful Hawksian opening scenes in which the hero settles smoothly and solidly in for the duration? No preliminaries, no expository devices: a door opens, and there he is in the first shot. The conversation gets going and quietly familiarizes us with his personal rhythm; after bumping into him like this, we can no longer leave his side. We are his companions all through the journey as it unwinds as surely and regularly as the film going through the projector. The hero moves with the litheness and constancy of a mountaineer who starts out with a steady gait and maintains it along the roughest trails, even to the end of the longest day's march.

From these first stirrings, we are not only sure that the heroes will never leave us, we also know that they will stick by their promises *to a fault*, and will never hesitate or quit: no one can put a stop to their marvellous stubbornness and tenacity. Once they have set out, they will go on to the end of their tether and carry the promises they have made to their logical conclusions, come what may. What is started must be finished. It doesn't matter that the heroes are often involved against their wills: by proving themselves, by achieving their ends, they win the right to be free and the honour of calling themselves men. To them, logic is not some cold intellectual activity, but proof that the body is a coherent whole, harmoniously following the consequences of an action out of loyalty to itself. The strength of the heroes' willpower is an assurance of the unity of the man and the spirit, tied together on behalf of that which both justifies their existence and gives it the highest meaning.

If it is true that we are fascinated by extremes, by everything which is bold and excessive, and that we find grandeur in a lack of moderation – then it follows that we should be intrigued by the clash of extremes, because they bring together the intellectual precision of abstractions with the elemental magic of the great earthly impulses, linking thunderstorms with equations in an affirmation of life. The beauty of a Hawks film comes from this kind of affirmation, staunch and serene, remorseless and resilient. It is a beauty which demonstrates existence by breathing and movement by walking. That which is, is.[7] □

Rivette's praise of Hawks is provocatively phrased in terms drawn from art and philosophy. Hawks's work can be seen as lyric, beautiful, heightened to the level of abstraction, expressionistic, rhythmic. It combines classical qualities of exactness and abstractness with a Romantic concern for extremes. Hawks can be compared, not only to more evidently 'artistic' directors – the Josef von Sternberg of *The Blue Angel*, F. W. Murnau – but also to two icons of French high culture, the seventeenth-century playwrights Pierre Corneille and Molière, and to two key twentieth-century writers, the poet Charles Péguy and the novelist Raymond Roussel. But it should also be stressed that Rivette's elevation of Hawks is combined with an analysis of the style of his films – for example, of their continuity and superficial monotony and of the way in which their drama is expressed in spatial terms – that could retain its validity even if the *auteur* is set aside: those stylistic features could still exist even if they were not attributed to a controlling author-director. One of the functions of the *auteur* approach, it could be said, was to encourage critics and cinema-goers to bestow on films by directors designated as *auteurs* the form of attention[8] more traditionally bestowed on the 'art film' or on traditional cultural forms such as painting and the novel. But the *auteur* approach is not essential to this form of attention.

In the 1950s, however, *Cahiers* was largely committed to an *auteur* approach; and its elevation of Hawks was exceeded by its elevation of Hitchcock. Hitchcock's reputation had been growing generally as the 1950s had advanced, and *Rear Window* (1954) had been especially well received. In *Rear Window*, L. B. Jefferies, a photographer confined to a wheelchair with a broken leg, observes what might be a murder in the block of flats opposite, and sends his girlfriend, Lisa Fremont, to undertake a hazardous investigation that he watches from a distance; the film would become a classic point of reference in film theory, since it seemed to provide an analogy of the very act of watching a film. In 1955, *Cahiers* published an analysis from one of its contributors whose own first film would be a thriller with Hitchcockian overtones, *Le Boucher* (*The Butcher*, 1969). In 'Serious Things', which first appeared in *Cahiers* no. 46 in April 1955, Claude Chabrol (born 1930) provides an interpretation of *Rear Window* in which he aims to look at elements that are 'less obvious, but even more interesting' than the 'culpability of the central character, a voyeur in the worst sense of the word':[9]

■ In its first few minutes *Rear Window* presents us with an assembly of rabbit hutches, each of them completely separate and observed from another closed, incommunicable, rabbit hutch. From there it is obviously just a step, made with no difficulty, to the conclusion that the behaviour of the rabbits is, or should be, the object of attention, since in fact there is nothing to contradict this interpretation of the elements before us. We merely have to acknowledge that the study of this behaviour is carried out by a rabbit essentially no different from the others. Which leads to the notion of a perpetual shift between the real behaviour of the rabbits and the interpretation that the observer-rabbit gives of it, ultimately the only one communicated to us, since any break or choice in the continuity of this behaviour, a continuity multiplied by the number of hutches observed, is imposed on us. While the observer-rabbit is himself observed with a total objectivity, for example that of a camera which restricts itself to the observer's hutch, we are obliged to acknowledge that all the other hutches and all the rabbits in them are the sum of a multiple distortion produced from the hutch and by the rabbit which is objectively, or directly, presented.

So in *Rear Window* the other side of the courtyard must be regarded as a multiple projection of James Stewart's amorous fixation [Stewart plays L.B. Jefferies].

The constitutive elements of this multiple projection are in fact a range of possible emotional relationships between two people of the opposite sex, from the absence of an emotional relationship, via the respective solitude of two people who are close neighbours, to a hate which ultimately turns to murder, by way of the sexual hunger of the first few days of love.

Once this is posited, another, essential element should be added: what might be called the position of the author, which, combined with the artistic factors imposed by the very nature of the enterprise, is developed through the characters directly presented and openly avowed by the strength of the evidence and the testimony of three biblical quotations, as Christian. [There seems to be only one direct Biblical quotation in *Rear Window*. This occurs about an hour and a half into the film, when L.B. Jefferies and Lisa Fremont (Grace Kelly) are discussing what Lisa calls 'rear window ethics', and Lisa says to L.B.: 'Whatever happened to that old saying, "Love thy neighbour"?' The film does, however, contain a number of possible Biblical allusions, rather than direct quotations.]

With these premises duly established, I leave to the reader the conclusion of that syllogism which definitively fixes the moral climate of the work, to pass on to what would properly be called its meaning.

The window which overlooks the courtyard consists of three sections, as stressed in the credit sequence. This trinity demands scrutiny. The work is in fact composed of three elements, three themes one could say, which are synchronic and in the end unified.

The first is a romantic plot, which by turns opposes and reunites James Stewart and Grace Kelly. Both are in search of an area of mutual understanding, for though each is in love with the other, their respective egos, only minimally divergent, constitute an obstacle.

The second theme is on the plane of the thriller. It is located on the other side of the courtyard, and consequently is of a rather complex, semi-obsessional character. Moreover it is very skilfully combined with a theme of indiscretion which runs through the whole work and confers on it a part of its unity. What is more, this thriller element presents all the stock characters of Hitchcock's earlier works, taken to their most extreme limits, since in the end one no longer knows whether the crime may not have been made a *reality* simply by Stewart's *willing* it.

The last theme reaches a complexity that cannot be defined in a single word: it is presented as a kind of realist painting of the courtyard, although 'realist' is a term that in the circumstances is a particularly bad choice, since the painting depicts beings which are, *a priori*, mental entities and projections. The aim is to illuminate, validate and affirm the fundamental conception of the work, its postulate: the egocentric structure of the world as it exists, a structure which the interlinking of themes seeks to represent faithfully. Thus the individual is the split atom, the couple is the molecule, the building is the body composed of x number of molecules, and itself split from the rest of the world. The two external characters have the double role of intelligent confidants, one totally lucid, the other totally mechanized, and of witnesses themselves incriminated. Thus generalizing the exposé.

Risking a musical comparison to illuminate the relationship between the themes, one might say that all three are composed with the same notes, but elaborated in a different order, and in different tonalities, each vying with the other and functioning in counterpoint. What is more, there is nothing presumptuous in such a comparison, since, within the rhythm of the work, it would be easy to determine four different constituent forms definable in musical jargon.

As one would expect in a work as structured as this one, there is in *Rear Window* a moment which crystallises the themes into a single lesson, an enormous, perfect harmony: the death of the little dog. This sequence, the only one treated peripherally to the position of the narrator as articulated above (the only one where the camera goes into the courtyard without the presence of the hero), though grounded in an incident that in itself is relatively undramatic, is of a tragic and overwhelming intensity. I can well understand how such vehemence and such gravity could seem rather inappropriate in the circumstances; a dog is only a dog and the death of a dog would seem an event whose tragic import bears no relation to the words spoken by the animal's owner. And these words themselves – 'You don't know the meaning of the word "neighbour"' – which encapsulate the film's moral significance, seem all too clumsy and too naïve to justify such a solemn style. But the displacement itself is destroyed, for the tone leaves no room for doubt and gives things and feelings their real intensity and their invective: in reality this is the massacre of an innocent, and a mother who bemoans her child.[10]

From then on the implications of this scene become vertiginous: responsibilities press upon one another at every imaginable level, to condemn a monstrously egocentric world, whose every element on every scale is immured in an ungodly solitude.

On the dramatic level, the scene presents the dual interest of a thriller plot development, aggravating suspicion, and an illustration of a theme dear to its author – the materialization of a criminal act that is indirectly willed (in this particular case, this death *confirms* Stewart's *hopes*).

From this point of view the confrontation between the murderer and the 'voyeur' is extremely interesting. The communication sought by the former – 'What do you want from me?' – whether blackmail or confession, involves the latter, who refuses from a recognition of its baseness, and in some way authenticates his responsibility. Stewart's refusal in this way illuminates the profound reason for the loneliness of the world, which is established as the absence of communication between human beings, in a word, the absence of love.

Other works of Hitchcock, like *Rebecca* (1940), *Under Capricorn* (1949) or *Notorious* (1946), have demonstrated the corollary of the problem: to know what the power of love can be. What is more, this aspect is not absent from *Rear Window*, where the embodiment of the Grace Kelly character draws her precious ambiguity from the opposition between her 'possible' and her 'being'. The possible is in fact the perceptible irradiation of her beauty and her charm, powerful enough to transform the oppressive and lonely atmosphere of the invalid's room into a flower garden with, in an unforgettable shot, James Stewart's head in repose. Simultaneously, with her appearance on the scene comes the inexpressible poetry which is the love of two human beings: more than justified by the knowing coquetry of the author in the work's construction, this poetry brings into the stifling atmosphere of *Rear Window*, which is the atmosphere of the sewers themselves, a fleeting vision of our lost earthly paradise.[11] ☐

In this account, Chabrol is not so much concerned to elevate Hitchcock in the ways that Rivette elevated Hawks by constructing him as an artist who combined classicism and Romanticism, and comparing him to esteemed cultural icons; his sense that Hitchcock's reputation was growing even among those whom he calls Anglo-Saxon critics perhaps allows him to set these strategies aside as unnecessary. Instead, he takes it for granted that Hitchcock can be treated as an 'author' with a 'point of view' – in this case, a Christian one – and with favourite themes (*Rear Window* exemplifies one of these themes, the occurrence in physical reality of a criminal act that is indirectly willed), and with a conscious flirtatiousness, a teasing of the audience, in the way he constructs his films. Chabrol's elevation of Hitchcock is implicit in his assumption that Hitchcock is an 'author' and in his interpretation of *Rear Window* in traditional aesthetic and moral terms as a thematically and dramatically complex work about isolation, egotism, and the absence and redemptive presence of love.

For *Cahiers* in the 1950s, Hawks and Hitchcock represented the best of the older generation of American *auteurs*; the key representative of a younger generation for *Cahiers* was Nicholas Ray (born Raymond Nicholas Kienzle, 1911–79). In 'Ajax or the Cid?', published in *Cahiers* no. 59 in May 1956, Eric Rohmer (born 1920) provided an assessment of what was to become Ray's best-known film, *Rebel Without a Cause* (1955), which helped to make a legend of its young star, James Dean (1931–55). Rohmer's account also helps to give a more general sense of the criteria for awarding a director the accolade of *auteur*:

■ *Cahiers* readers know that we deem Nicholas Ray to be one of the greatest ... of the new generation of American film-makers ... which only came on the scene after the [Second World War]. In spite of his obvious lack of pretensions, he is one of the few to possess his own style, his own vision of the world, his own poetry; he is an *auteur*, a great *auteur*. A discernible constant factor running all the way through someone's work is a double-edged weapon: it is proof of personality but also, in some cases, of meagreness. Yet the constraints exercised by the production companies on film-makers are such, the manpower, the managers and the good foremen so numerous, that the presence of a leitmotif [a leading motif, 'a frequently repeated ... image, symbol or situation' [12]] is *a priori* an auspicious sign. The diversity of themes handled by Nicholas Ray, and the richness of the variations which he adds to the beauty of the three or four great themes dearest to him, tend to make his originality somewhat less easy to pinpoint than that of any of his rivals. It is impossible to attach any convenient label to his position, as one can with John Huston (1906–87). It isn't problems that interest him, in the manner of a Richard Brooks (1912–92), but human beings. There is not a trace of the psychological subtleties so dear to Joseph L. Mankiewicz (1909–93). None of those instantly dazzling flashes of lyricism, as in Robert Aldrich (1918–83). His tempo is slow, his melody usually monochord, but its delineation is so precise, its progress so compulsive, that we cannot allow our attention to stray for a moment. The bravura set-pieces, brilliant as they are, only assume prominence after a slow crescendo. It is more an art of 'connections' than of 'brilliancies'.

The spirit of [*Rebel Without a Cause*] is similar to that of the earlier ones, but the situations themselves offer very specific analogies. The youth of the heroes, their stubborn intensity, is that of the characters in *Knock on Any Door* (1949) and *They Live by Night* (1948). We have already encountered the theme of violence in *On Dangerous Ground* (1951) and *In a Lonely Place* (1950). James Dean's futile heroism is Robert Mitchum's in *The Lusty Men* (1952) or James Cagney's in *Run for Cover* (1955). The character personified by Natalie Wood is not so dissimilar to the Joan Crawford character in *Johnny Guitar* (1953), despite the age difference. I'll go even further: without exception, all the heroines in his films – Cathy O'Donnell, Gloria Grahame, Susan Hayward, Ida Lupino, Viveca Lindfors, and the two already mentioned – under his direction take on a rather surprising air of physical resemblance. Just as he is the poet of violence, Nicholas Ray is perhaps the only poet of love; it is the fascination peculiar to both feelings that obsesses him, more than the study of their origins and their close or distant repercussions. Neither fury nor cruelty, but that special intoxication into which we are plunged by a violent physical act, situation or passion. Not desire, like the majority of his compatriots in the cinema, but the mysterious affinity that locks two human beings together. To all this I would add a feeling for nature, discernible in the background – in both the literal and the figurative sense – that is in harmony with his temperament as more of a colourist, even in his black and white films, than a plastic artist.

And then no other director knows how to give his characters so clearly the air of having a common genealogy. They are marked with the seal of the same fate, the same moral or physical disease that is not quite taint or decay. Look at the women's faces with their soft cheeks, but the eyes ringed with shadows and the heavy lips; those athletic male silhouettes, the Robert Ryans, the John Dereks, the Robert Mitchums, flattened, or rather drawn back into themselves. James Dean takes this even further; he is like a chrysalis badly folded out of its cocoon. Turned in on himself? A solitude that is suffered rather than willed, a tortured quest for affection, for love or friendship. I spoke just now of a linear development, but not as one of those fine straight lines which Hawks would trace, the wide epic road, the calm progressions, the noble bearing. Here everything is circular, from the gestures of love to the movement of the stars, from those devouring looks that envelop you in their intensity while they strive to avoid your eyes, to those wandering pursuits, those deaths that come full circle and return the heroes to their original state of innocence. Yes, that's it: what these men-children lack is the kind of virginity with which the adventure writer usually endows his characters. They do not have the resigned complacency, nor the will to self-abasement that belongs to the man of the modern novel. Nor are they entirely guilty ... [Rohmer's ellipsis]

Nicholas Ray is a poet, of that there is no doubt, but it is not only the lyrical character of his latest film I want to emphasize but its tragic character. First through its form, which may appear superficial but is not unimportant. *Rebel Without a Cause* is a genuine drama in five acts. *Act One*: exposition. Two youths and a young girl have just been picked up by the police. The parents intervene. The subject is immediately placed on the moral plane where it is to remain throughout the film: why the rebellion? It does not even have that depth proper to the intentionally absurd. Nor is it just the sudden leap of a restive young animal. It is the honour of these boys and girls which is at stake, an honour ill-conceived but which cannot be otherwise because its milieu and its circumstances leave it no more noble terrain. Certainly an excess of naïve psychoanalysis weighs down the argument. But I don't think it has to be seen as an explanation or an excuse: it is part of the setting of American life ... *Act Two*. Our main hero, personified by James Dean, has promised to behave, and goes back to school. His classmates make fun of his pretensions to 'toughness'. The first lyrical interlude, with the lesson in the planetarium, that apocalyptic evocation which barely succeeds in veiling with anxiety or feigned indifference the empty eyes of our high school kids. An idea that is over-simple on paper, but it has strength and depth in its execution, charged as it is with both gravity and derision, like everything that is to follow. As they leave, fresh provocations. Dean tries not to get involved, but his honour is at stake – not his honour as a small-town tough guy but, we feel, his honour in every sense – in not giving way. A knife fight, where the harshness and the beauty of the landscape against which it is projected make us forget that it is only a children's game. There is more: the second hand must be played that very evening in an even more absurd and dangerous exercise. This is *Act Three*. Don't forget that so far the will of the characters has been the principal mechanism of the plot; and so it will be until the end. The hero withdraws momentarily to his tent – namely, the family – to meditate. Then he presents himself for battle. A new set-piece, but this time it is at night. A peripeteia [sudden change of fortune] which makes the action resurge: the game is driving cars into the sea and jumping out at the last moment. The adversary is killed. Everyone takes to their heels. *Act Four*. Dean has saved his honour and won the love of the victim's girl-friend, the girl he met in the police station, played by Natalie Wood. He goes home and announces to his parents his intention of giving himself up to the police. They dissuade him. Their cowardice arouses his indignation. The father's weakness doesn't just 'explain' the presence of the honour 'complex' in the son, and his unhealthy notoriety, it justifies it, in the moral sense of the word, it calls out for it, demands it. Violence, unpleasant scenes handled with unusual candour. He goes to the police station but the police won't see him. Meanwhile his classmates, suspecting betrayal, search for him. His only friend, a little dark-haired kid strangely named 'Plato' ([played by] Sal Mineo), manages to join him after several incidents. This is the *Last Act*, at night, in a deserted house that recalls *On Dangerous Ground* or *Johnny Guitar*. The second lyrical interlude, when Natalie Wood joins the two boys. A love scene by candlelight in the empty room; torment and peace in the night; beyond childish cynicism comes the first uneasiness, the first shame

– the beauty of kisses and caresses. Before Woman, our erstwhile hero becomes the little boy that he could not be with his parents, but simultaneously he discovers his responsibility as a man. Ray's eroticism is, if it matters, as uneasy and equivocal as one could wish. There too the psychoanalyst will have plenty of scope. But he certainly won't be able to appreciate how much we, the audience, feel as we see the high school kids of that afternoon prepare for a physical and moral battle worthy of the name ... [Rohmer's ellipsis] And we *move*. Not just with events (which come thick and fast: the arrival of the other kids, the fight with Mineo, who gets scared and shoots, the police on the scene, the chase in the copse); nor with the theatrical grandeur, in the right sense of the term, of the *mise en scène* (the cars with their brilliant headlights encircling the planetarium, the police demands, the dialogue in the shadows with Dean trying to make his friend see reason); nor with the tragedy of the conclusion (when a policeman shoots 'Plato' as he appears at the top of the steps, nervously gripping the revolver that Dean had unloaded without his knowledge). We make an *absolute* move forward: we have eliminated that distance which we had so cautiously kept between the characters and ourselves. Their reasons are our reasons, their honour our honour, their madness ours. They have, to use a modern turn of phrase, emerged from inauthenticity. By merit they have acquired the dignity of tragic heroes, which we could not quite discern in them at first.

May I be forgiven my favourite vice, of evoking the memory of the ancient Greeks. I don't think, in all good faith, that in this case such a parallel would be artificial. The idea of fate is deep-rooted, in the works of every period and every nation. It alone is not enough for the foundation of tragedy; it needs the support of some great dissension between the forces present at every moment, in man and around him, between the individual's own pride and the society – or nature – that cannot allow it, and victimizes it, punishes it. A tragic hero is always in some sense a warrior awoken from the intoxication of battle, suddenly perceiving that he is a god no longer. Anyone who re-reads Greek tragedy for enjoyment, with schooldays over, will be struck by the presence of a theme which the commentators have hardly touched on and which, unhappily, has never inspired our classics – the theme of *violence* (that is how *hubris* [insolent pride or presumption] and *orgia* [drunken or licentious revels] should be understood), a violence that is dangerous, to be condemned but exhilarating and beautiful. The modern image of fate is no banal, stupid accident, like the one James Dean, the actor, died in at the height of his career. It is not the absurdity of chance, but of our condition or our will. It is the disproportion that exists between the measure of man – always a noble one – and the futility of the task that he often sets himself. It is not that earlier ages have been wiser than ours, or given more of themselves in the battle, they too without a cause; but more rigidly defined codes of honour always offered some pretext for the most absurd conduct. What I like about this film is that the word 'honour', out of the mouths of these apathetic, petit-bourgeois juveniles, is unchanged and loses none of its pure, dazzling brilliance, kept ablaze by these kids, these rodeo specialists, these outlaws of the prairie, even though their vanity and their foolish obstinacy are condemned by society, by morality, by whatever it is, in short by fate. They are not quite guilty, but not completely innocent either, only blighted by the defect of their century. It is the task of the politicians and the philosophers to show mankind horizons which are clearer than the ones it has chosen, but it is the poet's mission to doubt that optimism, to extract from the lees of his time the precious stone, to teach us to love without forbidding us to judge, to keep always alive in us the sense of *tragedy*. These thoughts came to me one day in a local cinema where they were showing *In a Lonely Place*. Each time I see a new Nicholas Ray film they come to mind again, and particularly with this one, his masterpiece.[13] □

In this article, Rohmer provides a useful definition of an *auteur* – a director who possesses his own style, vision and poetry. That style, vision and poetry is partly a matter of themes and situations that run through his films, partly a matter of rhythm, and partly a matter of connections. But Ray offers something more: in a comparison even more elevated than those which Rivette finds for Hawks, Rohmer sees him as keeping alive a sense of tragedy. In *The Death of Tragedy* (1961), the cultural critic George Steiner argued that, with the collapse of the religious sense, tragedy was no longer possible in the twentieth century; provocatively, Rohmer finds it in that supposedly most debased of cultural forms – Hollywood cinema. There could be no more arresting demonstration of the boldness of *Cahiers*' claims for the *auteur*.

The idea of the *auteur* was not universally acknowledged within *Cahiers*, however: one prominent voice which expressed dissent was that of André Bazin himself. In 'On the *politique des auteurs*', published in *Cahiers du Cinéma* no. 70 in April 1957, Bazin acknowledged that *Cahiers* had become identified with the '*politique des auteurs*' and accepted this as a general policy of the magazine, but also registered his own reservations. The extract below begins with his point that to see films as the work of an *auteur* may involve endowing an inferior film with undeserved merit and complexity, simply because it can be attributed to a particular director who has been granted *auteur* status:

■ Many a time I have felt uneasy at the subtlety of an argument, which was completely unable to camouflage the naïveté of the assumption whereby, for example, the intentions and the coherence of a deliberate and well thought out film are read into some little 'B' feature.

   And of course as soon as you state that the film-maker and his films are one, there can be no minor films, as the worst of them will always be in the image of their creator.[14] □

Bazin then moves on to a more general discussion that relates the idea of the *auteur* in the cinema to that of the *auteur* in the more traditional arts:

■ [T]he *politique des auteurs* is the application to the cinema of a notion that is widely accepted in the individual arts. François Truffaut likes to quote [Jean] Giraudoux's remark: 'There are no works, there are only *auteurs*' – a polemical sally which seems to me of limited significance. The opposite statement could just as well be set as an exam question. [The 'opposite statement' – there are no *auteurs*, only works (or texts) – could be seen as, effectively, the key proposition of the post-structuralist approach to film and literary studies.] The two formulae, like the maxims of La Rochefoucauld (1613–80) and Chamfort (1741–94), would simply reverse their proportion of truth and error. As for Eric Rohmer, he states (or rather asserts) that in art it is the *auteurs*, and not the works, that remain; and the programmes of film societies would seem to support this critical truth.

   But one should note that Rohmer's argument does not go nearly as far as Giraudoux's aphorism, for, if *auteurs* remain, it is not necessarily because of their production as a whole. There is no lack of examples to prove that the contrary is true. Maybe the name of Voltaire (1694–1778) is more important that his bibliography, but now that he has been put in perspective it is not so much his *Dictionnaire philosophique* (1764) that counts nowadays as his Voltairean wit, a certain *style* of thinking and writing. But today where are we to find the principle and the example? In his abundant and atrocious writings for the theatre? Or in the slim volume of short stories? And what about Beaumarchais (1732–99)? Are we to go looking in *La mère coupable* (*The Guilty Mother*, 1792)? [According to W. H. Barber, *La mère coupable* is 'an unconvincing sentimental melo-drama'.[15]]

In any case, the authors of that period were apparently themselves aware of the relativity of their worth, since they willingly disowned their works, and sometimes did not mind even being the subject of lampoons whose quality they took as a compliment. For them, almost the only thing that mattered was the work itself, whether their own or another's, and it was only at the end of the eighteenth century, with Beaumarchais in fact, that the concept of the *auteur* finally crystal-lized legally, with his royalties, duties and responsibilities. Of course I am making allowances for historical and social contingencies; polit-ical and moral censorship has made anonymity sometimes inevitable and always excusable. But surely the anonymity of the writings of the French Resistance in no way lessened the dignity and responsibility of the writer. It was only in the nineteenth century that copying or plagiarism really began to be considered a professional breach that disqualified its perpetrator.

The same is true of painting. Although nowadays any old splash of paint can be valued according to its measurements and the celebrity of the signature, the objective quality of the work itself was formerly held in much higher esteem. Proof of this is to be found in the difficulty there is in authenticating a lot of old pictures. What emerged from a studio might simply be the work of a pupil, and we are now unable to *prove* anything one way or the other. If one goes back even further, one has to take into consideration the anonymous works that have come down to us as the products not of an artist, but of an art, not of a man, but of a society.

I can see how I will be rebutted. We should not objectify our ignor-ance or let it crystallize into a reality. All these works of art, the Venus de Milo as well as the Negro mask, did in fact have an *auteur*; and the whole of modern historical science is tending to fill in the gaps and give names to these works of art. But did one really have to wait for such erudite addenda before being able to admire and enjoy them? Biographical criticism is one of many possible critical dimensions – people are still arguing about the identity of Shakespeare or Molière.

But that's just the point! People *are* arguing. So their identity is not a matter of complete indifference. The evolution of Western art towards greater personalization should definitely be considered as a step forward, as a refinement of culture, but only as long as this individualization remains only a final perfection and does not claim to *define* culture. At this point, we should remember that irrefutable commonplace we learnt at school: the individual transcends society, but society is also and above all *within* him. So there can be no definitive criticism of genius or talent which does not first take into consideration the social determinism, the historical combination of circumstances, and the technical background which to a large extent determine it. That is why the anonymity of a work of art is a handicap that impinges only very slightly on our understanding of it. In any case, much depends on the particular branch of art in question, the style adopted, and the sociological context. Negro art does not suffer by remaining anonymous – although of course it is unfortunate that we know so little about the societies that gave birth to it.

But Hitchcock's *The Man Who Knew Too Much* (1934; remade 1956), *Europa 51* (1952) directed by Roberto Rossellini (1906–77), and Nicholas Ray's *Bigger Than Life* (1956) are contemporary with the paintings of Pablo Picasso (1888–1973), Henri Matisse (1869–1954) and Gustave Singier (1909–84)! Does it follow that one should see in them the same degree of individualization? I for one do not think so.

If you will excuse yet another commonplace, the cinema is an art which is both popular and industrial. These conditions, which are necessary to its existence, in no way constitute a collection of hindrances – no more than in architecture – they rather represent a group of positive and negative circumstances which have to be reckoned with. And this is especially true of the American cinema, which the theoreticians of the *politique des auteurs* admire so much. What makes Hollywood so much better than anything else in the world is not only the quality of certain directors, but also the vitality and, in a certain sense, the excellence of a tradition. Hollywood's superiority is only incidentally technical; it lies much more in what one might call the American cinematic genius, something which should be analysed, then defined, by a sociological approach to its production. The American cinema has been able, in an extraordinarily competent way, to show American society just as it wanted to see itself; but not at all passively, as a simple act of satisfaction and escape, but dynamically, i.e. by participating with the means at its disposal in the building of this society. What is so admirable in the American cinema is that it cannot help being spontaneous. Although the fruit of free enterprise and capitalism – and harbouring their active or still only virtual defects – it is in a way the truest and most realistic cinema of all because it does not shrink from depicting even the contradictions of that society ...

But it follows that every director is swept along by this powerful surge; naturally his artistic course has to be plotted according to the currents – it is not as if he were sailing as his fancy took him on the calm waters of a lake.

In fact it is not even true of the most individual artistic disciplines that genius is free and always self-dependent. And what is genius anyway if not a certain combination of unquestionably personal talents, a gift from the fairies, and a moment in history? [Bazin then argues that authors of talent may fail if the historical situation is not favourable to their work, and that even the best writers will have weak moments.] ... ... Surely one can accept the permanence of talent without confusing it with some kind of artistic infallibility or immunity against making mistakes, which could only be divine attributes. But God, as Sartre has already pointed out, is not an artist![16] Were one to attribute to creative man, in the face of all psychological probability, an unflagging richness of inspiration, one would have to admit that this inspiration always comes up against a whole complex of particular circumstances which make the result, in the cinema, a thousand times more chancy than in painting or in literature.

Inversely, there is no reason why there should not exist – and sometimes there do – flashes in the pan in the work of otherwise mediocre film-makers. Results of a fortunate combination of circumstances in which there is a precarious moment of balance between talent and milieu, these fleeting brilliancies do not prove all that much about personal creative qualities; they are not, however, intrinsically inferior to others – and probably would not seem so if the critics had not begun by reading the signature at the bottom of the painting.

Well, what is true of literature is even truer of the cinema, to the extent that this art, the last to come on to the scene, accelerates and multiplies the evolutionary factors that are common to all the others. In fifty years the cinema, which started with the crudest forms of spectacle (primitive but not inferior), has had to cover the same ground as the play or the novel and is often on the same level as they are. Within this same period, its technical development has been of a kind that cannot compare with that of any traditional art within a comparable period (except perhaps architecture, another industrial art). Under such conditions, it is hardly surprising that the genius will burn himself out ten times as fast, and that a director who suffers no loss of ability may cease to be swept along by the wave. This was the case with Stroheim, Abel Gance and Orson Welles. We are now beginning to see things in enough perspective to notice a curious phenomenon: a film-maker can, within his own lifetime, be refloated by the following wave. This is true of Abel Gance or Stroheim, whose modernity is all the more apparent nowadays. I am fully aware that this only goes to prove their quality of *auteur*, but their eclipse still cannot be entirely explained away by the contradictions of capitalism or the stupidity of producers. If one keeps a sense of proportion, one sees that the same thing has happened to men of genius in the cinema as would have happened to a 120-year-old Jean Racine (1639–99) writing Racinian plays in the middle of the 18th century. Would his tragedies have been better than Voltaire's? The answer is by no means clear-cut; but I bet they would not have been.

One can justifiably point to Chaplin, Renoir or René Clair (1898–1981). But each of them was endowed with further gifts that have little to do with genius and which were precisely the ones that enabled them to adapt themselves to the predicament of film production. Of course, the case of Chaplin was unique since, as both *auteur* and producer, he has been able to be both the cinema and its evolution.

It follows, then, according to the most basic laws of the psychology of creation that, as the objective factors of genius are much more likely to modify themselves in the cinema than in any other art, a rapid maladjustment between the film-maker and the cinema can occur, and this can abruptly affect the quality of his films as a result. Of course I admire Welles's *Confidential Report* (1955; aka *Mr Arkadin*), and I can see the same qualities in it as I see in *Citizen Kane*. But *Citizen Kane* opened up a new era of American cinema, and *Confidential Report* is a film of only secondary importance.

But let's pause a moment on this assertion – it may, I feel, allow us to get to the heart of the matter. I think that not only would the supporters of the *politique des auteurs* refuse to agree that *Confidential Report* is an inferior film to *Citizen Kane*;[17] they would be more eager to claim the contrary, and I can well see how they would go about it. As *Confidential Report* is Welles's sixth film, one can assume that a certain amount of progress has already been made. Not only did the Welles of 1953 have more experience of himself and of his art than in 1941, but however great was the freedom he was able to obtain in Hollywood[,] *Citizen Kane* cannot help remaining to a certain extent an RKO product. The film would never have seen the light of day without the co-operation of some superb technicians and their just as admirable technical apparatus. Gregg Toland, to mention only one, was more than a little responsible for the final result. [Gregg Toland (1904–48) was the director of photography on *Citizen Kane* who, according to David A. Cook, 'perfected for Welles a method of deep-focus photography capable of achieving an unprecedented depth of field'.[18]] On the other hand, *Confidential Report* is completely the work of Welles. Until it can be proved to the contrary, it will be considered *a priori* a superior film because it is more personal and because Welles's personality can only have matured as he grew older.

As far as this question is concerned, I can only agree with my young firebrands when they state that age as such cannot diminish the talent of a film-maker, and react violently to that critical prejudice which consists in always finding the works of a young or mature film-maker superior to the films of an old man ... A great talent matures but does not grow old. There is no reason why this law of artistic psychology should not also be valid for the cinema ... From this point of view, the bias of the *politique des auteurs* is very fruitful ... ... But, always remembering this, one has nevertheless to accept that certain indisputable 'greats' have suffered an eclipse or a loss of their powers. I think what I have already said in this article may point to the reason for this [see pp. 122–3 above]. The drama does not reside in the growing old of men but in that of the cinema: those who do not know how to grow old *with* it will be overtaken by its evolution. This is why it has been possible for there to have been a series of failures leading to complete catastrophe without it being necessary to suppose that the genius of yesterday has become an imbecile. Once again, it is simply a question of the appearance of a clash between the subjective inspiration of the creator and the objective situation of the cinema, and this is what the *politique des auteurs* refuses to see. To its supporters *Confidential Report* is a more important film than *Citizen Kane* because they justifiably see more of Orson Welles in it. In other words, all they want to retain[,] in the equation *auteur* plus *subject* [equals] *work*[,] is the *auteur*, while the subject is reduced to zero. Some of them will pretend to grant me that, all things being equal as far as the *auteur* is concerned, a good subject is naturally better than a bad one, but the more outspoken and foolhardy among them will admit that it very much looks as if they prefer small 'B' films, where the banality of the scenario leaves more room for the personal contribution of the author.

Of course I will be challenged on the very concept of *auteur*. I admit that the equation I just used was artificial, just as much so, in fact, as the distinction one learnt at school between form and content. To benefit from the *politique des auteurs* one has first to be worthy of it, and as it happens this school of criticism claims to distinguish between true *auteurs* and directors, even talented ones: Nicholas Ray is an *auteur*, John Huston is supposed to be only a director; Robert Bresson (1907–82) and Roberto Rossellini are *auteurs*, René Clément (1913–96) is only a great director, and so on. So this conception of the author is not compatible with the *auteur*/subject distinction, because it is of greater importance to find out if a director is worthy of entering the select group of *auteurs* than it is to judge how well he has used his material. To a certain extent at least, the *auteur* is a subject to himself; whatever the scenario, he always tells the same story, or, in case the word 'story' is confusing, let's say he has the same attitude and passes the same moral judgments on the action and on the characters. Jacques Rivette has said that an *auteur* is someone who speaks in the first person. It's a good definition; let's adopt it.

The *politique des auteurs* consists, in short, of choosing the personal factor in artistic creation as a standard of reference, and then assuming that it continues and even progresses from one film to the next. It is recognized that there do exist certain important films of quality that escape this test, but these will systematically be considered inferior to those in which the personal stamp of the *auteur*, however run-of-the-mill the scenario, can be perceived even minutely.

It is far from being my intention to deny the positive attitude and methodological qualities of this bias. First of all, it has the great merit of treating the cinema as an adult art and of reacting against the impressionistic relativism that still reigns over the majority of film reviews. I admit that the explicit or admitted pretension of a critic to reconsider the production of a film-maker with every new film in the light of his judgment has something presumptuous about it that recalls Ubu [the grotesque protagonist of the play *Ubu Roi* (*King Ubu*, 1896) by Alfred Jarry (1873–1907)]. I am also quite willing to admit that if one is human one cannot help doing this, and, short of giving up the whole idea of actually criticizing, one might as well take as a starting point the feelings, pleasant and unpleasant, one feels personally when in contact with a film. Okay, but only on condition that these first impressions are kept in their proper place. We have to take them into consideration, but we should not use them as a basis. In other words, every critical act should consist of referring the film in question to a scale of values, but this reference is not merely a matter of intelligence; the sureness of one's judgment arises also, or perhaps even first of all (in the chronological sense of the word), from a general impression experienced during a film. I feel there are two symmetrical heresies, which are (*a*) objectively applying to a film a critical all-purpose yardstick, and (*b*) considering it sufficient simply to state one's pleasure or disgust. The first denies the role of taste, the second presupposes the superiority of the critic's taste over that of the author. Coldness ... or presumption! [Bazin's ellipsis]

What I like about the *politique des auteurs* is that it reacts against the impressionist approach while retaining the best of it. In fact the scale of values it proposes is not ideological. Its starting-point is an appreciation largely composed of taste and sensibility: it has to discern the contribution of the artist as such, quite apart from the qualities of the subject or the technique: i.e. the man behind the style. But once one has made this distinction, this kind of criticism is doomed to beg the question, for it assumes at the start of its analysis that the film is automatically good as it has been made by an *auteur* ... For it is objectively speaking safer to trust in the genius of the artist than in one's own critical intelligence. And this is where the *politique des auteurs* falls in line with the system of 'criticism by beauty'; in other words, when one is dealing with genius, it is always a good method to presuppose that a supposed weakness in a work of art is nothing other than a beauty that one has not yet managed to understand. But ... this method had its limitations even in traditionally individualistic arts such as literature, and all the more so in the cinema where the sociological and historical cross-currents are countless ...

Another point is that as the criteria of the *politique des auteurs* are very difficult to formulate the whole thing becomes highly hazardous. It is significant that our finest writers on *Cahiers* have been practising it for three or four years now and have yet to produce the main corpus of its theory. Nor is one particularly likely to forget how Rivette suggested we should admire Hawks: 'The evidence on the screen is the proof of Hawks's genius: you only have to watch *Monkey Business* to know that it is a brilliant film. Some people refuse to admit this, however; they refuse to be satisfied by proof. There can't be any other reason why they don't recognize it …'[19] [For a comment on the implications of Bazin's citation of Rivette in this context, see p. 102 of this Critical History.] You can see the danger: an aesthetic personality cult.

But that is not the main point, at least to the extent that the *politique des auteurs* is practised by people of taste who know how to watch their step. It is its negative side that seems the most serious to me. It is unfortunate to praise a film that in no way deserves it, but the dangers are less far-reaching than when a worthwhile film is rejected because its director has made nothing good up to that point. I am not denying that the champions of the *politique des auteurs* discover or encourage a budding talent when they get the chance. But they do systematically look down on anything in a film that comes from a common fund and which can sometimes be entirely admirable, just as it can be utterly detestable. Thus, a certain kind of popular American culture lies at the basis of *Lust for Life* (1956), directed by Vicente Minnelli (1903–86), but another more spontaneous kind of culture is also the principle of American comedy, the Western, and the gangster film. And its influence here is beneficial, for it is this that gives these cinematic genres their vigour and richness, resulting as they do from an artistic evolution that has always been in wonderfully close harmony with its public. And so one can read a review in *Cahiers* of a Western by Anthony Mann (1906–67) (and God knows I like Anthony Mann's Westerns!)[20] as if it were not above all a Western, i.e. a whole collection of conventions in the script, the acting, and the direction. I know very well that in a film magazine one may be permitted to skip such mundane details; but they should at least be implied, whereas what in fact happens is that their existence is glossed over rather sheepishly, as though they were a rather ridiculous necessity that it would be incongruous to mention. In any case, [*auteur* critics] will look down on, or treat condescendingly, any Western by a director who is not yet approved, even if it is as round and smooth as an egg. Well, what is *Stagecoach* if not an ultra-classical Western in which the art of John Ford consists simply of raising characters and situations to an absolute degree of perfection;[21] and while sitting on the Censorship Committee I have seen some admirable Westerns, more or less anonymous and off the beaten track, but displaying a wonderful knowledge of the conventions of the genre and respecting the style from beginning to end.

Paradoxically, the supporters of the *politique des auteurs* admire the American cinema, where the restrictions of production are heavier than anywhere else. It is also true that it is the country where the greatest technical possibilities are offered to the director. But the one does not cancel out the other. I do however admit that freedom is greater in Hollywood than it is said to be, as long as one knows how to detect its manifestations, and I will go so far as to say that the tradition of genres is a base of operations for creative freedom. The American cinema is a classical art, but why not then admire in it what is most admirable, i.e., not only the talent of this or that film-maker, but the genius of the system, the richness of its ever-vigorous tradition, and its fertility when it comes into contact with new elements – as has been proved, if proof there need be, in such films as Minnelli's *An American in Paris* (1951), *The Seven Year Itch* (1955), directed by Billy Wilder (born 1906), and *Bus Stop* (1956), directed by Joshua Logan (1908–88). True, Logan is lucky enough to be considered an *auteur*, or at least a budding *auteur*. But then when Logan's *Picnic* (1955) or *Bus Stop* get good reviews the praise does not go to what seems to me to be the essential point, i.e. the social truth, which of course is not offered as a goal that suffices in itself but is integrated into a style of cinematic narration just as pre-war America was integrated into American comedy.

To conclude: the *politique des auteurs* seems to me to hold and defend an essential critical truth that the cinema needs more than the other arts, precisely because an act of true artistic creation is more uncertain and vulnerable in the cinema than elsewhere. But its exclusive practice leads to another danger: the negation of the film to the benefit of praise of its *auteur*. I have tried to show why mediocre *auteurs* can, by accident, make admirable films, and how, conversely, a genius can fall victim to an equally accidental sterility. I feel that this useful and fruitful approach, quite apart from its polemical value, should be complemented by other approaches to the cinematic phenomenon which will restore to a film its quality as a work of art. This does not mean one has to deny the role of the *auteur*, but simply give him back the preposition without which the noun *auteur* remains but a halting concept. *Auteur*, yes, but what *of*?[22] □

Bazin's criticisms of the *auteur* approach remain forceful and largely valid. As he observes, the idea of the *auteur* is not essential even in the traditional arts – a point that, in respect of literature, was to be made famously by Roland Barthes in his essay 'The Death of the Author' (1968).[23] In contrast to Barthes, however, Bazin is willing to let the author live and even to see him/her as an index of cultural advance and refinement, provided that the constraints on authorial autonomy, especially in the cinema, are taken into consideration and acknowledged as potentially positive in some respects. Whereas Eric Rohmer saw the artistic triumph of the *auteur*-director as a victory over the constraints of Hollywood, Bazin sees those constraints as contributions to that artistic triumph, and to other cinematic triumphs that are unrecognised because they cannot be attributed to an *auteur*. Bazin identifies and questions certain assumptions that, in his view, go along with an *auteur* approach – for example, that an *auteur*-director's work improves with time since his personality becomes more mature and his artistic experience increases; that the subject or story of a film is unimportant compared to the opportunity it provides for the director to express himself; that an apparent weakness in an *auteur*'s work is a strength that one has yet to grasp. In sum, the *auteur* approach, for Bazin, is flawed in both its evaluative and explanatory critical practice and in its theory. In evaluative terms, its critical practice may constrict its capacity both to acknowledge flaws in films by established *auteurs* and to recognise strengths in films by those on whom *auteur* status has not yet been conferred; in explanatory terms, it pays too little attention to genre and to the cinema industry. As for a real *theory* of the *auteur*, that has yet to appear as an explicit and coherent body of ideas.

In a sense, Bazin's remarks can be seen as the beginning of the end for the *auteur* approach as a dominant critical and (quasi-)theoretical position. It was an approach that had undoubtedly had a strong strategic importance, in the way in which it drew on an entrenched cultural assumption – that great works in literature and painting were the product of authors of genius – in order to elevate the status of film as a cultural form worthy of admiration and analysis; and the analyses that it generated were often very insightful. But, as was suggested by the comments earlier in this chapter on Rivette's discussion of Hawks, the idea of the *auteur*, while it may have been *enabling* in the sense that it provided a justification for taking hitherto neglected films seriously, was not *essential*: much of the analysis produced by Rivette, Chabrol or Rohmer could survive the death of the *auteur*. But is this to say that the idea of the *auteur* is now superfluous? Hardly: it remains, as Bazin said, a useful and fruitful approach – and a fascinating and intellectually challenging one – to explore the ways in which a particular director, working within all the constraints of the medium and the industry, may have made films marked by a distinctive vision and style. But it is still the case that the contribution of the director remains under-theorised; *auteur* theory in the 1950s perhaps needed its Jean-Paul Sartre, who would have applied to film directors a combination of biographical, stylistic, psychological, sociological and philosophical perspectives similar to that employed in Sartre's 'existential biographies' of Baudelaire, Genet and Flaubert.[24] A revival of *auteur* theory today would need both to study specific directors and to develop its own combination of investigative approaches, perhaps starting from Sartre. But as the 1960s accelerated, *auteur* theory, as championed by *Cahiers*, and the idea of realism, as variously expressed by Bazin and Kracauer, were to come under challenge and would be, for a time, swept aside by a heady combination of politics, semiotics, psycho-analysis and post-structuralism. In the aftermath of the turbulent events of 1968, *Cahiers* would apply this shifting kaleidoscope of political, semi-ological, psychoanalytical and post-structuralist perspectives to film theory: but the kaleidoscope would reveal its richest cinematic patterns in the British journal *Screen*.

CHAPTER FOUR

Storming the Reality Studios: *Screen*

In the 1970s, *Screen* would become the major forum for the dissemination and development of the semiotic, post-structuralist, psycho-analytical and politicised film theory that would displace the realist and *auteur* approaches to film. It might seem surprising that such a journal should emerge in Britain, a culture notoriously resistant to theory; but a concatenation of circumstances led to a magazine that had originally been concerned with film education in a relatively practical way turning into a theoretical platform for a range of young intellectuals, most notably Stephen Heath and Colin MacCabe. MacCabe was to become the centre of a controversy that became national news when Cambridge University refused to confirm his probationary appointment as a lecturer in English – a refusal that was related to his theoretical interests and, MacCabe believed, to his work on television and film.[1]

Screen, generously funded by the British Film Institute in the early 1970s, had, as MacCabe observes, a 'strong material base' that enabled it to pursue its theoretical concerns without too much practical worry.[2] Those theoretical concerns were closely linked with educational, cultural and political engagements, as Stephen Heath recalls:

■ I have instant physical memories of long evening hours spent in the office we had in Old Compton Street, with Soho lights and street noise as backdrop to the intensity of our debates. There was a sense of inventing a cultural politics around education and the media, of thinking about what the critique and transformation of film and then television might be. *Screen* had a marginal institutional position as a subsidiary part of the Society for Education in Film and Television which was itself an outpost of the British Film Institute; at the same time, it interconnected in various ways with the educational sector, with various cultural and radical bodies, with a number of independent film-making groups, and so on. These interconnections were often difficult, contradictory, and tense, which was the point, the impetus in the working through of the issues. More than a journal, *Screen* was also meetings, weekend schools, interventions in different kinds of event, a whole educational process sharply centred on matters of cultural-political analysis. How do you think about, analyse, understand, effectively criticize and change such powerful and widely received social productions of meaning as film and television?[3] □

One important approach that *Screen* employed to try to understand, criticise and change received productions of meaning in film and television was the critique of classic realism derived from the French literary and cultural critic Roland Barthes (1915–80) and, more distantly, from the German Marxist playwright Bertolt Brecht (1898–1956) – a critique that drew on structuralism, Marxism and the psychoanalysis of Freud and Jacques Lacan (1901–81). In this critique, classic realism, especially in the novel, was characterised by a hierarchy of discourses in which the dominant discourse delivers the supposed truths of human nature and helps to produce a falsely satisfying sense of closure, an imaginary resolution of real contradictions that disables political perception and action. Colin MacCabe's 'Realism and the Cinema: Notes on some Brechtian Theses', first published in *Screen* 15:2 in Summer 1974, begins by discussing the classic realist text as exemplified by a scene in George Eliot's *Middlemarch* (1871–2); he then suggests that, with a slight adaptation, the notion of the classic realist text can also be applied to film:

■ The narrative prose [in the classic realist novel] achieves its position of dominance because it is in the position of knowledge and this function of knowledge is taken up in the cinema by the narration of events. Through the knowledge we gain from the narrative we can split the discourses of the various characters from their situation and compare what is said in these discourses with what has been revealed to us through narration. The camera shows us what happens – it tells the truth against which we can measure the discourses. A good example of this classical realist structure is to be found in *Klute* (1971) [a film made by Alan J. Pakula (born 1928)]. This film is of particular interest because it was widely praised for its realism on its release. Perhaps even more significantly, it tended to be praised for its realistic presentation of the leading woman, Bree (played by Jane Fonda).

In *Klute* the relationship of dominance between discourses is peculiarly accentuated by the fact that the film is interspersed with

fragments of Bree talking to her psychiatrist. This subjective discourse can be exactly measured against the reality provided by the
unfolding of the story. Thus all her talk of independence is portrayed
as finally an illusion as we discover, to no great surprise but to our
immense relief, what she really wants is to settle down in the mid-
West with John Klute (the detective played by Donald Sutherland)
and have a family. The final sequence of the film is particularly telling
in this respect. While Klute and Bree pack their bags to leave, the
soundtrack records Bree at her last meeting with her psychiatrist. Her
own estimate of the situation is that it most probably won't work but
the reality of the image [assures] us that this is the way it will really be.
Indeed Bree's monologue is even more interesting – for in relation to
the reality of the image it marks a definite advance on her previous
statements. She has gained insight through the plot development and
like many good heroines of classic realist texts her discourse is more
nearly adequate to the truth at the end of the film than at the beginning. But if a progression towards knowledge is what marks Bree, it
is possession of knowledge which marks the narrative, the reader of
the film and John Klute himself. For Klute is privileged by the narrative as the one character whose discourse is also a discourse of
knowledge. Not only is Klute a detective and thus can solve the problem of his friend's disappearance – he is also a man, and a man who
because he has not come into contact with the city has not had his
virility undermined. And it is as a full-blooded man that he can know
not only the truth of the mystery of the murders but also the truth of
the woman Bree. Far from being a film which goes any way to portraying a woman liberated from male definitions (a common critical
response), *Klute* exactly guarantees that the real essence of woman
can only be discovered and defined by a man.

The analysis sketched here is obviously very schematic but what,
hopefully, it does show is that the structure of the classic realist text
can be found in film as well. That narrative of events – the knowledge
which the film provides of how things really are – is the metalanguage
in which we can talk of the various characters in the film. What would
still remain to be done in the elaboration of the structure of the classic realist text in cinema is a more detailed account of the actual
mechanisms by which the narrative is privileged (and the way in
which one or more of the characters within the narrative can be
equally privileged) and also a history of the development of this dominant narrative. On the synchronic level it would be necessary to

attempt an analysis of the relationship between the various types of shot and their combination into sequences – are there for example certain types of shot which are coded as subjective and therefore subordinate to others which are guaranteed as objective? In addition how does music work as the guarantee or otherwise of truth? On the diachronic level it would be necessary to study how this form was produced – what relationship obtains between the classic realist text and technical advances such as the development of the talkie? What ideological factors were at work in the production and dominance of the classic realist text?

To return, however, to the narrative discourse. It is necessary to attempt to understand the type of relations that this dominant discourse produces. The narrative discourse cannot be mistaken in its identifications because the narrative discourse is not present as discourse – as articulation. The unquestioned nature of the narrative discourse entails that the only problem that reality poses is to go and look and see what *Things* there are. The relationship between the reading subject and the real is placed as one of pure specularity [looking]. The real is not articulated – it is. These features imply two essential features of the classic realist text:

1. The classic realist text cannot deal with the real as contradictory.
2. In a reciprocal movement the classic realist text ensures the position of the subject in a relation of dominant specularity ... ...

It may be objected that the account I have given of the classic [realist] text is deficient in the following extremely important fashion. It ignores what is the usual criterion for realism, that is to say subject matter. The category of the classic realist text lumps together in book and film *The Grapes of Wrath* (1939) and *The Sound of Music* (1965), *L'Assommoir* (1877) and *Toad of Toad Hall* (1930).[4] In order to find a criterion with which to make distinctions within the area of the classic realist text it is necessary to reflect on contradiction. I have stated that the classic realist text cannot deal with the real in its contradiction because of the unquestioned status of the representation at the level of the dominant discourse. In order to understand how contradiction can be dealt with[,] it is necessary to investigate the workings of an operation that is often opposed to representation, namely montage ... ... Eisenstein thinks of the world as being composed of basic objects available to sight which are then linked together in various ways by the perceiving subject with the aid of his past experiences ...

Montage is ... for Eisenstein, in [his theoretical writings] (which must not be confused with Eisenstein's cinematic practice), the manipulation of definite representations to produce images in the mind of the spectator. But now it can be seen that this definition of montage does not contradict representation at all. If we understand by representation the rendering of identities in the world then Eisenstein's account of montage is not opposed to representation but is simply a secondary process which comes after representation. Eisenstein would have montage linking onto representation but not in any sense challenging it. The representation starts from an identity in the world which it re-presents, the montage starts from representations, identities, and combines them to form an image.

Eisenstein's acceptance of representation can be seen in those passages where representation is contrasted with montage. For Eisenstein the opposite to montage is ['*affidavit-exposition*'] which he defines as 'in film terms, *representations shot from a single set-up*'.[5] Thus montage is the showing of the same representation from different points of view. And it is from this point that we can begin to challenge Eisenstein's conception of montage. A point of view suggests two things. Firstly a view – something that is seen – and secondly a location from which the view may be had, the sight may be seen. Thus the suggestion is that there are different locations from which we can see. But in all cases the sight remains the same – the activity of representation is not the determining factor in the sight seen but simply the place from where it is seen. The inevitable result of this is that there is something the same which we all see but which appears differently because of our position. But if there is identity; if there is something over and above the views which can be received at different points then this identity must be discern[i]ble from some other 'point of view'. And this neutral point of view is exactly the '*representations shot from a single set-up*'.

What is at work in Eisenstein's argument is the idea that there is some fixed reality which is available to us from an objective point of view (the single set-up). Montage is simply putting these fixed elements together in such a way that the subject [the person who perceives, the spectator of the film] brings forth other elements in his experience – but without any change in the identities, the elements that are being rendered. It is essential to realise that this account leaves both subject [the person who perceives] and object [what is perceived] unchallenged and that montage becomes a kind of super-representation which is more effective at demonstrating the real qualities of the object through the links it can form within the subject ... What Eisenstein ignores is that the method of representation (the language: verbal or cinematic) determines in its structural activity (the oppositions which can be articulated) both the places where the object 'appears' and the 'point' from which the object is seen. It is this point which is exactly the place allotted to the reading subject ... ...

[O]pposed to Eisenstein's concept of montage resting on the juxta-positions of identities already rendered, we could talk of montage as the effect generated by a conflict of discourse in which the oppositions available in the juxtaposed discourses are contradictory and in conflict.

... [T]he classic realist text (a heavily 'closed' discourse) cannot deal with the real in its contradictions and ... in the same movement it fixes the subject in a point of view from which everything becomes obvious. There is, however, a level of contradiction into which the classic realist text can enter. This is the contradiction between the dominant discourse of the text and the dominant ideological discourses of the time. Thus a classic realist text in which a strike is represented as a just struggle in which oppressed workers attempt to gain some of their rightful wealth would be in contradiction with certain contemporary ideological discourses and as such might be classified as progressive. It is here that subject matter enters into the argument and where we can find the justification for Marx and Engels's praise of Balzac and Lenin's texts on the revolutionary force of Tolstoy's texts which ush-ered the Russian peasant on to the stage of history. Within contempo-rary films one could think of the films of Constantine Costa-Gavras (born 1933) or such television documentaries as *Cathy Come Home* (1966). What is, however, still impossible for the classic realist text is to offer any perspectives for struggle due to its inability to investigate contradiction. It is thus not surprising that these films tend either to be linked to a social democratic conception of progress – if we reveal injustices then they will go away – or certain *ouvrieriste* ['workerist'] tendencies which tend to see the working class, outside any dialecti-cal movement, as the simple possessors of truth. It is at this point that Brecht's demand that literary and artistic productions be regarded as social events gains its force. The contradictions between the dominant discourse in a classic realist text and the dominant ideological dis-courses at work in a society are what provide the criteria for discrim-inating within the classic realist text. And these criteria will often resolve themselves into questions of subject matter.[6] □

MacCabe draws on psychoanalysis to offer an account of moments and strategies of textual subversion that go beyond the representation of progressive subject matter within a realist framework:

■ Freud's theory is a theory of the construction of the subject: the entry of the small infant into language and society and the methods by which it learns what positions, as subject, it can take up. This entry into the symbolic [order] (the whole cultural space which is structured, like language[,] through a set of differences and oppositions) is most easily traced in the analytic situation through that entry which is finally determining for the infant – the problem of sexual difference. Freud's insight is that the unproblematic taking up of the position of the subject entails the repression of the whole mechanism of the subject's construction. The subject is seen as the founding source of meanings – unproblematically standing outside an articulation in which it is, in fact, defined. This view of the subject as founding source is philosophically encapsulated in Descartes' *cogito*: I think, therefore I am – the I in simple evidence to itself provides a moment of pure presence which can found the enterprise of analysing the world. Jacques Lacan, the French psychoanalyst, has read Freud as reformulating the Cartesian *cogito* and destroying the subject as source and foundation – Lacan rewrites the *cogito*, in the light of Freud's discoveries[,] as, I think where I am not and I am where I do not think. We can understand this formulation as the indicating of the fundamental misunderstanding (*méconnaissance*) which is involved in the successful use of language (or any other area of the symbolic which is similarly structured) in which the subject is continually ignored as being caught up in a process of articulation to be taken as a fixed place founding the discourse. The unconscious is that effect of language which escapes the conscious subject in the distance between the act of signification[,] in which the subject passes from signifier to signifier[,] and what is signified[,] in which the subject finds himself in place as, for example, the pronoun 'I'. The importance of phenomena like verbal slips is that they testify to the existence of the unconscious through the distance between what was said and what the conscious subject intended to say. They thus testify to the distance between the subject of the act of signification and the conscious subject (the ego). In this distance there is opened a gap which is the area of desire. What is essential to all of those psychic productions which Freud uses in the analytic interpretation is that they bear witness to the lack of control of the conscious subject over his dis courses. The mechanisms of the unconscious can indeed be seen as the mechanisms of language. Condensation is the work of metaphor which brings together two signifieds under one signifier and displacement is the constant process along the signifying chain. The ego is constantly caught in this fundamental misunderstanding (*méconnaissance*) about language in which from an illusory present it attempts to read only one signified as present in the metaphor and attempts to bring the signifying chain to an end in a perpetually deferred present.

The relationship between the unconscious and desire, the subject and language is concisely summarised by Lacan in the following passage:

There is not *an* unconscious because then there would be an unconscious desire which was obtuse, heavy, caliban like, even animal like, an unconscious desire lifted up from the depths which would be primitive and would have to educate itself to the superior level of consciousness. Completely on the contrary there is desire because there is unconsciousness (*de l'inconscient*) – that's to say language which escapes the subject in its structure and in its effects and there is always at the level of language something which is beyond consciousness and it is there that one can situate the function of desire.[7]

It is clear that the classic realist text ... guarantees the position of the subject exactly outside any articulation – the whole text works on the concealing of the dominant discourse as articulation – instead the dominant discourse presents itself exactly as the presentation of objects to the reading subject. But within the classic realist text the dominant discourse can be subverted, brought into question – the position of the subject may be rendered problematic ... [There is] the possibility of *moments* within a classical realist text which subvert it and its evident status for subject and object. We are relatively fortunate in already possessing this kind of analysis within the cinema in the *Cahiers du Cinéma*'s reading of John Ford's *Young Mr Lincoln* (1939).[8] These *moments* are those elements which escape the control of the dominant discourse in the same way as a neurotic symptom or a verbal slip attest to the lack of control of the conscious subject. They open up another area than that of representation – of subject and object caught in an eternal paralysed fixity – in order to investigate the very movement of articulation and difference – the movement of desire ... Over and above these *moments* of subversion, however, there are what one might call *strategies* of subversion. Instead of a dominant discourse which is transgressed at various crucial moments we can find a systematic refusal of any such dominant discourse. One of the best examples of a cinema which practises certain strategies of subversion are the films of Roberto Rossellini. In *Germany Year Zero* (1947), for example, we can locate a multitude of ways in which the reading subject finds himself without a position from which the film can be regarded. Firstly, and most importantly, the fact that the narrative is not privileged in any way with regard to the characters' discourses. The narrative does not produce for us the knowledge with which we can then judge the truth of those discourses. Rather than the narrative providing us with knowledge – it provides us with various settings. Just as in Brecht the 'fable' serves simply as a procedure to produce the various *gests*, so in Rossellini the story simply provides a framework for various scenes which then constitute the picture of Germany in year zero. [A '*gest*' or '*gestus*' is 'an expression in words and movement of basic attitudes. It demonstrates a relationship cut to essentials.'[9]] ... Indeed the narrative of *Germany Year Zero* can be seen as a device to introduce the final *gest* of Edmund's suicide – and in this it closely resembles the first reel of Brecht's own *Kuhle Wampe* (1932, aka *Whither Germany?* and *To Whom Does the World Belong?*) [scripted by Brecht, directed by Slatan Dudow (1903–63)]. Secondly, Rossellini's narrative introduces many elements which are not in any sense resolved and which deny the possibility of regarding the film as integrated through a dominant discourse. The Allied soldiers, the street kids, the landlord, the Teacher's house – all these provide elements which stretch outside the narrative of the film and deny its dominance.

The result of these two strategies is that the characters themselves cannot be identified in any final way. Instead of their discourses, clothes, mannerisms being the punctual expressions of an identity fixed by the narrative – each element is caught up in a complex set of differences. The whole problematic of inside and outside which preoccupies the classic realist text is transformed into a series of relationships in which word, dress, action and gesture interact to provide a never-finished series of significant differences which is the character.

It may be objected that it is deliberately perverse to tear Rossellini away from realism with which he has been firmly connected both through his own statements and through critical reception. The realist element in Rossellini is not simply located in the subject matter, the traditional criterion of realism, for I have already argued that the subject matter is a secondary condition for realism. What typifies the classic realist text is the way the subject matter is ordered and articulated rather than its origins. To deal with the facts of the world is, in itself, not only a realist but also a materialist viewpoint. The materialist, however, must regard these materials as ordered within a certain mode of production, within which they find their definition. And it is here that one could begin to isolate that element of realist ideology which does figure in Rossellini's films as a certain block. If the reading subject is not offered any certain mode of entry into what is presented on the screen, he is offered a certain mode of entry to the screen itself. For the facts presented by the camera, if they are not ordered in fixed and final fashion amongst themselves, *are* ordered in themselves. The camera, in Rossellini's films[,] is not articulated as part of the productive process of the film. What it shows is in some sense beyond argument and it is here that Rossellini's films show the traditional realist weakness of being unable to deal with contradiction. In *Viva l'Italia* (1960) the glaring omission of the film is the absence of Cavour [Camillo Cavour (1810–61) was the liberal architect of the Risorgimento, the nineteenth-century movement for Italian independence and unification]. It is wrong to attack this omission on purely political grounds for it is an inevitable result of a certain lack of questioning of the camera itself. Garibaldi can be contrasted with Francisco II of Naples because their different conceptions of the world are so specifically tied to different historical eras that the camera can cope with their contradictions within an historical perspective. [Giuseppe Garibaldi (1807–82) was the soldier-hero of the Risorgimento.] Here is the way the world is now – there is the way the world was then. But to introduce Cavour would involve a simultaneous contradiction – a class contradiction. At this point the camera itself, as a neutral agent, would become impossible. For it would have to offer two present contradictory articulations of the world and thus reveal its own presence. This cannot happen within a Rossellini film where if we are continually aware of our presence in the cinema (particularly in his historical films) – that presence itself is not questioned in any way. We are not allowed any particular position to read the film but we are allowed the position of a reader – an unproblematic viewer – an eternally human nature working on the material provided by the camera.

A possible way of advancing on Rossellini's practice (there are no obvious films which have marked such an advance although some of Godard's early films might be so considered) would be to develop the possibility of articulating contradiction. Much in the way that James Joyce in *Ulysses* and *Finnegans Wake* (1939) investigated the contradictory ways of articulating reality through an investigation of the different forms of language, one could imagine a more radical strategy of subversion than that practised by Rossellini in which the possibilities of the camera would be brought more clearly into play. What would mark such a cinema and indeed any cinema of subversion would be ... that it would be ill at ease in the class struggle, always concerned with an area of contradiction beyond the necessity of the present revolution – the ineliminable contradictions of the sexes, the eternal struggle between Desire and Law, between articulation and position.[10] □

MacCabe then outlines the possibility of what he would see as a truly revolutionary text. Once more, he draws on psychoanalysis, this time on the concept of fetishism:

■ The fetish is that object which places the subject in a position of security outside of that terrifying area of difference opened up by the perception of the mother's non-possession of the phallus. Although most popular accounts of fetishism concentrate on the fetishised objects, it is exemplary for Roland Barthes as a structure which holds both subject and object in place – it is the fetish above all that holds the subject in position. What is essential to Barthes's argument is the idea that the subject must always be the same – caught in the same position vis-à-vis the world. Within this view a revolutionary work of art can do no more than provide a correct representation (provided by the [Communist] Party) of the world. It may be helpful[, in order] to attain this goal[,] to subvert the position of the subject so that his acceptance of the new representation is facilitated but finally the revolutionary artist is committed (condemned) to the world of representation.

Within the framework I have constructed in this article one could say that the revolutionary artist may practice certain strategies of subversion but must finally content himself with the production of a progressive realist text. The question I want to raise here, and it must be emphasized that it can only be raised, is the possibility of *another* activity which rather than the simple subversion of the subject or the representation of different (and *correct*) identities, would consist of the displacement of the subject within ideology – a different constitution of the subject ... ... What Brecht suggests in his comments on the spectator in the cinema is that the very position offered to the spectator is one that guarantees the necessary re-production of labour power. It is the cinema's ability to place the spectator in the position of a unified subject that ensures the contradiction between his working activity which is productive and the leisure activity in which he is constantly placed as consumer. Louis Althusser (1918– 90) makes the very important point in his essay ['Ideology and Ideological State Apparatuses' (1971)] that ideology is not a question of ideas circulating in people's heads but is inscribed in certain material practices.[11] The reactionary practice of the cinema is that which involves this petrifaction of the spectator in a position of pseudo-dominance offered by the metalanguage. This metalanguage, resolving as it does all contradictions, places the spectator outside the realm of contradiction and of action – outside of production.

Two films which suggest a way of combating this dominance of the metalanguage, without falling into an agnostic position vis-à-vis all discourses (which would be the extreme of a subversive cinema – intent merely on disrupting any position of the subject) are *Kuhle Wampe* (the film in which Brecht participated) and Godard–Gorin's *Tout Va Bien* (1972) [directed by Jean-Luc Godard, scripted by Jean-Pierre Gorin]. In both films the narrative is in no way privileged as against the characters. Rather the narrative serves simply as the method by which various situations can be articulated together. The emphasis is on the particular scenes and the knowledge that can be gained from them rather than the providing of a knowledge which requires no further activity – which just is there on the screen. Indeed the presentation of the individual's discourses is never stripped away from the character's actions but is involved in them. Whether it is a question of the petit-bourgeois and the workers discussing the waste of coffee in the S-Bahn or the various monologues in *Tout Va Bien* – it is not a question of the discourses being presented as pure truth content which can be measured against the truth provided by the film. Rather the discourses are caught up in certain modes of life which are linked to the place of the agent in the productive process. The unemployed workers know that waste is an inevitable part of the capitalist process because they experience it every day in their search for work. Equally the workers in the meat factory know that the class struggle is not finished for they experience the exploitation of their labour in such concrete details as the time that is allowed them to go to the toilet. The film does not provide this knowledge ready-made in a dominant discourse but in the contradictions offered, the reader has to produce a meaning for the film (it is quite obvious in films of this sort that the meaning produced will depend on the class-positions of the reader). It is this emphasis on the reader as producer (more obvious in *Tout Va Bien* which is in many ways more Brechtian than *Kuhle Wampe*) which suggests that these films do not just offer a different representation for the subject but a different set of relations to both the fictional material and 'reality'.

Very briefly this change could be characterized as the introduction of time (history) into the very area of representation so that it is included within it. It is no accident that both films end with this same emphasis on time and its concomitant change. 'But who will change the world' (*Kuhle Wampe*) – 'We must learn to live historically' (*Tout Va Bien*) – this emphasis on time and change embodied both within the film and in the position offered to the reader suggests that a revolutionary socialist ideology might be different in form as well as content. It also throws into doubt Barthes's thesis that revolutionary art is finally caught in the same space of representation that has persisted for 2,000 years in the West. This monolithic conception of representation ignores the fact that post-Einsteinian physics offers a conception of representation in which both subject and object are no longer caught in fixed positions but caught up in time.

It might be thought that this possibility of change, of transformation – in short, of production – built into the subject–object relation (which could no longer be characterized in this simple fashion) simply reduplicates the Hegelian error of final reconciliation between the orders of being and consciousness. But this is not so in so far as this possibility of change built into the relation does not imply the inevitable unfolding of a specific series of changes but simply the possibility of change – an area of possible transformations contained within the relation.

It seems that some such account must be offered if one wishes to allow the possibility of a revolutionary art. Otherwise it seems inevitable that art can simply be progressive or subversive and Brecht's whole practice would be a marriage of the two, in which subversive effects were mechanically used simply to aid the acceptance of the progressive content of his work.[12] □

MacCabe's analysis remains lucid and forceful and its conceptual arsenal and aggressive tone exemplify a particular moment, not only in the development of *Screen*, but also in film theory more generally – a moment when film theory was linked to post-structuralism and to potential revolution. There are a number of problems with MacCabe's account, however. His reading of *Klute* leaves little room for alternative interpretations, and in particular it implicitly proscribes the possibility of any positive feminist response to Bree by taking a faintly patronising tone, when Bree is compared to 'many good heroines of classic realist texts' and when the idea that the film might portray a partly liberated woman is defined as a 'common' – and erroneous – critical response. As he himself acknowledges, his analysis of *Klute* is 'very schematic' and could be seen to oversimplify a rather more complex and contradictory narrative – a narrative which would unsettle his claim that the classic realist text cannot deal with the real as contradictory and that it provides a secure subject position from which the world can be clearly viewed. MacCabe's model here is the combination of political and textual radicalism developed by the group around the magazine *Tel Quel* that included Barthes, Philippe Sollers and Julia Kristeva, and with which MacCabe, and even more so Stephen Heath, were associated. The idea was that conventionally realistic cinematic or literary texts had no part to play in political revolution and that, even where their content was progressive, their adherence to unproblematic representation made them inevitably reactionary. Truly revolutionary texts subverted representation and coherence. But there were difficulties with this position: how many people would be likely to watch or read such texts? How could such texts relate to political action beyond the initial shattering of an illusion of coherence and verisimilitude? And was there not, behind the supposed radicalism of such texts, the sense of a universal, unchanging truth – what MacCabe himself, in the above extract, calls 'the ineliminable contradictions of the sexes, the eternal struggle between Desire and Law, between articulation and position' – that could prove disabling?

MacCabe's work was closely linked with that of Stephen Heath. In the 1970s, Heath produced a number of essays, published in *Screen* and elsewhere, that covered a range of aspects of film theory as seen through post-structuralist and semiotic perspectives. In the following extract from 'On Screen, in Frame: Film and Ideology', he provides concise

Potemkin (Sergei Eisenstein, Soviet Union, 1925): 'Three short shots: a stone lion asleep; a stone lion with open eyes; a rampant stone lion. … [O]ne of Eisenstein's most striking visual metaphors. A stone lion rises to its feet and roars. This amazing image [is] impossible ... outside the limitations of the silent screen.' (Roger Scruton)

TOP: *Citizen Kane* (Orson Welles, USA, 1941): 'Thanks to the depth of field, whole scenes are covered in one take, the camera remaining motionless. Dramatic effects for which we had formerly relied on montage were created out of the movements of the actors within a fixed framework.' (André Bazin)

BOTTOM: *Rear Window* (Alfred Hitchcock, USA, 1954): '[T]he individual is the split atom, the couple is the molecule, the building is the body composed of x number of molecules, and itself split from the rest of the world. ... [T]he profound reason for the loneliness of the world ... is established as the absence of communication between human beings, in a word, the absence of love.' (Claude Chabrol)

Rebel Without a Cause (Nicholas Ray, USA, 1955): 'James Dean
… is like a chrysalis badly folded out of its cocoon. Turned in on
himself? A solitude that is suffered rather than willed, a tortured
quest for affection, for love or friendship.' (Eric Rohmer)

Klute (Alan J. Pakula, USA, 1971): 'Far from being a film which goes any way to portraying a woman liberated from male definitions (a common critical response), *Klute* exactly guarantees that the real essence of woman can only be discovered and defined by a man.' (Colin MacCabe)

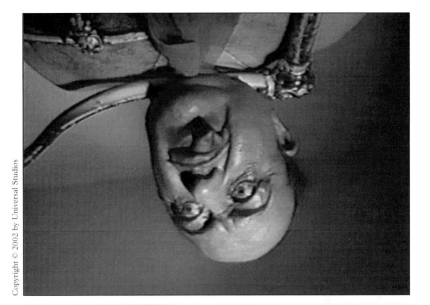

TOP: *Touch of Evil* (Orson Welles, USA, 1958): 'The scenery is photographed from odd, often low, angles, with a climax in the subjective shot which shows how the wife wakes up from her drugged condition and sees the weird and bloody head of a murdered man turned upside-down above her.' (Torben Grodal)

BOTTOM: *Pat Garrett and Billy the Kid* (Sam Peckinpah, USA, 1973): 'Significantly, Kris Kristofferson as Billy ..., the ultimate incarnation of omnipotent male narcissism in Peckinpah's films, is spared any bloody and splintered death. Shot by Pat Garrett, his body shows no sign either of wounds or blood: narcissism transfigured (rather than destroyed) by death.' (Steve Neale)

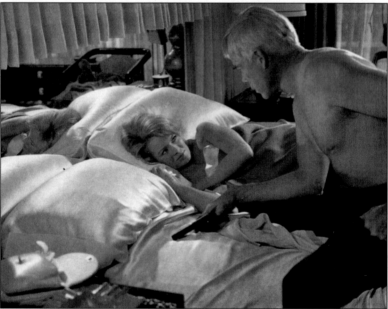

TOP: *Vertigo* (Alfred Hitchcock, USA, 1958): '[T]he look is central to the plot, oscillating between voyeurism and fetishistic fascination. ... The power to subject another person to the will sadistically or to the gaze voyeuristically is turned onto the woman as the object of both.' (Laura Mulvey)

BOTTOM: *Point Blank* (John Boorman, USA, 1967): '[D]irect displays of the male body can be found, though they tend ... to be fairly brief ... Examples ... would include ... some of the images of Lee Marvin in *Point Blank*.' (Steve Neale)

TOP: *All About Eve* (Joseph L. Mankiewicz, USA, 1950): '*All About Eve* is … precisely about the pleasures and dangers of spectatorship for women. One of its central themes is the construction and reproduction of feminine identities, and the activity of looking is highlighted as an important part of these processes.' (Jackie Stacey)

BOTTOM: *Le Samouraï* (Jean-Pierre Melville, France, 1967): '[N]arcissism is stressed in particular through his obsessive concern with his appearance … omnipotence, silence and inviolability are all under threat. … The kind of image that Delon here embodies … is one marked not only by emotional reticence, but also by silence, a reticence with language. Theoretically, this silence, this absence of language can further be linked to narcissism and to the construction of an ideal ego.' (Steve Neale)

Once Upon a Time in the West (Sergio Leone, Italy/USA, 1972): '[M]ale struggle becomes pure spectacle. Perhaps the most extreme examples [of voyeuristic looking] are to be found in Leone's Westerns, where the exchange of aggressive looks … is taken to the point of fetishistic parody through the use of extreme and repetitive close-ups. At which point the look begins to oscillate between voyeurism and fetishism as the narrative starts to freeze and spectacle takes over.' (Steve Neale)

definitions of an array of terms that are crucial to thinking about film and cinema in those perspectives:

- The distinction can be made between industry, machine and text. *Industry* refers to the direct economic system of cinema, the organization of the structure of production, distribution and consumption. Studies have shown that such organization has, at least in Britain and America, by and large conformed to typical patterns of capitalist activity [Heath does not give references here for these studies]. The *text*, the film, is a particular product of that industry. Currency is occasionally given to the idea that the film industry is one of 'prototypes' ('every film a new film'), but it is clear that the optimal exploitation of the production apparatus, which ties up considerable amounts of capital, requires the containment of creative work within established frameworks and that genres, film kinds, even so-called 'studio styles', are crucial factors here. As for the *machine*, this is cinema itself seized exactly between industry and product as the stock of constraints and definitions from which film can be distinguished as *specific signifying practice*. That formulation in turn needs to be opened out a little. *Signifying* indicates the recognition of film as system or series of systems of meanings, film as articulation. *Practice* stresses the process of this articulation, which it thus refuses to hold under the assumption of notions such as 'representation' and 'expression'; it takes film as a work of production of meanings and in so doing brings into the analysis the question of the positionings of the subject within that work. *Specific* is the necessity for the analysis to understand film in the particularity of the work it engages, the difference of its conjuncture with other signifying practices. This last does not entail pulling film as specific signifying practice towards some aesthetic idea of a pure cinematicity …; specificity here is semiotic, and a semiotic analysis of film – of film as signifying practice – is the analysis of a heterogeneity, the range of codes and systems at work in the film-text; specificity, that is, is at once those codes particular to cinema (codes of articulation of sound and image, codes of scale of shot, certain codes of narrative arrangement, etc.) *and* the heterogeneity in its particular effects, its particular inscriptions of subject and ideology, of the subject in ideology.[13] □

The conceptual tools for the analysis of the film-text are developed further in 'Film, System, Narrative', with particular relation to a specific example of such a film-text – Orson Welles's *Touch of Evil* (1958):

■ It is as though the film – a film – presented itself in the form of a *narrative image*, a kind of static portrait in which it comes together, on the basis of which it is talked about (the production stills displayed outside a cinema are so many incitements to such an image). 'Unity', 'work', the fiction film is defined by its closure: the consistency (this is well and truly the realm of the imaginary) or again the coalescence (the signified which fills the signifier) of this image which is in fact the film's currency, that on which it can be bought and sold, marketed (by criticism, for instance). This being so, the detail of the film – the possible chance of the signifier – matters little. Sure enough (but the observation is no doubt banal), working 'in detail' on *Touch of Evil*, I have often been confronted by critical summaries that are unashamedly false to the manifest discourse – the body of the film … but which none the less (and it is this [which] is significant) answer exactly to the narrative image, to the negotiable meaning: errors then, but correct errors, perfectly in accordance with the hold of the film, helping it to achieve and sustain consistency, coalescence.

The film must hang together: the narrative, therefore, must work. Hence the requirement of practicability so constantly held to by the unfolding – the resolving progress – of the narrative film. Every element introduced must be practicable in the development of the narrative, must be taken up again and be 'finished off' as an evident function in its progress, its resolution (the fiction film follows very much an order of *evidence*). While talking on the telephone, Vargas (Charlton Heston), the hero of *Touch of Evil*, opens his briefcase, takes out a gun and checks that it is in good working condition; later, he finds the briefcase, entrusted to his wife who has been kidnapped, opens it and discovers the gun to be missing; the gun finally reappears in the hands of his enemy. The example is typical of this 'taking up again', this 'finishing off': the gun was not introduced for nothing, is *of use*. The narrative, that is, strives to gather up the elements it puts forward in order with them to go forward *evidently*.

This, however, is never simple, never without slippage: the narrative cannot contain *everything*. Except by resorting to a scrupulous – 'abstract' – construction of profilmic space (in the manner of the scene in *An Actor's Revenge* (1963), directed by Kon Ichikawa (born 1915) which utilizes only three actors, a tree and a rope against a black back-cloth, but this is a very different economy to that of the films of the dominant Western cinema), the narrative film can only seek to maintain a tight balance between the photographic image as a reproduction of reality and the narrative as the sense, the intelligibility, of that reality (a balance which is the ideological good fortune of the fiction film, simultaneously sense and reality, naturalizing the one from the other). The film picks up – indicating by framing, shot angle, lighting, dialogue mention, musical underscoring, and so on – the notable elements (to be noted in and for the progress of the narrative which in return defines their notability) without for all that giving up what is thus left aside and which it seeks to retain – something of an available reserve of insignificant material – in order precisely to ring 'true', true *to reality*. In short, the film-narrative is a *regulated* loss, that loss becoming the *sign* of the real.

Yet it happens too that this regulation runs into its own loss, goes off in evasions and abandonments. Abandonment: taken to a hotel on the promise of information concerning her husband, Susan (Janet Leigh), Vargas's wife, is tricked into having her photograph taken in front of the entrance with a young Mexican, the start perhaps of a plan to blackmail or compromise her in some way; but though she is later sent the photo, nothing comes of it, it has no finish; the narrative lets it drop, abandons. Evasion: near the beginning and near the end of the film are two great scenes between Quinlan (Orson Welles), an unscrupulous cop ready for any kind of deal or scheme that will enable him to convict a suspect and who is being pursued by Vargas for just such a frame-up (I am borrowing here from the version of the narrative image provided by André Bazin),[14] and Tanya (Marlene Dietrich), owner of a *maison close* [brothel] that Quinlan used to visit in days long gone; scenes that are oblique to the narrative, that do not have its sense, its direction; scenes that stop, evade the action of the film, and that bring with them moreover a whole mythology or nostalgia of the past: of Quinlan and Tanya, of Welles and Dietrich (*Follow the Boys*, the film-review in which they played together in 1944), of cinema (the richly Sternbergian décor of Tanya-Dietrich's house); scenes in which the narrative slips, drifts.

'That festival of affects [emotional experiences] that is called a film', writes Barthes.[15] The narrative takes care of this affectivity (which it thus also sets out), places it (comes to an end of the free circulation, constructs positions for the subject). Finally, the narrative is the very triumph of *framing* (the links between conventions of framing and the demands of the narrative have often been stressed); the frame is what holds tight against movement and slippage, cuts short the interminable play of the signifier, the subject in process, imposes a coherence and a continuity of representation.[16] □

Heath then offers a definition of action in a story, a narrative, as a series of elements that brings about a transformation from one state of things to another. In this perspective, a story starts with what is, in effect, a violent disruption of a given state of affairs (though that state may not so much be given directly in the narrative as reconstructed retrospectively – from what we see now, as the story begins, we infer how things were before the story began). In *Touch of Evil*, the violent disruption of a given state of affairs is literally an act of violence: the explosion of a bomb planted in a car kills its driver and passenger. The job of the story, the narrative, is to resolve this violent disruption, to replace it with a state of affairs that is new but that reassembles the elements that were scattered by the initial disruption into a different configuration. Heath declares that '[i]deally, a narrative would be the perfect symmetry of this move-ment' from one state of affairs to another, and points to the symmetry in *Touch of Evil*: 'the kiss [that] the explosion postpones is resumed in the kiss of the close of the film as Susan is reunited with Vargas – the same kiss, but delayed, set into a narrative':[17]

■ The explosion of the car interrupts the kiss between Susan and Vargas, separates them; henceforth, Vargas's action as hero of the nar-rative is the desire to get things back into place: re-establish Law in the light of Justice (defeat Quinlan); have his wife returned to him 'clean' (as a result of Quinlan's schemes, she has been arrested on drugs and murder charges). This action is accomplished in the exchange of Menzies (Joseph Calleia), who passes from Quinlan, whose devoted associate he had been until then, to Vargas, whom he helps to reveal the truth. The exchange is stressed: Menzies, who lov-ingly finds his identity in Quinlan[,] *becomes* Mike Vargas, the instru-ment – the 'mike' – with which the latter records the confessions of the unscrupulous cop; moreover, this transference has its 'magic' token: Menzies gives Vargas Quinlan's stick – the rod of power and the key to the crime, to Quinlan's guilt.

What the action restores, what the exchanges are for, is Susan, *the woman*, the very object of the Law. Logic of the narrative (of *Touch of Evil*): the Law is out of order, *therefore* the woman is no longer there, in her place; or again, the woman is a heat, a fire, a conflagration (this is the guiding metaphor of the film), *therefore* the Law is no longer assured, in order; this being the 'evil' of the title, as well as the task of the narrative: find the woman, the (legal) place of desire. The narrative allows the problem to be posed in terms of images of the Law (Vargas against Quinlan, Vargas as representative of a just – 'democratic' – law) in order to resolve *thereby* the excess of desire (Vargas as husband, the right limit – equally 'democratic' – of sexuality); the first serves as a cover for the second which is called upon to resorb [*sic*] itself in it ['resorb' means 'to absorb again']. Indeed, following that psychology vaguely coloured with 'psychoanalycity' – or 'traumaticity', since it is a matter of bringing everything down to an explanatory trauma – of which the American cinema has been so fond, if Quinlan is crooked, it is because the murderer of his own wife escaped justice and punishment; thus if the Law is out of order, it is finally a personal problem (a drama), in no way implicating the question of the Law itself.

The woman must be restored, but the woman as good object, that is to say, as object, which is to say in turn – and the circle is closed – as 'the woman', Vargas's woman, his wife. Blind spot of the film, the woman is put for an impossible pleasure, in violation of the order: on the one hand, the woman as focus of desire; on the other, the desire to know nothing of that desire, to wipe it out as the memory of a different economy, that of sexual *contradiction*, of a sexuality in excess of its established reduction to a simple genitality, the order of the phallus: a body crossed with differences, a subject divided, not 'one', in process. Turned towards restoration, the film, in the very development of its narrative (the woman set aside: expelled from the main action until she can be brought back into place), goes through the figures of the repression it operates, swerves to systems – fragments of systematicity – that do not *quite* fit into the narrative unity, its direction of the film. This gives, for example, simultaneous with the wish to restore Susan as good object, the necessity of demonstrating her, the woman, as *bad* object: object of panic (the scene in the motel between Susan and the 'Night Man', a hysterical neurotic, jumpy at her body, her presence as other); object of assault (captured by a gang of youths, target of Quinlan's hatred and attacks); fetish object (Susan is at one point caught as she is undressing in the beam of light from the torch of an aggressor, is held there, stripteased). It gives too, in a kind of symbolic discrepancy from this demonstration, a whole mass of 'propositions' – stirrings of stories, of other exchanges – constantly running out of phase with the narrative purpose: thus, where the psychologizing explanation has it that Quinlan's wife was strangled long ago by a killer who evaded the police and that therefore Quinlan will stop at nothing in his pursuit of those whom he takes to be guilty of crimes, the film – the twist of its relations – says clearly that the killer can only be Quinlan himself; he who strangles Grandi (Akim Tamiroff, the head of a local mafia, presented as an intolerable sexual confusion, another transgression of the Law) over Susan's body stretched out on a huge hotel bed: frenzied music, neon lights flashing on and off outside, rapid cutting from Quinlan pulling tight to Susan moaning, everything coming to a frantic climax.

These propositions, these returns on the sense of the narrative, work over different matters of expression, straddling them like so many shifters from code to code ... A quick example: in the car explosion, Zita (Joi Lansing), the woman passenger, is burnt alive; in front of the cabaret where she was employed as a striptease dancer, a sign announces 'Twenty Sizzling Strippers'; while following Quinlan at the beginning of the investigation of the explosion, Vargas is intercepted by one of Grandi's 'nephews' who aims a bottle of vitriol at him, misses his target (or hits it, the narrative miss made good in the mesh of the symbolic) and splatters a photo of Zita on a poster that is held for a moment in close shot: Zita burns a second time, with, on the soundtrack, the sizzling of the vitriol over the poster. Thus is set going a chain which mobilizes writing, the photographic image and recorded sound, specific cinematic codes (the car blows up in a violent rhythm created by a pattern of cutting and shifts in framing) and codes that are not specifically cinematic (the English language – 'sizzling').

That chain set going touches on what is at issue in the textual system, condensed in an alternative the terms of which, although not the sole property of film (they are found elsewhere) are figures that are filmic properties – a whole 'cinema'. As was said, the narrative must serve to restore the woman as good object (the narrative image depends on this); which obliges it to envisage her as bad object (the other side of the restoration that it seeks to accomplish). Given which, there are two resources: either the woman truly posed as an object in order that sexuality be put at her distance as such – this is the woman stripteased, Susan fixed as spectacle under the beam of light ..., or again the pin-up, the star (always the essential luminosity), Susan as Janet Leigh, the only way known *to the narrative* to admit desire ...; or the woman obliterated, extinguished (like a fire) – captured by the Grandi gang, nothing happens to Susan, simply she is faded out ...; recourses that the chain ceaselessly picks up to mark the points of their excess, the terms they engage. It is as though the film – the textual system – followed *literally* the stereotype-metaphor of an 'explosive' sexuality, the woman as 'dynamite' ... ...

Barthes: 'As fiction, the Oedipus complex served at least some purpose: that of producing good novels, of telling good stories (this is written after having seen Murnau's *City Girl* (1930))'.[18] Is it conceivable that the film narrative will always provide the clues of this fiction? The fact remains that I note in the course of Welles's film the scattered signs of its oedipal logic: the swollen foot (Quinlan hobbles along as a result of his 'gammy' leg), the stick of the riddle[19] (the key to the crime), the man who uncovers the truth of himself as the criminal (Quinlan ends up a murderer), the theme of blindness (wanting to phone Susan, Vargas enters a shop kept by a blind woman), the baby left to die (Susan lets herself be photographed because a baby is suddenly held up in front of her and which she turns to admire: it is the symbolic that reasserts its dominance in this abandonment of the narrative, the baby that is given no life in its development: before he enters the blind woman's shop, Vargas finds another baby in his path – he puts on dark glasses, refuses to see clearly).

Ceaselessly, the film puts off 'something else' into the past, makes a screen against it; the indefinite memory of a far-off time, the *novel* of Quinlan: murder of the woman, his wife, *and* fairy universe – a cinematic dream (a dream of cinema) of Tanya (Ti*tania*, the Queen of the Fairies in Shakespeare's *A Midsummer Night's Dream* (1600), this in a film which multiplies Shakespearian references). Something else outside the narrative which, from its order, its sense, can see it only as death, as the image of a paradise lost; an image to which criticism does not fail to respond: 'Tanya's piano, the only pure rhythm in this syncopated film, like a heart still beating in an agonising organism, is the last burst of life, an unbearable tenderness in the face of death ... the momentary appearance of the lost happiness that music alone is capable of depicting on the threshold of hell'.[20] A perfect response to the mode of the narrative – the Law is established, stands against the horizon of an inevitably *tragic* sexuality. Simply, something else comes too, another return through the narrative sense, the chain continues: from Tanya to Zita (Zi – ta – nya) to Susan – what wipes out, again, here too at the end, the honeymoon kiss ... figures emptiness in Susan's expected place, is Tanya, the fantasy of this 'past', the shadow-mother of the 'something else'.[21] □

In concluding his analysis of *Touch of Evil,* Heath makes the general point that specific films draw on the codes of the overall signifying system of 'cinema', but also depart from them. Here he echoes the quotation from Christian Metz that began his essay: 'Every film shows us the cinema and also its death.'[22] As Heath later put it in 1991:

- [E]very film is *in* cinema, within or in relation to this dominant and defining institution, but it is always also *more than* cinema, is an operation of cinema that has its own particular material complexity, that realizes, redeploys, recasts the institutional terms.[23] □

Heath's excellent analysis of *Touch of Evil* demonstrates how a specific film employs and mixes the codes of cinema in a distinctive way that cannot wholly be analysed in terms of an overall system – rather, elements or fragments of a range of systems come into play. If his close attention to detail owes something to the kind of textual analysis practised by Roland Barthes in his critique of Balzac's *Sarrasine* in *S/Z* (1970), it owes another debt to the tradition, in Cambridge English studies, of 'close reading' that developed from the work of I. A. Richards, William Empson and F. R. Leavis in the later 1920s and the 1930s. In a sense, one of the results of Heath's approach is to free a specific filmic text from being merely the exemplification of a set of codes and to allow it to be addressed in its particularity – not a particularity that is wholly free of pre-existing codes, but not one that is wholly determined by them. It would be going too far to claim that this marks the return, in a different idiom, of the idea – again very crucial to 'Cambridge English' and to the more general development of mid-twentieth-century literary criticism – that the specific text has a uniqueness that escapes exhaustive definition in general terms and can only be partly grasped by attention to detail; but there is an element of this. To a qualified extent, Heath's 'close reading' of *Touch of Evil* could be seen as a continuation of Cambridge English by other means, an extension of its techniques to the analysis of the filmic text. In this respect, it is exemplary: it demonstrates how a good close reading of a film can be done, and remains a model. To suggest this underlying continuity, however, is not to deny the difference in Heath's approach that is due to his use of semiotics and psychoanalysis. The issue is: how far does the strength of the close reading depend on semiotics and psychoanalysis? It is arguable that the strength of this reading depends on its attention to detail and its capacity to make connections, rather than to its semiotic and psychoanalytic framework. This framework is *enabling*, but it is not *essential*.

Nonetheless, it was semiotics and psychoanalysis that were to dominate film theory in the later 1970s and the 1980s, especially in its feminist aspect. Indeed, the most influential essay in the history of film theory to date draws heavily on those perspectives: this is Laura Mulvey's 'Visual Pleasure and Narrative Cinema', written in 1973 and first published in *Screen* in 1975.[24] The article emerged at a significant cultural moment in the UK: as Mulvey herself observed in another essay, the 1960s 'had seen a massive growth of interest in French theory (initiated by the *New Left Review*), both Marxist and psychoanalytic, and also in US popular culture, movies and music ... It is to this background, under the catalyst of feminism, that I owe my starting-point.'[25] 'Visual Pleasure and Narrative Cinema' brings together French theory, Hollywood film and feminism in a forceful analysis of narrative cinema, the dominant cinema whose very structures tell a patriarchal story.

'Visual Pleasure and Narrative Cinema' declares that it is using psycho-analysis 'as a political weapon' that demonstrates 'the way the unconscious of patriarchal society has structured film form'. Armed with this weapon, the essay seeks 'to discover where and how the fascination of film is reinforced by pre-existing patterns of fascination already at work within the individual subject and the social formations that have moulded him'. Its starting-point is 'the way film reflects, reveals and even plays on the straight, socially established interpretation of sexual difference which controls images, erotic ways of looking and spectacle'. An understanding of how the 'magic' of cinema has worked in the past is helpful in the attempt to produce 'a theory and a practice which will challenge this cinema of the past'.[26] It is important to stress that Mulvey is a film-maker herself, and that her essay was originally concerned not only with theoretical analysis but also with the possibility of making films that would be 'radical in both a political and an aesthetic sense' and that would challenge 'the basic assumptions of the mainstream film'.[27]

Mulvey's analysis of the 'magic' of cinema focuses on visual pleasure:

■ The magic of the Hollywood style at its best (and of all the cinema which fell within its sphere of influence) arose, not exclusively, but in one important aspect, from its skilled and satisfying manipulation of visual pleasure. Unchallenged, mainstream cinema coded the erotic into the language of the dominant patriarchal order. In the highly developed Hollywood cinema it was only through these codes that the alienated subject, torn in his imaginary memory by a sense of loss, by the terror of potential lack in fantasy, came near to finding a glimpse of satisfaction: through its formal beauty and its play on his own formative obsessions. This article will discuss the interweaving of that erotic pleasure in film, its meaning and, in particular, the central place of the image of woman.[28] □

Mulvey then anticipates a possible objection and counters it in a striking and, at the time, unexpected way:

■ It is said that analysing pleasure, or beauty, destroys it. That is the intention of this article. The satisfaction and reinforcement of the ego that represent the high point of film history hitherto must be attacked. Not in favour of a reconstructed new pleasure, which cannot exist in the abstract, nor of intellectualised unpleasure, but to make way for a total negation of the ease and plenitude of the narrative fiction film. The alternative is the thrill that comes from leaving the past behind without simply rejecting it, transcending outworn or oppressive forms, and daring to break with normal pleasurable expectations in order to conceive a new language of desire.[29] □

It can be seen here why Mulvey's article was so exciting when it first appeared. It throws down the gauntlet, uncompromisingly, to traditional narrative fiction film and posits an alternative that involves nothing less than a reconfiguration of desire. These absolute positions belong to the moment in which the article emerged: a moment in which it was still possible to believe, in the wake of the 1960s, that a total transformation of humanity and society might take place, might even be just around the corner. At the same time, the article does not advocate a total rejection of what Mulvey sees as 'the past', and indeed takes that 'past' as an object of analysis. Thus, the analysis that it provides is able to survive the disappearance of the utopian, revolutionary moment in which it first appeared, and can be – and has been – assimilated into the academic study of film. The transformative aim may have faded, but the analysis remains. Mulvey starts that analysis with a discussion headed 'Pleasure in Looking/Fascination with the Human Form':[30]

■ The cinema offers a number of possible pleasures. One is scopophilia (pleasure in looking ['scopophilia' is the word used to translate the German term *Schaulust*, or visual pleasure[31]]). There are circumstances in which looking itself is a source of pleasure, just as, in the reverse formation, there is pleasure in being looked at. Originally, in his *Three Essays on Sexuality* (1905), Freud isolated scopophilia as one of the component instincts of sexuality which exist as drives quite independently of the erotogenic zones.[32] At this point he associated scopophilia with taking other people as objects, subjecting them to a controlling and curious gaze ... At the extreme, it can become fixated into a perversion, producing obsessive voyeurs and Peeping Toms whose only sexual satisfaction can come from watching, in an active controlling sense, an objectified other.

At first glance, the cinema would seem to be remote from the undercover world of the surreptitious observation of an unknowing and unwilling victim. What is seen on the screen is so manifestly shown. But the mass of mainstream film, and the conventions within which it has consciously evolved, portray a hermetically sealed world which unwinds magically, indifferent to the presence of the audience, producing for them a sense of separation and playing on their voyeuristic fantasy. Moreover the extreme contrast between the darkness in the auditorium (which also isolates the spectators from one another) and the brilliance of the shifting patterns of light and shade on the screen helps to promote the illusion of voyeuristic separation. Although the film is really being shown, is there to be seen, conditions of screening and narrative conventions give the spectator an illusion of looking in on a private world. Among other things, the position of the spectators in the cinema is blatantly one of repression of their exhibitionism and projection of the repressed desire onto the performer.

The cinema satisfies a primordial wish for pleasurable looking, but it also goes further, developing scopophilia in its narcissistic aspect. The conventions of mainstream film focus attention on the human form. Scale, space, stories are all anthropomorphic. Here, curiosity and the wish to look intermingle with a fascination with likeness and recognition: the human face, the human body, the relationship between the human form and its surroundings, the visible presence of the person in the world. Jacques Lacan has described how [the mirror phase,] the moment when a child recognises its own image in the mirror[,] is crucial for the constitution of the ego[33] ... The mirror phase occurs at a time when children's physical ambitions outstrip their motor capacity, with the result that their recognition of themselves is joyous in that they imagine their mirror image to be more complete, more perfect than they experience in their own body. Recognition is thus overlaid with misrecognition: the image recognised is conceived as the reflected body of the self, but its misrecognition as superior projects this body outside itself as an ideal ego, the alienated subject which, reintrojected [taken back into oneself] as an ego ideal, prepares the way for identification with others in the future. This mirror moment predates language for the child.

[Thus,] it is an image that constitutes the matrix of the imaginary, of recognition/misrecognition and identification, and hence of the first articulation of the I, of subjectivity. This is a moment when an older fascination with looking (at the mother's face, for an obvious example) collides with the initial inklings of self-awareness. Hence it is the birth of the long love affair/despair between image and self-image which has found such intensity of expression in film and such joyous recognition in the cinema audience. Quite apart from the extraneous similarities between screen and mirror (the framing of the human form in its surroundings, for instance), the cinema has structures of fascination strong enough to allow temporary loss of ego while simultaneously reinforcing it. The sense of forgetting the world as the ego has come to perceive it (I forgot who I am and where I was) is nostalgically reminiscent of that pre-subjective moment of image recognition. While at the same time, the cinema has distinguished itself in the production of ego ideals, through the star system for instance. Stars provide a focus or centre both to screen space and screen story where they act out a complex process of likeness and difference (the glamorous impersonates the ordinary).[34] □

Mulvey then proceeds to sum up the 'two contradictory aspects of the pleasurable structures of looking in the conventional cinematic situation'[35] that she has set out:

■ The first, scopophilic, arises from pleasure in using another person as an object of sexual stimulation through sight. The second, developed through narcissism and the constitution of the ego, comes from identification with the image seen. Thus, in film terms, one implies a separation of the erotic identity of the subject from the object on the screen (active scopophilia), the other demands identification of the ego with the object on the screen through the spectator's fascination with and recognition of his like. The first is a function of the sexual instincts, the second of ego libido. This dichotomy was crucial for Freud. Although he saw the two as interacting and overlaying each other, the tension between instinctual drives and self-preservation polarises in terms of pleasure. But both are formative structures, mechanisms without intrinsic meaning. In themselves they have no signification, unless attached to an idealisation. Both pursue aims in indifference to perceptual reality, and motivate eroticised phantasmagoria that affect the subject's perception of the world to make a mockery of empirical objectivity.

During its history, the cinema seems to have evolved a particular illusion of reality in which this contradiction between libido and ego has found a beautifully complementary fantasy world. In *reality* the fantasy world of the screen is subject to the law which produces it. Sexual instincts and identification processes have a meaning within the symbolic order which articulates desire. Desire, born with language, allows the possibility of transcending the instinctual and the imaginary, but its point of reference continually returns to the traumatic moment of its birth: the castration complex. Hence the look, pleasurable in form, can be threatening in content, and it is woman as representation/image that crystallises this paradox.[36] □

In Mulvey's analysis, woman crystallises the paradox that the look can be pleasurable in form but threatening in content because of the way in which 'the representation of the female form' in a phallocentric symbolic order 'speaks castration':[37]

■ [T]he function of woman in forming the patriarchal unconscious is twofold: she firstly symbolises the castration threat by her real lack of a penis and secondly thereby raises her child into the symbolic. Once this has been achieved, her meaning in the process is at an end. It does not last into the world of law and language except as a memory, which oscillates between memory of maternal plenitude and memory of lack. Both are posited on nature (or on anatomy in Freud's famous phrase ['Anatomy is destiny'[38]]). Woman's desire is subjugated to her image as bearer of the bleeding wound; she can exist only in relation to castration and cannot transcend it. She turns the child into the signifier of her own desire to possess a penis (the condition, she imagines, of entry into the symbolic). Either she must gracefully give way to the word, the name of the father and the law, or else struggle to keep her child down with her in the half-light of the imaginary. Woman then stands in patriarchal culture as a signifier for the male other, bound by a symbolic order in which man can live out his fantasies and obsessions through linguistic command by imposing them on the silent image of woman still tied to her place as bearer, not maker, of meaning.[39] □

It is this view of the function of the image of woman in the patriarchal unconscious that informs the next stage of Mulvey's analysis, which is headed 'Woman as Image, Man as Bearer of the Look':[40]

■ In a world ordered by sexual imbalance, pleasure in looking has been split between active/male and passive/female. The determining male gaze projects its fantasy onto the female figure, which is styled accordingly. In their traditional exhibitionist role women are simultaneously looked at and displayed, with their appearance coded for strong visual and erotic impact so that they can be said to connote *to-be-looked-at-ness*. Woman displayed as sexual object is the *leitmotif* of erotic spectacle: from pin-ups to strip-tease, from Ziegfeld[41] to Busby Berkeley,[42] she holds the look, and plays to and signifies male desire. Mainstream film neatly combines spectacle and narrative. (Note, however, how in the musical song-and-dance numbers interrupt the flow of the diegesis [the main story[43]].) The presence of woman is an indispensable element of spectacle in normal narrative film, yet her visual presence tends to work against the development of a story-line, to freeze the flow of action in moments of erotic contemplation. This alien presence then has to be integrated into cohesion with the narrative ... ...

Traditionally, the woman displayed has functioned on two levels: as erotic object for the characters within the screen story, and as erotic object for the spectator within the auditorium, with a shifting tension between the looks on either side of the screen. For instance, the device of the show-girl allows the two looks to be unified technically without any apparent break in the diegesis. A woman performs within the narrative; the gaze of the spectator and that of the male characters in the film are neatly combined without breaking narrative verisimilitude [a story's appearance of being true]. For a moment the sexual impact of the performing woman takes the film into a no man's land outside its own time and space. Thus Marilyn Monroe's first appearance in *The River of No Return* (1954) and Lauren Bacall's songs in *To Have and Have Not*. Similarly, conventional close-ups of legs (Dietrich, for instance) or a face (Garbo) integrate into the narrative a different mode of eroticism. One part of a fragmented body destroys the Renaissance space, the illusion of depth demanded by the narrative; it gives flatness, the quality of a cut-out or icon, rather than verisimilitude, to the screen.

An active/passive heterosexual division of labour has similarly controlled narrative structure. According to the principles of the ruling ideology and the psychical structures that back it up, the male figure cannot bear the burden of sexual objectification [of being looked at as a sexual object]. Man is reluctant to gaze at his exhibitionist like. Hence the split between spectacle and narrative supports the man's role as the active one of advancing the story, making things happen. The man controls the film fantasy and also emerges as the representative of power in a further sense: as the bearer of the look of the spectator, transferring it behind the screen to neutralise the extra-diegetic tendencies represented by woman as spectacle ['extra-diegetic' means 'standing outside of the sphere of the main story';[44] Mulvey has suggested earlier that the 'visual presence' of woman in a film 'tends to work against the development of a story-line',[45] that is, of a diegesis, a main story; the 'visual presence' of woman tends to stand outside the story, to move towards the extra-diegetic]. This is made possible through the processes set in motion by structuring the film around a main controlling figure with whom the spectator can identify. As the spectator identifies with the main male protagonist, he projects his look onto that of his like, his screen surrogate, so that the power of the male protagonist as he controls events coincides with the active power of the erotic look, both giving a satisfying sense of omnipotence. A male movie star's glamorous characteristics are thus not those of the erotic object of the gaze, but those of the more perfect, more complete, more powerful ideal ego conceived in the original moment of recognition in front of the mirror. The character in the story can make things happen and control events better than the subject/spectator, just as the image in the mirror was more in control of motor co-ordination.

In contrast to woman as icon, the active male figure (the ego ideal of the identification process) demands a three-dimensional space corresponding to that of the mirror recognition, in which the alienated subject internalised his own representation of his imaginary existence. He is a figure in a landscape. Here the function of film is to reproduce as accurately as possible the so-called natural conditions of human perception. Camera technology (as exemplified by deep-focus in particular) and camera movements (determined by the action of the protagonist), combined with invisible editing (demanded by realism), all tend to blur the limits of screen space. The male protagonist is free to command the stage, a stage of spatial illusion in which he articulates the look and creates the action ...

[There is] a tension between a mode of representation of woman in film and conventions surrounding the diegesis. Each is associated with a look: that of the spectator in direct scopophilic contact with the female form displayed for his enjoyment (connoting male fantasy) and that of the spectator fascinated with the image of his like set in an illusion of natural space, and through him gaining control and possession of the woman within the diegesis. (This tension and the shift from one pole to the other can structure a single text[, as in] *Only Angels Have Wings* and in *To Have and Have Not* ...)

But in psychoanalytic terms, the female figure poses a deeper problem. She also connotes something that the look continually circles around but disavows: her lack of a penis, implying a threat of castration and hence unpleasure. Ultimately, the meaning of woman is sexual difference, the visually ascertainable absence of the penis, the material evidence on which is based the castration complex essential for the organisation of entrance to the symbolic order and the law of the father. Thus the woman as icon, displayed for the gaze and enjoyment of men, the active controllers of the look, always threatens to evoke the anxiety it originally signified. The male unconscious has two avenues of escape from this castration anxiety: preoccupation with the re-enactment of the original trauma (investigating the woman, demystifying her mystery), counterbalanced by the devaluation, punishment or saving of the guilty object (an avenue typified by the concerns of the *film noir*); or else complete disavowal of castration by the substitution of a fetish object or turning the represented figure itself into a fetish so that it becomes reassuring rather than dangerous (hence overvaluation, the cult of the female star).

This second avenue, fetishistic scopophilia, builds up the physical beauty of the object, transforming it into something satisfying in itself. The first avenue, voyeurism, on the contrary, has associations with sadism: pleasure lies in ascertaining guilt (immediately associated with castration), asserting control and subjugating the guilty person through punishment or forgiveness. This sadistic side fits in well with narrative. Sadism demands a story, depends on making something happen, forcing a change in another person, a battle of will and strength, victory/defeat, all occurring in a linear time with a beginning and an end. Fetishistic scopophilia, on the other hand, can exist outside linear time as the erotic instinct is focused on the look alone. These contradictions and ambiguities can be illustrated more simply by using works by Hitchcock and Sternberg, both of whom take the look almost as the content or subject matter of many of their films. Hitchcock is the more complex, as he uses both mechanisms. Sternberg's work, on the other hand, provides many pure examples of fetishistic scopophilia.

Sternberg once said he would welcome his films being projected upside-down so that story and character involvement would not interfere with the spectator's undiluted appreciation of the screen image.[46] This statement is revealing but ingenuous: ingenuous in that his films do demand that the figure of the woman (Dietrich, in the cycle of films with her, as the ultimate example [*The Blue Angel*; *Morocco* (1930); *Dishono[u]red* (1931)]) should be identifiable; but revealing in that it emphasises the fact that for him the pictorial space enclosed by the frame is paramount, rather than narrative or identification processes. While Hitchcock goes into the investigative side of voyeurism, Sternberg produces the ultimate fetish, taking it to the point where the powerful look of the male protagonist (characteristic of traditional narrative film) is broken in favour of the image in direct erotic rapport with the spectator. The beauty of the woman as object and the screen space coalesce; she is no longer the bearer of guilt but a perfect product, whose body, stylised and fragmented by close-ups, is the content of the film and the direct recipient of the spectator's look.

Sternberg plays down the illusion of screen depth; his screen tends to be one-dimensional, as light and shade, lace, steam, foliage, net, streamers and so on reduce the visual field. There is little or no mediation of the look through the eyes of the main male protagonist. On the contrary, shadowy presences like La Bessière in *Morocco* act as surrogates for the director, detached as they are from audience identification. Despite Sternberg's insistence that his stories are irrelevant, it is significant that they are concerned with situation, not suspense, and cyclical rather than linear time, while plot complications revolve around misunderstanding rather than conflict. The most important absence is that of the controlling male gaze within the screen scene. The high point of emotional drama in the most typical Dietrich films, her supreme moments of erotic meaning, take place in the absence of the man she loves in the fiction. There are other witnesses, other spectators watching her on the screen, their gaze is one with, not standing in for, that of the audience. At the end of *Morocco*, Tom Brown has already disappeared into the desert when Amy Jolly kicks off her gold sandals and walks after him. At the end of *Dishono[u]red*, Kranau is indifferent to the fate of Magda. In both cases, the erotic impact, sanctified by death, is displayed as a spectacle for the audience. The male hero misunderstands and, above all, does not see.

In Hitchcock, by contrast, the male hero does see precisely what the audience sees. However, although fascination with an image through scopophilic eroticism can be the subject of the film, it is the role of the hero to portray the contradictions and tensions experienced by the spectator. In *Vertigo* (1958) in particular, but also in *Marnie* (1964) and *Rear Window*, the look is central to the plot, oscillating between voyeurism and fetishistic fascination. Hitchcock has never concealed his interest in voyeurism, cinematic and non-cinematic.[47] His heroes are exemplary of the symbolic order and the law – [an ex-]policeman (*Vertigo*), a dominant male possessing money and power (*Marnie*) – but their erotic drives lead them into compromised situations. The power to subject another person to the will sadistically or to the gaze voyeuristically is turned onto the woman as the object of both. Power is backed by a certainty of legal right and the established guilt of the woman (evoking castration, psycho-analytically speaking). True perversion is barely concealed under a shallow mask of ideological correctness – the man is on the right side of the law, the woman on the wrong. Hitchcock's skilful use of identification processes and liberal use of subjective camera from the point of view of the male protagonist draw the spectators deeply into his position, making them share his uneasy gaze. The spectator is absorbed into a voyeuristic situation within the screen scene and diegesis, which parodies his own in the cinema.

In an analysis of *Rear Window*, Jean Douchet takes the film as a metaphor for the cinema.[48] Jefferies[49] is the audience, the events in the apartment block opposite correspond to the screen. As he watches, an erotic dimension is added to his look, a central image to the drama. His girlfriend Lisa had been of little sexual interest to him, more or less a drag, so long as she remained on the spectator side. When she crosses the barrier between his room and the block opposite, their relationship is reborn erotically. He does not merely watch her through the lens, as a distant meaningful image, he also sees her as a guilty intruder exposed by a dangerous man threatening her with punishment, and thus finally giving him the opportunity to save her. Lisa's exhibitionism has already been established by her obsessive interest in dress and style, in being a passive image of visual perfection; Jefferies's voyeurism and activity have also been established through his work as a photo-journalist, a maker of stories and captor of images. However, his enforced inactivity, binding him to his seat as a spectator, puts him squarely in the fantasy position of the cinema audience.

In *Vertigo*, subjective camera predominates. Apart from one flashback from Judy's point of view, the narrative is woven around what Scottie [the ex-police detective, played by James Stewart] sees or fails to see. The audience follows the growth of his erotic obsession and subsequent despair precisely from his point of view. Scottie's voyeurism is blatant: he falls in love with a woman he follows and spies on without speaking to. Its sadistic side is equally blatant: he has chosen (and freely chosen, for he had been a successful lawyer) to be a policeman, with all the attendant possibilities of pursuit and investigation. As a result, he follows, watches and falls in love with a perfect image of female beauty and mystery. Once he actually confronts her, his erotic drive is to break her down and force her *to tell* by persistent cross-questioning.

In the second part of the film, he re-enacts his obsessive involvement with the image he loved to watch secretly. He reconstructs Judy as Madeleine, forces her to conform in every detail to the actual physical appearance of his fetish. Her exhibitionism, her masochism, make her an ideal passive counterpart to Scottie's active sadistic voyeurism. She knows her part is to perform, and only by playing it through and then replaying it can she keep Scottie's erotic interest. But in the repetition he does break her down and succeeds in exposing her guilt. His curiosity wins through; she is punished.

Thus, in *Vertigo*, erotic involvement with the look boomerangs: the spectator's own fascination is revealed as illicit voyeurism as the narrative content enacts the processes and pleasures that he is himself exercising and enjoying. The Hitchcock hero here is firmly placed within the symbolic order, in narrative terms. He has all the attributes of the patriarchal superego. Hence the spectator, lulled into a false sense of security by the apparent legality of his surrogate, sees through his look and finds himself exposed as complicit, caught in the moral ambiguity of looking. Far from being simply an aside on the perversion of the police, *Vertigo* focuses on the implications of the active/looking, passive/looked-at split in terms of sexual difference and the power of the male symbolic encapsulated in the hero. Marnie, too, performs for Mark Rutland's gaze and masquerades as the perfect to-be-looked-at image. He, too, is on the side of the law until, drawn in by obsession with her guilt, her secret, he longs to see her in the act of committing a crime, make her confess and thus save her. So he, too, becomes complicit as he acts out the implications of his power. He controls money and words; he can have his cake and eat it.[50] ☐

It could be argued that Mulvey, in order to support her idea of an active-male/passive-female dichotomy, overemphasises the passivity of Lisa in *Rear Window* and the active power of Scottie in *Vertigo*. As Elise Lemire suggests: '[T]o the extent that Lisa is what Mulvey terms an "image", she is not a passive one but rather a self-made and self-directed image ... "loaded to her fingertips", as Stella (Thelma Ritter) says, not only with love for Jeff, but with her own agency [in the sense of 'power of action'].' When Lisa 'enters wearing her nightgown like a model walking on a fashion show runway, striking poses that alternate with twirls[, s]he is not the "passive image" ... Mulvey imagines but, rather, purposefully makes herself a show'.[51] In *Vertigo*, Scottie is not, as Mulvey implies, still a policeman when the film begins; it is quickly made clear that he had to 'quit the force' because of his 'fear of heights', his 'acrophobia'. He starts to follow Madeleine, not in any official police capacity, but as the result of a request from her husband, an apparent friend of Scottie's who is in fact using him as an unwitting pawn in a plot to murder her. Far from being a secure embodiment of legality and authority, he is a vulnerable and suffering figure, as Marian E. Keane argues:

■ Mulvey describes [Scottie] as possessing, brandishing, and relishing a position of active power in relation to the woman, but the truth is that he suffers throughout *Vertigo*. He suffers from the moment he painfully discovers his acrophobia on the rooftop, through his involvement with Madeleine, under the condescending and barbed censure of the court officer at the hearing [after the real Madeleine's death], and up to his dream, the final nightmare of his life until the end of the film. His dream renders him a catatonic in a sanat[o]rium, immobilized by depression ... ... When Stewart/Scottie emerges from the hospital, his suffering continues. A series of short sequences shows him retracing the steps of his relationship with Madeleine. Each blonde woman in the distance causes his heart to leap as he believes, for an instant, that she has returned. But he is looking for a woman who had died, a ghost.

When he finds Judy, his suffering is not over. He will not be satisfied until the ghost is made flesh, until he has created a living woman out of the dead one. Mulvey claims that Scottie 'reconstructs Judy as Madeleine, forces her to conform in every detail to the actual physical appearance of his fetish'. 'Fetish' and 'fetishism' are important terms in Mulvey's understanding of how sexuality functions and is contained in classical films. Mulvey's concept of 'fetishism', however, is too extended or metaphorical to bear the weight she puts upon it, as for example when she claims that Scottie is 'reconstructing a fetish' when he insists that Judy's clothes and hair style and color match Madeleine's. Stewart/Scottie is not reconstructing a fetish; he is creating a woman in fulfillment of his *vision*. This construction of Judy as Madeleine is, with terrible irony, destructive; it may be even more brutal than Mulvey's idea of 'fetish'. What is shown to be brutal in *Vertigo* is the nature of human desire and need, not some function of a particular phase of male development whose correction it is fairly simple to imagine.[52] □

The points made by Keane and Lemire are important challenges to Mulvey, but they are also testimony to the stimulus of 'Visual Pleasure and Narrative Cinema'. Mulvey concludes her famous article with a succinct summary of its argument that begins by drawing together the psychoanalytical concepts she has employed and then develops into a call to action based on her analysis:

■ The scopophilic instinct (pleasure in looking at another person as an erotic object) and, in contradistinction, ego libido (forming identification processes) act as formations, mechanisms, which mould [the] formal attributes [of traditional narrative film]. The actual image of woman as (passive) raw material for the (active) gaze of man takes the argument a step further into the content and structure of representation, adding a further layer of ideological significance demanded by the patriarchal order in its favourite cinematic form – illusionistic narrative film ... [W]omen in representation can signify castration, and activate voyeuristic or fetishistic mechanisms to circumvent this threat. Although none of these interacting layers is intrinsic to film, it is only in the film form that they can reach a perfect and beautiful contradiction, thanks to the possibility in the cinema of shifting the emphasis of the look. The place of the look defines cinema, the possibility of varying it and exposing it. This is what makes cinema quite different in its voyeuristic potential from, say, strip-tease, theatre shows and so on. Going far beyond highlighting a woman's to-be-looked-at-ness, cinema builds the way she is to be looked at into the spectacle itself. Playing on the tension between film as controlling the dimension of time (editing, narrative) and film as controlling the dimension of space (changes in distance, editing), cinematic codes create a gaze, a world and an object, thereby producing an illusion cut to the measure of desire. It is these cinematic codes and their relationship to formative external structures that must be broken down before mainstream film and the pleasure it provides can be challenged.

To begin with (as an ending), the voyeuristic-scopophilic look that is a crucial part of traditional filmic pleasure can itself be broken down. There are three different looks associated with cinema: that of the camera as it records the pro-filmic event, that of the audience as it watches the final product, and that of the characters at each other within the screen illusion. The conventions of narrative film deny the first two and subordinate them to the third, the conscious aim being always to eliminate intrusive camera presence and prevent a distancing awareness in the audience. Without these two absences (the material existence of the recording process, the critical reading of the spectator), fictional drama cannot achieve reality, obviousness and truth. Nevertheless ... the structure of looking in narrative fiction film contains a contradiction in its own premises: the female image as a castration threat constantly endangers the unity of the diegesis and bursts through the world of illusion as an intrusive, static, one-dimen[s]ional fetish. Thus the two looks materially present in time and space are obsessively subordinated to the neurotic needs of the male ego. The camera becomes the mechanism for producing an illusion of Renaissance space, flowing movements compatible with the human eye, an ideology of representation that revolves around the perception of the subject; the camera's look is disavowed in order to create a convincing world in which the spectator's surrogate can perform with verisimilitude. Simultaneously, the look of the audience is denied an intrinsic force: as soon as fetishistic representation of the female image threatens to break the spell of illusion, and the erotic image on the screen appears directly (without mediation) to the spectator, the fact of fetishisation, concealing as it does castration fear, freezes the look, fixates the spectator and prevents him from achieving any distance from the image in front of him.

This complex interaction of looks is specific to film. The first blow against the monolithic accumulation of traditional film conventions (already undertaken by radical film-makers) is to free the look of the camera into its materiality in time and space and the look of the audience into dialectics and passionate detachment. There is no doubt that this destroys the satisfaction, pleasure and privilege of the 'invisible guest', and highlights the way film has depended on voyeuristic active/passive mechanisms. Women, whose image has continually been stolen and used for this end, cannot view the decline of the traditional film form with anything much more than sentimental regret.[53] □

The 'traditional film form' was, of course, to prove rather more durable than Mulvey's use of the term 'decline' suggests, and her belittling of 'sentimental regret' as an unimportant emotion was to be implicitly challenged by the revaluations of melodrama and the 'women's film' that would develop in the 1980s and 90s. It might be suggested, provocatively, that the influence her essay assumed demonstrates the poverty of film theory at this time; but, as the next chapter will show, there can be no doubt that it generated a wide range of responses and revisions, not least from Mulvey herself, even if its framework was finally to prove constricting.

CHAPTER FIVE

Gender Agenda: Images of Women and Men

The semiotic, post-structuralist and psychoanalytic film theory that became prominent in the 1970s, primarily in *Screen*, was buoyed up by a belief that revolutionary social transformation was imminent, and that abstruse radical theory and minority forms of cultural practice would play a key role in bringing it about. It now seems that this belief, like Hegel's famous Owl of Minerva,[1] took wing not in bright day, but at dusk, in the twilight of radical hopes that would thicken into darkness with the collapse of Soviet and Eastern European Communism at the end of the 1980s – an event that, even for those who had long lost faith in such states, nonetheless brought a strong sense of an ending. The great expectations of change that had grown in the 1960s and survived for much of the 1970s were not, of course, wholly wrong, as indeed the collapse of Communism showed. The 1980s and the 1990s would certainly see large transformations, but those transformations were to create a very different world from that of any projected revolutionary utopia.

As these changes began to gather pace in the 1980s, film theory became both more parochial, losing its global ambitions, and more open to the developing perspectives of feminism. It was, however, not so much a period of generating new theories as of developing, questioning and refining old ones – and in this respect, as the last chapter observed, Laura Mulvey's 'Visual Pleasure and Narrative Cinema' played a key role. The closing implication of that essay – that 'the monolithic accumulation of traditional film conventions' could be toppled – was characteristic of mid-1970s over-confidence; and pleasure, like the 'traditional film form', proved more persistent than Mulvey's polemics supposed. As she later acknowledged herself, one matter that was 'shelved' (might one say 'repressed'?) in 'Visual Pleasure and Narrative Cinema' was her 'own love of Hollywood melodrama'. Another matter that was 'equally shelved' in the article was· "'[W]hat about the women in the audience?'" Mulvey notes that she was often asked why she 'only used the *male* third person singular' – he – 'to stand in for the spectator'.[2] 'Afterthoughts on "Visual Pleasure and Narrative Cinema" inspired by King Vidor's *Duel in the Sun* (1946)', a paper first published in 1981, pursues these two issues, initially defining them in the following ways:

■ First (the 'women in the audience' issue), whether the female spectator is carried along, as it were by the scruff of the text, or whether her pleasure can be more deep-rooted and complex. Second (the 'melodrama' issue), how the text and its attendant identifications are affected by a *female* character occupying the centre of the narrative arena. So far as the first issue is concerned, it is always possible that the female spectator may find herself so out of key with the pleasure on offer, with its 'masculinisation', that the spell of fascination is broken. On the other hand, she may not. She may find herself secretly, unconsciously almost, enjoying the freedom of action and control over the diegetic world that identification with a hero provides. It is *this* female spectator that I want to consider here. So far as the second issue is concerned, I want to limit the area under consideration in a similar manner. Rather than discussing melodrama in general, I am concentrating on films in which a woman central protagonist is shown to be unable to achieve a stable sexual identity, torn between the deep blue sea of passive femininity and the devil of regressive masculinity.

There is an overlap between the two areas, between the unacknowledged dilemma faced in the auditorium and the dramatic double bind up there on the screen. Generally it is dangerous to elide these two separate worlds. In this case, the emotions of those women accepting 'masculinisation' while watching action movies with a male hero are illuminated by the emotions of a heroine of a melodrama whose resistance to a 'correct' feminine position is the critical issue at stake. Her oscillation, her inability to achieve stable sexual identity, is echoed by the woman spectator's masculine 'point of view'. Both create a sense of the difficulty of sexual difference in cinema that is missing in the undifferentiated spectator of 'Visual Pleasure [and Narrative Cinema]'.[3] □

Mulvey develops her discussion by combining psychoanalytic concepts with studies of the folk-tale. She points out that 'the conventional equation of activity and masculinity', as Freud called it,[4] 'structures most popular narratives, whether film, folk-tale or myth ..., where his metaphoric usage is acted out literally in the story' – that is, the narrative equates the active with the masculine. In the classical Greek myth of Perseus, for example, Andromeda, the female, 'stays tied to the rock, a victim, in danger', until Perseus, the male, 'slays the monster and saves her'. In this respect, the representation perpetuates an image of female passivity. But 'the "grammar" of the story places the reader, listener or spectator *with* the hero'. A film may work in the same way: the 'woman spectator in the cinema can make use of an age-old cultural tradition adapting her to this convention, which eases a transition out of her own sex into another'. Whereas 'Visual Pleasure and Narrative Cinema' aimed 'to identify a pleasure that was specific to cinema, ... the eroticism and cultural conventions surrounding the look', this article emphasises 'the way that popular cinema inherited traditions of story-telling that are common to other forms of folk and mass culture, with attendant fascinations other than those of the look'.[5]

Mulvey draws on 'a concept of character function based on' Vladimir Propp's *Morphology of the Folk Tale* (1929) 'to argue for a chain of links and shifts in narrative pattern, showing up the changing function of "woman"'. She suggests that the Western, as a film genre, 'bears a residual imprint of the primitive narrative structure analysed by ... Propp in folk-tales'. Moreover, the 'traditional invulnerability' of the Western hero closely relates to Freud's remarks on day-dreaming.[6] Thus 'the Western genre provides a crucial node in a series of transformations that *comment* on the function of "woman" (as opposed to "man") as a narrative signifier and sexual difference as personification of "active" or "passive" elements in a story'.[7] Mulvey develops her account of the relationship between Propp's analysis of the folk-tale, the Western, and the function of 'woman', by pointing out that, in Propp's account, an important feature of narrative closure – of the way a story ends – is 'marriage', and that this narrative function is the only one that is specific to one gender, since it is characterised by a 'princess' or the equivalent. In the Western, 'marriage' also makes a key contribution to concluding the story, but it can be complicated by its opposite: 'not marriage'. The social integration that marriage represents is crucial to the folk-tale; in the Western, however, it can be accepted or rejected, and the Western hero's rejection of the 'princess' may redound to his credit. Mulvey translates this into psychoanalytic terms: the acceptance of marriage represents the resolution of the Oedipus complex by an integration into the symbolic order, while the rejection of marriage is a regression to a phallic narcissism and imaginary omnipotence that cannot be easily fitted into the Oedipal scenario. This creates a contradiction in the Western:

- The tension between two points of attraction, the symbolic (social integration and marriage) and nostalgic narcissism, generates a common splitting of the Western hero into two, something unknown in the Proppian tale. Here two functions emerge, one celebrating integration into society through marriage, the other celebrating resistance to social demands and responsibilities, above all those of marriage and the family, the sphere represented by woman. A story such as *The Man Who Shot Liberty Valance* (1962) juxtaposes these two points of attraction, and spectator fantasy can have its cake and eat it too. This particular tension between the double hero also brings out the underlying significance of the drama, its relation to the symbolic, with unusual clarity. A folk-tale story revolves around conflict between hero and villain. The flashback narration in *Liberty Valance* seems to follow these lines at first. The narrative is generated by an act of villainy (Liberty rampages, dragon-like, around the countryside). However the development of the story acquires a complication. The issue at stake is no longer how the villain will be defeated, but how the villain's defeat will be inscribed into history, whether the *upholder* of law as a symbolic system (Ranse) will be seen to be victorious or the *personification* of law in a more primitive manifestation (Tom), closer to the good or the right. *Liberty Valance*, as it uses a flashback structure, also brings out the poignancy of this tension. The 'present-tense' story is precipitated by a funeral, so that the story is shot through with nostalgia and sense of loss. Ranse Stoddart mourns Tom Doniphon.

  This narrative structure is based on an opposition between two irreconcilables. The two paths cannot cross. On one side there is an encapsulation of power, and phallic attributes, in an individual who has to bow himself out of the way of history; on the other, an individual impotence rewarded by political and financial power, which, *in the long run*, in fact becomes history. Here the function 'marriage' is as crucial as it is in the folk-tale. It plays the same part in creating narrative resolution, but is even more important in that 'marriage' is an integral attribute of the upholder of the law. In this sense Hallie's choice between the two men is predetermined. Hallie equals princess equals Oedipal resolution rewarded, equals repression of narcissistic sexuality in marriage.[8] □

In a Western that employs these conventions, 'marriage' thus functions to sublimate 'the erotic into a final, closing, social ritual'.[9] This ritual is 'the main rationale for any female presence in this strand of the genre',[10] and this 'narrative function restates the propensity for "woman" to signify "the erotic"', as it does in *visual* representation. But 'introducing a woman as central to a story shifts its meanings, producing another kind of narrative discourse'.[11] *Duel in the Sun* exemplifies this:

- While the film remains visibly a 'Western', the generic space seems to shift. The landscape of action, although present, is not the dramatic core of the film's story, rather it is the interior drama of a girl caught between two conflicting desires. The conflicting desires, first of all, correspond closely with Freud's argument about ... an oscillation between 'passive' femininity and regressive 'masculinity' [in *Female Sexuality*]. [Compare Freud, in 'Femininity', quoted earlier in Mulvey's article: '[T]he development of femininity remains exposed to disturbance by the residual phenomena of the early masculine period. Regressions to the fixations of the pre-Oedipus phases very frequently occur; in the course of some women's lives there is a repeated alternation between periods in which masculinity or femininity gains the upper hand.'[12]] Thus, the symbolic equation, woman equals sexuality, still persists, but now rather than being an image or a narrative function, the equation opens out a narrative area previously suppressed or repressed. Woman is no longer the signifier of sexuality (function 'marriage') in the 'Western' type of story. Now the female presence as centre allows the story to be actually, *overtly*, about sexuality: it becomes a melodrama. It is as though the narrational lens had zoomed in and opened up the neat function 'marriage' ('and they lived happily ...' [Mulvey's ellipsis]) to ask 'what next?' and to focus on the figure of the princess, waiting in the wings for her one moment of importance, to ask 'what does *she* want?'. Here we find the generic terrain for melodrama, in its woman-orientated strand. The second question ('what does *she* want?') takes on greater significance when the hero function is split, as described above in the case of *Liberty Valance*, where the heroine's choice puts the seal of married grace on the upholder of the law. *Duel in the Sun* opens up this question.

In *Duel in the Sun* the iconographical attributes of the two male (oppositional) characters, Lewt and Jesse, conform very closely to those of Tom and Ranse in *Liberty Valance*. But now the opposition between Ranse and Tom (which represents an abstract and allegorical conflict over Law and history) is given a completely different twist of meaning. As Pearl is at the centre of the story, caught between the two men, their alternative attributes acquire meaning *from* her, and represent different sides of her desire and aspiration. They personify the split in *Pearl*, not a split in the concept of *hero*, as previously argued for *Liberty Valance*.

However, from a psychoanalytic point of view, a strikingly similar pattern emerges[:] Jesse (attributes: books, dark suit, legal skills, love of learning and culture, destined to be Governor of the State, money, and so on) signposts the 'correct' path for Pearl, towards learning a passive sexuality, learning to 'be a lady', above all sublimation into a concept of the feminine that is socially viable. Lewt (attributes: guns, horses, skill with horses, Western get-up, contempt for culture, destined to die an outlaw, personal strength and personal power) offers sexual passion, not based on maturity but on a regressive, boy/girl mixture of rivalry and play. With Lewt, Pearl can be a tomboy (riding, swimming, shooting). Thus the Oedipal dimension persists, but now illuminates the sexual ambivalence it represents for femininity.

In the last resort, there is no more room for Pearl in Lewt's world of misogynist machismo than there is room for her desires as Jesse's potential fiancée. The film consists of a series of oscillations in her sexual identity, between alternative paths of development, between different desperations. Whereas the regressive phallic male hero (Tom in *Liberty Valance*) had a place (albeit a doomed one) that was stable and meaningful, Pearl is unable to settle or find a 'femininity' in which she and the male world can meet. In this sense, although the male characters personify Pearl's dilemma, it is their terms that make and finally break her. Once again, however, the narrative drama dooms the phallic, regressive resistance to the symbolic. Lewt, Pearl's masculine side, drops out of the social order. Pearl's masculinity gives her the 'wherewithal' to achieve heroism and kill the villain. The lovers shoot each other and die in each other's arms. Perhaps, in *Duel*, the erotic relationship between Pearl and Lewt also exposes a dyadic interdependence between hero and villain in the primitive tale, now threatened by the splitting of the hero with the coming of the Law. [A dyad is a group of two elements, or a couple; 'dyadic interdependence' thus means, in this context, that the 'hero' and 'villain' of the primitive tale form a couple in which each depends for its identity on (its difference from) the other. When the function of the 'hero' is split between two characters, however, as in *Duel*, it introduces a third term into the two-part grouping or dyad, thus complicating it and making it more difficult to sustain.]

In *Duel in the Sun*, Pearl's inability to become a 'lady' is highlighted by the fact that the perfect lady appears, like a phantasmagoria of Pearl's failed aspiration, as Jesse's perfect future wife. Pearl recognises her and her rights over Jesse, and sees that she represents the 'correct' road. In an earlier film by King Vidor (1894–1982), *Stella Dallas* (1937), narrative and iconographic structures similar to those outlined above make the dramatic meaning of the film[,] although it is not a Western. Stella, as central character, is flanked on each side by a male personification of her instability, her inability to accept correct, married 'femininity' on the one hand, or find a place in a macho world on the other. Her husband, Stephen, demonstrates all the attributes associated with Jesse, with no problems of generic shift. Ed Munn, representing Stella's regressive 'masculine' side, is considerably emasculated by the loss of the Western's accoutrements and its terrain of violence. (The fact that Stella is a mother, and that her relationship to her child constitutes the central drama, undermines a possible sexual relationship with Ed.) He does retain residual traces of Western iconography. His attributes are mapped through associations with horses and betting, the racing scene. However, more importantly, his relationship with Stella is regressive, based on 'having fun', most explicitly in the episode in which they spread itching powder among the respectable occupants of a train carriage. In *Stella Dallas*, too, a perfect wife appears for Stephen, representing the 'correct' femininity that Stella rejects (very similar to Helen, Jesse's fiancée in *Duel in the Sun*).

I have been trying to suggest a series of transformations in narrative pattern that illuminate, but also show shifts in, Oedipal nostalgia. The 'personifications' and their iconographical attributes do not relate to parental figures or reactivate an actual Oedipal moment. On the contrary, they represent an internal oscillation of desire, which lies dormant, waiting to be 'pleasured' in stories of this kind. Perhaps the fascination of the classic Western, in particular, lies in its rather raw touching on this nerve. However, for the female spectator the situation is more complicated and goes beyond simple mourning for a lost fantasy of omnipotence. The masculine identification, in its phallic aspect, reactivates for her a fantasy of 'action' that correct femininity demands should be repressed. The fantasy 'action' finds expression through a metaphor of masculinity. Both in the language used by Freud and in the male personifications of desire flanking the female protagonist in the melodrama, this metaphor acts as a strait-jacket, becoming itself an indicator, a litmus paper, of the problems inevitably activated by any attempt to represent the feminine in patriarchal society. The memory of the 'masculine' phase has its own romantic attraction, a last-ditch resistance, in which the power of masculinity can be used as postponement against the power of patriarchy. Thus Freud's comments illuminate both the position of the female spectator and the image of oscillation represented by Pearl and Stella:

> ... in the course of some women's lives there is a repeated alternation between periods in which masculinity or femininity gains the upper hand.[13]

> ... the phallic phase ... ... succumbs to the momentous process of repression whose outcome, as has so often been shown, determines the fortunes of a woman's femininity.[14]

I have argued that Pearl's position in *Duel in the Sun* is similar to that of the female spectator as she temporarily accepts 'masculinisation' in memory of her 'active' phase. Rather than dramatising the success of masculine identification, Pearl brings out its sadness. Her 'tomboy' pleasures, her sexuality, are not fully accepted by Lewt, except in death. So, too, is the female spectator's fantasy of masculinisation at cross-purposes with itself, restless in its transvestite clothes.[15] □

Mulvey's focus in these 'Afterthoughts' on films 'in which a woman central protagonist is ... torn between the deep blue sea of passive femininity and the devil of regressive masculinity'[16] opens up another avenue that has proved fruitful – that of masculinity itself in relation to film. This was pursued by Steve Neale in a contribution to *Screen* in 1983 called 'Masculinity as Spectacle: Reflections on Men and Mainstream Cinema', which takes Mulvey's essay on 'Visual Pleasure and Narrative Cinema' as 'a central, structuring reference point'[17] and explores 'the process of narcissistic identification':[18]

■ Inasmuch as films *do* involve gender identification, and inasmuch as current ideologies of masculinity involve so centrally notions and attitudes to do with aggression, power and control, it seems to me that narcissism and narcissistic identification may be especially significant ... ... Narcissism and narcissistic identification both involve phantasies of power, omnipotence, mastery and control ... ... [Mulvey points out] the extent to which [the male protagonist's image] is dependent upon narcissistic phantasies, phantasies of the 'more perfect, more complete, more powerful ideal ego'[19] ... ... It is easy enough to find examples of films in which these fantasies are heavily prevalent, in which the male hero is powerful and omnipotent to an extraordinary degree: the Clint Eastwood character in [the films directed by Sergio Leone (1921–89):] *A Fistful of Dollars* (1964), *For a Few Dollars More* (1965) and *The Good, the Bad and the Ugly* (1966), the Tom Mix westerns, Charlton Heston in *El Cid* (1961), the *Mad Max* films (1979; 1981; 1985), the Steve Reeves epics, *Superman* (1978; 1981; 1983; 1987), *Flash Gordon* (1980) and so on. There is generally, of course, a drama in which that power and omnipotence [is] tested and qualified (*Superman 2* is a particularly interesting example[,] as are Howard Hawks'[s] westerns and adventure films), but the Leone trilogy, for example, is marked by the extent to which the hero's powers are rendered almost godlike, hardly qualified at all. Hence, perhaps, the extent to which they are built around ritualised scenes which in many ways are devoid of genuine suspense. [On the other hand, a film like *Le Samouraï* (*The Samurai*, 1967; aka *The Godson* in the USA), directed by Jean-Pierre Melville (1917–73),] starts with the image of self-possessed, omnipotent masculinity and traces its gradual and eventual disintegration. Alain Delon plays a lone gangster, a hit-man. His own narcissism is stressed in particular through his obsessive concern with his appearance, marked notably by a repeated and ritualised gesture he makes when putting on his hat, a sweep of the hand across the rim. Delon is sent on a job, but is spotted by a black female singer in a club. There is an exchange of looks. From that point on his omnipotence, silence and inviolability are all under threat. He is shot and wounded; his room is broken into and bugged; he is nearly trapped on the Metro. Eventually, he is gunned down, having returned to the club to see the singer again. The film is by no means a critique of the male image it draws upon. On the contrary, it very much identifies (and invites us to identify) with Delon. Nevertheless, the elements both of that image and of that to which the image is vulnerable are clearly laid out. It is no accident that Delon's downfall is sym[p]tomatically inaugurated in his encounter with the black woman. Difference (double difference) is the threat. An exchange of looks in which Delon's cold commanding gaze is troubled, undermined and returned is the mark of that threat.

The kind of image that Delon here embodies, and that Eastwood and the others mentioned earlier embody too, is one marked not only by emotional reticence, but also by silence, a reticence with language. Theoretically, this silence, this absence of language can further be linked to narcissism and to the construction of an ideal ego. The acquisition of language is a process profoundly challenging to the narcissism of early childhood. It is productive of what has been called 'symbolic castration'. Language is a process (or set of processes) involving absence and lack, and these are what threaten any image of the self as totally enclosed, self-sufficient, omnipotent. The construction of an ideal ego, meanwhile, is a process involving profound contradictions. While the ideal ego may be a 'model' with which the subject identifies and to which it aspires, it may also be a source of further images and feelings of castration, inasmuch as that ideal is something to which the subject is never adequate.[20]

If this is the case, there can be no simple and unproblematic identification on the part of the spectator, male or female, with Mulvey's 'ideal ego' on the screen ... ...

Taking a cue from Mulvey's remarks about nostalgia in *Liberty Valance*, one could go on to discuss a number of nostalgic westerns ... in terms of the theme of lost or doomed male narcissism. The clearest example would be [the] westerns of Sam Peckinpah (1925–84): *Guns in the Afternoon* (1962; *Ride the High Country* in the USA), *Major Dundee* (1964) (to a lesser extent), *The Wild Bunch* (1969) and, especially, *Pat Garrett and Billy the Kid* (1973). These films are shot through with nostalgia, with an obsession with images and definitions of masculinity and masculine codes of behaviour, and with images of male narcissism and the threats posed to it by women, society and the Law. The threat of castration is figured in the wounds and injuries suffered by Joel McCrea in *Guns in the Afternoon*, Charlton Heston in *Major Dundee* and William Holden in *The Wild Bunch*. The famous slow-motion violence, bodies splintered and torn apart, can be viewed at one level at least as the image of narcissism in its moment of disintegration and destruction. Significantly, Kris Kristofferson as Billy in *Pat Garrett and Billy the Kid*, the ultimate incarnation of omnipotent male narcissism in Peckinpah's films, is spared any bloody and splintered death. Shot by Pat Garrett, his body shows no sign either of wounds or blood: narcissism transfigured (rather than destroyed) by death.

I want now to move on from identification and narcissism to discuss in relation to images of men and masculinity the two modes of looking addressed by Mulvey in 'Visual Pleasure', voyeuristic looking, on the one hand, and fetishistic looking on the other ... ... In discussing these two types of looking, both fundamental to the cinema, Mulvey locates them solely in relation to a structure of activity/passivity in which the look is male and active and the object of the look female and passive. Both are considered as distinct and variant means by which male castration anxieties may be played out and allayed.

Voyeuristic looking is marked by the extent to which there is a distance between spectator and spectacle, a gulf between the seer and the seen. This structure is one which allows the spectator a degree of power over what is seen. It hence tends constantly to involve sado-masochistic phantasies and themes ... ... [Mulvey discusses the sadistic] characteristics of voyeuristic looking in terms of the *film noir* and of Hitchcock's movies, where the hero is the bearer of the voyeuristic look, engaged in a narrative in which the woman is the object of its sadistic components. However, if we take some of the terms used in her description – 'making something happen', 'forcing a change in another person', 'a battle of will and strength', 'victory/defeat'[21] – they can immediately be applied to 'male' genres, to films concerned largely or solely with the depiction of relations between men, to any film, for example, in which there is a struggle between a hero and a male villain. War films, westerns and gangster movies, for instance, are all marked by 'action', by 'making something happen'. Battles, fights and duels of all kinds are concerned with struggles of 'will and strength', 'victory/defeat', between individual men and/or groups of men. All of which implies that male figures on the screen are subject to voyeuristic looking, both on the part of the spectator and on the part of other male characters ... ...

... The rep[r]ession of any explicit avowal of eroticism in the act of looking at the male seems structurally linked to a narrative content marked by sado-masochistic phantasies and scenes. Hence both forms of voyeuristic looking, infra- and extra-diegetic [that is, the voyeuristic looks of the characters *in* the film, and the voyeuristic look of the spectator *at* the film], are especially evident in those moments of contest and combat referred to above, in those moments at which a narrative outcome is determined through a fight or gun-battle, at which male struggle becomes pure spectacle. Perhaps the most extreme examples are to be found in Leone's Westerns, where the exchange of aggressive looks marking most western gun-duels is taken to the point of fetishistic parody through the use of extreme and repetitive close-ups. At which point the look begins to oscillate between voyeurism and fetishism as the narrative starts to freeze and spectacle takes over ... ...

[In] Leone's shoot-outs, we can see that some elements of the fetishistic look ... are present, others not. We are offered the spectacle of male bodies, but bodies unmarked as objects of erotic display. There is no trace of an acknowledgment or recognition of those bodies as displayed solely for the gaze of the spectator. They are on display, certainly, but there is no cultural or cinematic convention which would allow the male body to be presented in the way that Dietrich so often is in Sternberg's films. We see male bodies stylised and fragmented by close-ups, but our look is not direct, it is heavily mediated by the looks of the characters involved. And those looks are marked not by desire, but rather by fear, or hatred, or aggression. The shoot-outs are moments of spectacle, points at which the narrative hesitates, comes to a momentary halt, but they are also points at which the drama is finally resolved, a suspense in the culmination of the narrative drive. They thus involve an imbrication of *both* forms of looking, their inter-twining designed to minimise and displace the eroticism they each tend to involve, to disavow any explicitly erotic look at the male body.

There are other instances of male combat which seem to function in this way. Aside from the western, one could point to the epic as a genre, to the gladiatorial combat in *Spartacus* (1960), to the fight between Christopher Plummer and Stephen Boyd at the end of *The Fall of the Roman Empire* (1964), to the chariot race in *Ben-Hur* (1959). More direct displays of the male body can be found, though they tend either to be fairly brief or else to occupy the screen during credit sequences and the like (in which case the display is mediated by another textual function). Examples of the former would include the extraordinary shot of Gary Cooper lying under the hut toward the end of *Man of the West* (1958), his body momentarily filling the Cinemascope screen. Or some of the images of Lee Marvin in *Point Blank* (1967), his body draped over a railing or framed in a doorway. Examples of the latter would include the credit sequence of *Man of the West* ..., and *Junior Bonner* (1972).

The presentation of Rock Hudson in [the] melodramas [of

Douglas Sirk (born Detlef Sierck, 1900–87)] is a particularly interesting case. There are constantly moments in these films [*Magnificent
Obsession* (1954), *All That Heaven Allows* (1955)] in which Hudson is
presented quite explicitly as the object of an erotic look. The look is
usually marked as female. But Hudson's body is *feminised* in those
moments, an indication of the strength of those conventions which
dictate that only women can function as the objects of an explicitly
erotic gaze. Such instances of 'feminisation' tend also to occur in the
musical, the only genre in which the male body has been unashamedly put on display in mainstream cinema in any consistent
way. (A particularly clear and interesting example would be the presentation of John Travolta in *Saturday Night Fever* (1977)).

It is a refusal to acknowledge or make explicit an eroticism that
marks all three of the psychic functions and processes discussed here
in relation to images of men: identification, voyeuristic looking and
fetishistic looking. It is this that tends above all to differentiate the
cinematic representation of images of men and women. Although I
have sought to open up a space within Laura Mulvey's arguments
and theses, to argue that the elements she considers in relation to
images of women can and should also be considered in relation to
images of men, I would certainly concur with her basic premise that
the spectatorial look in mainstream cinema is implicitly male: it is one
of the fundamental reasons why the erotic elements involved in the
relations between the spectator and the male image have constantly
to be repressed and disavowed. Were this not the case, mainstream
cinema would have openly to come to terms with the male homosexuality it so assiduously seeks either to denigrate or deny. As it is,
male homosexuality is constantly present as an undercurrent, as a
potentially troubling aspect of many films and genres, but one that is
dealt with obliquely, symptomatically, and that has to be repressed.
While mainstream cinema, in its assumption of a male norm, perspective and look, can constantly take women and the female image
as its object of investigation, it has rarely investigated men and the
male image in the same kind of way: women are a problem, a source
of anxiety, of obsessive enquiry; men are not. Where women are investigated, men are tested. Masculinity, as an ideal, at least, is implicitly
known. Femininity is, by contrast, a mystery. This is one of the reasons
why the representation of masculinity, both inside and outside the
cinema, has been so rarely discussed. Hopefully, this article will contribute towards such a discussion.[22] □

Neale's hope that his article would contribute towards a discussion of the representation of masculinity inside and outside the cinema has certainly been fulfilled, and such representations – and the 'troubling undercurrent of male homosexuality' in many films and genres – have today become key topics of inquiry for film, gender and cultural studies. Closer attention to the representation of masculinity has, however, called into question Neale's concluding argument that masculinity is implicitly known and in some sense secure, at least as an ideal. A challenge might also be made today to the way in which Neale remains within the psychoanalytical terms of reference set out by Mulvey – identification, narcissism, voyeurism, fetishism – and treats them as if they offered access to a 'deeper' level of truth than would be available to a critic who responded to a film in a more straightforward way. But faced, for example, with Neale's claim that the wounds and injuries suffered by certain characters in Peckinpah's films figure the threat of castration, might it not be said, more simply, that they figure the threat of wounds and injuries (which might include, but are not confined to, castration)? Similarly, one could take issue with the claim that the slow motion violence 'can be viewed at one level at least as the image of narcissism in its moment of disintegration and destruction'. The 'at one level at least' qualifies the statement, of course, though one would like to know what those implied other levels are; but it might be asked why bodies splintered and torn apart should primarily be interpreted as images of disintegrating male narcissism rather than an image of the disintegrating physical body that is disturbing on a more primal level than that of a threat to an illusory self-image? There is also a notable lack of historical perspective in Neale's discussion of Peckinpah: he does not register the way in which Peckinpah is part of a movement, in the later 1960s, on to a new level of graphic violence on the screen. To do so might raise the issue of whether psychoanalytical concepts formed in a period when the display of sexuality, like the display of violence, was strongly controlled are applicable, without considerable modification, to a period when such displays are more overt. When the display of violence is overt in the Peckinpah manner, does a psychoanalytic concept such as narcissism provide the most relevant means of analysis?

Possibly not; and it is feasible to pursue the areas of concern that Neale had indicated without a psychoanalytical vocabulary, though such a vocabulary has continued to be dominant in such explorations. If Neale had raised the issue of the representation of masculinity and of male homosexuality in film, Jackie Stacey, in her essay 'Desperately Seeking

Difference', which appeared in *Screen* in 1987, explored the question of 'the specifically homosexual pleasures of female spectatorship' and aimed to suggest some theoretical reasons for its neglect. Like Neale, she took Mulvey's 'Visual Pleasure and Narrative Cinema' – the 'springboard for much feminist film criticism during the last decade'[23] – as her point of departure, but proposed a more flexible and contradictory model of spectatorship in her analysis of 'the pleasures of two narrative films which develop around one woman's obsession with another woman', *All About Eve* (1950), directed by Joseph L. Mankiewicz, and *Desperately Seeking Susan* (1984), directed by Susan Seidelman (born 1952). While not claiming them as 'lesbian films',[24] Stacey argues that 'these films offer particular pleasures to the women in the audience which cannot simply be reduced to a masculine heterosexual equivalent':[25]

■ I want to explore the representation of forms of desire and identification in these films in order to consider their implications for the pleasures of female spectatorship. My focus is on the relations between women on the screen, and between these representations and the women in the audience. Interestingly, the fascinations which structure both narratives are precisely about difference – forms of otherness between women characters which are not merely reducible to sexual difference, so often seen as the sole producer of desire itself ... ... *All About Eve* is ... precisely about the pleasures and dangers of spectatorship for women. One of its central themes is the construction and reproduction of feminine identities, and the activity of looking is highlighted as an important part of these processes. The narrative concerns two women, a Broadway star and her most adoring spectator, Eve. In its course, we witness the transformation of Eve Butler (Anne Baxter) from spectator to star herself. The pleasures of spectatorship are emphasised by Eve's loyal attendance at every one of Margot Channing's (Bette Davis) performances. Its dangers are also made explicit as an intense rivalry develops between them. Eve emerges as a greedy and ambitious competitor, and Margot steps down from stardom into marriage, finally enabling her protégée to replace her as 'actress of the year' in a part written originally for Margot.

Eve's journey to stardom could be seen as the feminine equivalent to the masculine Oedipal trajectory ... Freud's later descriptions of the feminine Oedipal journey[26] contradict his previous symmetrical model wherein the girl's first love object is her father, as the boy's is his mother. In his later arguments, Freud also posited the mother as the girl's first love object. Her path to heterosexuality is therefore difficult and complex, since it requires her not only to relinquish her first object, like the boy, but to transform both its gender (female to male) and the aim (active to passive) directed at it. Up to this point, active desire towards another woman is an experience of all women, and its re-enactment in *All About Eve* may constitute one of the pleasures of spectatorship for the female viewer.

Eve is constantly referred to as innocent and childlike in the first half of the film and her transformation involves a process of maturation, of becoming a more confident adult. First she is passionately attached to Margot, but then she shifts her affection to Margot's lover Bill, attempting unsuccessfully to seduce him. Twice in the film she is shown interrupting their intimacy: during their farewell at the airport and then during their fierce argument about Margot's jealousy, shortly before Bill's welcome-home party. Eve's third object of desire, whom she actively pursues, is the married playwright, Lloyd Richards, husband to Margot's best friend. In both cases the stability of the older heterosexual couples, Margot and Bill, Karen and Lloyd, is threatened by the presence of the younger woman who completes the Oedipal triangle. Eve is finally punished for her desires by the patriarchal power of the aptly named Addison de Wit, who proves to be one step ahead of her manipulations.

The binary opposition between masculinity and femininity offers a limited framework for the discussion of Eve's fascination with Margot, which is articulated actively through an interplay of desire and identification during the film. In many ways, Margot is Eve's idealised object of desire. She follows Margot from city to city, never missing any of her performances. Her devotion to her favourite Broadway star is stressed at the very start of the film.

Karen   But there are hundreds of plays on Broadway ...
Eve   Not with Margot Channing in them!

Margot is moved by Eve's representation of her 'tragic' past, and flattered by her adoration, so she decides to 'adopt' her.

Margot (*voice over*) We moved Eve's few pitiful possessions into my apartment ... Eve became my sister, mother, lawyer, friend, psychiatrist and cop. The honeymoon was on!

Eve acts upon her desire to become more like her ideal. She begins to wear Margot's cast-off clothes, appearing in Margot's bedroom one morning in her old black suit. Birdie, Margot's personal assistant, responds suspiciously to Eve's behaviour.

Margot   She thinks only of me.

Birdie   She thinks only *about* you – like she's studying you – like you was a book, or a play, or a set of blueprints – how you walk, talk, eat, think, sleep.

Margot   I'm sure that's very flattering, Birdie, and I'm sure there's nothing wrong with it.

The construction of Bette Davis as the desirable feminine ideal in this narrative has a double significance here. As well as being a 'great star' for Eve, she is clearly the same for the cinema audience. The film offers the fictional fulfilment of the spectator's dreams as well as Eve's, to be a star like Bette Davis, like Margot. Thus the identifications and desires of Eve, to some extent, narrativise [make a story of] a traditional pleasure of female spectatorship.

Margot is not only a star, she is also an extremely powerful woman who intimidates most of the male characters in the film. Her quick wit and disdain for conventional politeness, together with her flair for drama offstage as much as on, make her an attractive figure for Eve, an 'idealistic dreamy-eyed kid', as Bill describes her. It is this *difference* between the two women which motivates Eve, but which Eve also threatens. In trying to 'become as much like her ideal as possible', Eve almost replaces Margot in both her public and her private lives. She places a call to Bill on Margot's behalf, and captures his attention when he is on his way upstairs to see Margot before his coming home party. Margot begins to feel dispensible.

Margot   I could die right now and nobody would be confused. My inventory is all in shape and the merchandise all put away.

Yet even dressed in Margot's costume, having taken her role in the evening's performance, Eve cannot supplant her in the eyes of Bill, who rejects her attempt at seduction. The difference between the two women is repeatedly stressed and complete identification proves impossible.

All About Eve offers some unusual pleasures for a Hollywood film, since the active desire of a female character is articulated through looking at the female star. It is by watching Margot perform on the stage that Eve becomes intoxicated with her idol. The significance of active looking in the articulation of feminine desire is foregrounded at various points in the narrative. In one scene, we see Eve's devoted spectatorship in progress during one of Margot's performances. Eve watches Margot from the wings of the stage, and Margot bows to the applause of her audience. In the next scene the roles are reversed, and Margot discovers Eve on the empty stage bowing to an imaginary audience. Eve is holding up Margot's costume to sample the pleasures of stardom for herself. This process is then echoed in the closing scene of the film with Eve, now a Broadway star herself, and the newly introduced Phoebe, an adoring schoolgirl fan. The final shot shows Phoebe, having covertly donned Eve's bejewelled evening cloak, holding Eve's award and gazing at her reflection in the mirror. The reflected image, infinitely multiplied in the triptych of the glass, creates a spectacle of stardom that is the film's final shot, suggesting a perpetual regeneration of intra-feminine fascinations through the pleasure of looking ... ...

Like *All About Eve*, *Desperately Seeking Susan* concerns a woman's obsession with another woman. But instead of being punished for acting upon her desires, like Eve, Roberta (Rosanna Arquette) acts upon her desires, if in a rather more haphazard way, and eventually her initiatives are rewarded with the realisation of her desires. Despite her classic feminine behaviour, forgetful, clumsy, unpunctual and indecisive, she succeeds in her quest to find Susan (Madonna).

Even at the very beginning of the film, when suburban housewife Roberta is represented at her most dependent and childlike, her actions propel the narrative movement. Having developed her own fantasy narrative about Susan by reading the personal advertisements, Roberta acts upon her desire to be 'desperate' and becomes entangled in Susan's life. She anonymously attends the romantic reunion of Susan and Jim, and then pursues Susan through the streets of Manhattan. When she loses sight of her quarry in a second-hand shop, she purchases the jacket which Susan has just exchanged. The key found in its pocket provides an excuse for direct contact, and Roberta uses the personals to initiate another meeting.

Not only is the narrative propelled structurally by Roberta's desire, but almost all the spectator sees of Susan at the beginning of the film is revealed through Roberta's fantasy. The narrativisation of her desires positions her as the central figure for spectator identification: through her desire we seek, and see, Susan. Thus, in the opening scenes, Susan is introduced by name when Roberta reads the personals aloud from under the dryer in the beauty salon. Immediately following Roberta's declaration 'I wish I was desperate', there is a cut to the first shot of Susan.

The cuts from the Glass's party to Susan's arrival in New York City work to the same effect. Repelled by her husband's TV commercial for his bathroom wares, Roberta leaves her guests and moves towards the window, as the ad's voice-over promises 'At Gary's Oasis, all your fantasies can come true'. Confronted with her own image in the reflection, she pushes it away by opening the window and looking out longingly onto Manhattan's skyline. The ensuing series of cuts between Roberta and the bridge across the river to the city link her desiring gaze to Susan's arrival there via the same bridge.

At certain points within *Desperately Seeking Susan*, Roberta explicitly becomes the bearer of the look. The best illustration of this transgression of traditional gender positionalities occurs in the scene in which she first catches sight of Susan. The shot sequence begins with Jim seeing Susan and is immediately followed with Roberta seeing her. It is, however, Roberta's point of view which is offered for the spectator's identification. Her look is specified by the use of the pay-slot telescope through which Roberta, and the spectator, see Susan.

In accordance with classic narrative cinema, the object of fascination in *Desperately Seeking Susan* is a woman – typically, a woman coded as a sexual spectacle. As a star Madonna's image is saturated in sexuality. In many ways she represents the '80s 'assertive style' of heterosexual spectacle, inviting masculine consumption. This is certainly emphasised by shots of Susan which reference classic pornographic poses and camera angles; for example, the shot of Susan lying on Roberta's bed reading her diary, which shows Susan lying on her back, wearing only a vest and a pair of shorts over her suspenders and lacy tights. (Although one could argue that the very next shot, from Susan's point of view, showing Gary upside down, subverts the conventional pornographic codes.) My aim is not to deny these meanings in *Desperately Seeking Susan*, in order to claim it as a 'progressive text', but to point to cinematic pleasures which may be available to the spectator *in addition* to those previously analysed by feminist film theory. Indeed, I believe such a project can only attempt to work within the highly contradictory constructions of femininity in mainstream films.

Susan is represented as puzzling and enigmatic to the protagonist, and to the spectator. The desire propelling the narrative is partly a desire to become more like her, but also a desire to know her, and to solve the riddle of her femininity. The protagonist begins to fulfil this desire by following the stranger, gathering clues about her identity and her life, such as her jacket, which, in turn, produces three other clues, a key, a photograph and a telephone number. The construction of her femininity as a riddle is emphasised by the series of intrigues and misunderstandings surrounding Susan's identity. The film partly relies on typical devices drawn from the mystery genre in constructing the protagonist's, and thus the spectator's, knowledge of Susan through a series of clues and coincidences. Thus, in some ways, Susan is positioned as the classic feminine enigma; she is, however, investigated by another woman.

One line of analysis might simply see Roberta as taking up the position of the masculine protagonist in expressing a desire to be 'desperate', which, after all, can be seen as identifying with Jim's position in relation to Susan, that of active desiring masculinity. Further legitimation for this reading could be seen in Jim's response to Roberta's advertisement to Susan in the personals. He automatically assumes it has been placed there by another man, perhaps a rival. How can we understand the construction of the female protagonist as the agent and articulator of desire for another woman in the narrative within existing psychoanalytic theories of sexual difference? The limitations of a dichotomy which offers only two significant categories for understanding the complex interplay of gender, sexual aim and object choice, is clearly demonstrated here … …

The difference which produces the narrative desire in *Desperately Seeking Susan* is not sexual difference, but the difference between two women in the film. It is the difference between suburban marriage and street credibility. Two sequences contrast the characters using smoking as a signifier of difference. The first occurs in Battery Park, where Roberta behaves awkwardly in the unfamiliar territory of public space. She is shown sitting on a park bench, knees tightly clenched, looking around nervously for Susan. Jim asks her for a light, to which she timidly replies that she does not smoke. The ensuing cut shows Susan, signalled by Jim's shout of recognition. Susan is sitting on the boat rail, striking a match on the bottom of her raised boot to light a cigarette.

Smoking is used again to emphasise difference in a subsequent sequence. This time, Roberta, having by now lost her memory and believing she may be Susan, lights a cigarette from Susan's box. Predictably, she chokes on the smoke, with the unfamiliarity of an adolescent novice. The next cut shows us Susan, in prison for attempting to skip her cab fare, taking a light from the prison matron and blowing the smoke defiantly straight back into her face. The contrast in their smoking ability is only one signifier of the characters' very different femininities. Roberta is represented as young, inexperienced and asexual, while Susan's behaviour and appearance are coded as sexually confident and provocative. Rhyming sequences are used to emphasise their differences even after Roberta has taken on her new identity as Susan. She ends up in the same prison cell, but her childlike acquiescence to authority contrasts with Susan's defiance of the law.

Susan transgresses conventional forms of feminine behaviour by appropriating public space for herself. She turns the public lavatory into her own private bathroom, drying her armpits with the hand blower, and changing her clothes in front of the mirror above the washbasins as if in her own bedroom. In the streets, Susan challenges the patronising offer of a free newspaper from a passerby by dropping the whole pile at his feet and taking only the top copy for herself. In contrast to Susan's supreme public confidence, Roberta is only capable in her own middle class privacy. Arriving home after her day of city adventures, she manages to synchronise with a televised cooking show, catching up on its dinner preparations with confident dexterity in her familiar domestic environment.

As soon as Roberta becomes entangled in Susan's world, her respectable sexuality is thrown into question. First she is assumed to be having an affair, then she is arrested for suspected prostitution, and finally Gary asks her if she is a lesbian. When the two photographs of Roberta, one as a bride and one as a suspected prostitute, are laid down side by side at the police station, her apparent transformation from virgin to whore shocks her husband. The ironic effect of these largely misplaced accusations about Roberta's sexuality works partly in relation to Susan, who is represented as the epitome of opposition to acceptable bourgeois feminine sexuality. She avoids commitment, dependency or permanence in her relationships with men, and happily takes their money, while maintaining an intimate friendship with the woman who works at the Magic Box.

Roberta's desire is finally rewarded when she meets Susan in an almost farcical chase scene at that club during the chaotic film finale. Gary finds Roberta, Des finds 'Susan' (Roberta), Jim finds Susan, the villain finds the jewels (the earrings which Susan innocently pocketed earlier in the film), Susan and Roberta catch the villain, and Susan and Roberta find each other ... [Stacey's ellipsis] The last shot of the film is a front-page photograph of the two women hand in hand, triumphantly waving their reward cheque in return for the recovery of the priceless Nefertiti earrings. In the end, both women find what they were searching for throughout the narrative: Roberta has found Susan, and Susan has found enough money to finance many future escapades.

Roberta's desire to become more like her ideal – a more pleasingly coordinated, complete and attractive feminine image[27] – is offered temporary narrative fulfilment. However, the pleasures of this feminine desire cannot be collapsed into simple identification, since difference and otherness are continuously played upon, even when Roberta 'becomes' her idealised object. Both *Desperately Seeking Susan* and *All About Eve* tempt the woman spectator with the fictional fulfilment of becoming an ideal feminine other, while denying complete transformation by insisting upon differences between women. The rigid distinction between *either* desire *or* identification, so characteristic of psychoanalytic film theory, fails to address the construction of desires which involve a specific interplay of both processes.[28] □

Whereas Steve Neale largely accepted Mulvey's terms and extended them to consider representations of masculinity, Stacey, as her conclusion to the above extract emphasises, takes a greater distance from Mulvey, and more generally from a psychoanalytical approach to film theory and analysis. It is true that, across the whole of her essay, she continues to use words that are associated with psychoanalysis, semiotics, structuralism and post-structuralism, such as identification, desire, construction, diegesis, narrativisation, representation, the bearer of the look, gender positionalities, object choice, signifier, difference, otherness. But these are not intellectually crucial to her argument; she offers, in effect, an interesting content analysis of films that appear to present, whatever other negative and reactionary meanings they may carry, positive and pleasurable models of varieties of female desire. Stacey's essay exemplifies four aspects of a more general development in film theory and criticism in the later 1980s: there is a welcome interrogation of the more rigid and dogmatic aspects of semiotic film theory; there is a questionable move away from abstract questions of theory to specific analyses that use theoretical terms in a relatively loose and light way, as a kind of *lingua franca* of critical discourse; there is a greater emphasis on the contra-dictoriness of filmic texts, the clashing of reactionary and progressive positions that they offer; and, again questionably, there is a blurring of the distinction between theoretical and political correctness – a theory is rejected partly because it is held to be intellectually invalid but also partly because it is politically unacceptable. In a section of her article that precedes the above extract, for example, Stacey observes that the theories of Mulvey, Raymond Bellour and Mary Anne Doane offer the female spectator 'only the three rather frustrating options of masculini-sation, masochism or marginality'.[29] Stacey's rejection of those theories is, in part, based on what she regards as their inadequacy to account for the relevant data, 'the complex interplay of gender, sexual aim and object choice'; but to reject a theory because of its 'frustrating' effect is to invoke another kind of criterion. A theory might be 'frustrating' but still true.

Despite Neale's modifications of Mulvey, and Stacey's greater reser-vations about her approach, and in spite of a range of other responses, 'Visual Pleasure and Narrative Cinema' continued to exercise a dis-proportionate dominance in film studies in the 1980s and into the 1990s. The most radical objections to the essay came from a theorist who refused the terms that Stacey, while registering her disagreements with Mulvey, was still willing to employ: Noël Carroll. In *Mystifying Movies* (1988), Carroll, who was to become one of the leading exponents of what has come to be called cognitive film theory, had already launched a sustained attack on the kind of psychoanalytical, post-structuralist and semiotic theory associated with *Screen* and exemplified, in this Critical History, by the extracts from the essays of MacCabe, Heath and Mulvey. In 'The Image of Women in Film', first published in the *Journal of Aesthetics and Art Criticism* in Fall 1990, and collected in *Theorizing the Moving Image* (1996), Carroll focuses on Mulvey's essay in order to develop his 'objections to psychoanalytic-feminism in contemporary [i.e. 1980s] film studies'. That this will be a rather stronger attack than those of others who have taken issue with Mulvey is indicated by Carroll's claim that 'many of the theoretical tendencies which [he intends] to crit-icize in Mulvey's essay continue to plague psychoanalytic film feminism, even in those cases where other psychoanalytically inclined feminists may explicitly wish to modify Mulvey's approach'.[30] Carroll then develops his argument:

■ According to Mulvey, one place to look for a theoretical framework that will enable an interrogation of patterns of visual fascination is psychoanalysis. Psychoanalysis has a theory of visual pleasure or scopophilia; so it is at least a candidate for answering questions about cinematic visual pleasure. However, it must be noted that Mulvey's embrace of psychoanalysis seems to be unargued. Rather, she announces the need for theoretical vocabularies and generalizations, and then she endorses psychoanalysis simply because it has them. She does not ask whether there are rival theoretical frameworks to psychoanalysis which might also serve her purposes; she does not consider any problems concerning the scientific status of psychoanalysis; she does not weigh the shortcomings of psychoanalysis against the advantages of competing models. Her acceptance of psychoanalysis appears almost uncritically pragmatic: we need a theory of visual pleasure; psychoanalysis has one; so let's use it.

This unquestioning acceptance of the *scientific* authority of psychoanalysis is a continuing feature of epistemologically dubious merit in contemporary feminist film criticism.[31] [By 'epistemologically dubious', Carroll means that it is doubtful whether psychoanalysis provides a scientifically acceptable foundation for and method of acquiring knowledge; epistemology is the theory of the grounds and/or the methods of knowledge.] Where psychoanalytic hypotheses are not marred by obvious sexism, psychoanalytic feminists tend to be willing to accept them without exploring their possible logical flaws, empirical shortcomings, or relative disadvantages with respect to other theoretical frameworks. In this, they follow Mulvey's lead ... I believe that this methodological oversight, in the opening moves of psychoanalytic-feminism, with respect to theory choice, compromises feminist-psychoanalytic film criticism fundamentally.[32]

From psychoanalysis, Mulvey inherits the observation that scopophilia is targeted at the human form. To this, then, she adds an empirical generalization, presumably one independent of psychoanalysis, that in film there is a division of labour in terms of the portrayal of the human form.[33] Men are characterized as active agents; women are objects of erotic contemplation – so many pin-ups or arrested images of beauty ... ...

... Mulvey situates the visual pleasure in Hollywood cinema in the satisfaction of the male's desire to contemplate the female form erotically. This contemplation itself is potentially unpleasurable, however, since contemplation of the female form raises the prospect of castration anxiety. Cinematic strategies corresponding to fetishism and voyeurism – and emblematized respectively by the practices of von Sternberg and Hitchcock – provide visual and narrative means to protect the structure of male visual pleasure, obsessively opting for cinematic conventions and schemata that are subordinated to the neurotic needs of the male ego. Feminist film practice of the sort Mulvey champions seeks to subvert the conventions that support the system of visual pleasure deployed in Hollywood and to depose the hegemony of the male gaze.

... [A]part from her psychoanalytic commitments, Mulvey's theory of visual pleasure rests on some highly dubitable empirical suppositions. On Mulvey's account, male characters in cinema are active; females are passive, primarily functioning to be seen. She writes that a male movie star's glamorous characteristics are not those of an erotic object of the gaze.[34] It is hard to see how anyone could come to believe this. In our own time, we have Sylvester Stallone and Arnold Schwarzenegger whose star vehicles slow down and whose scenes are blocked and staged precisely to afford spectacles of bulging pectorals and other parts. Nor are these examples from contemporary film new developments in film history. Before Stallone, there were Steve Reeves and Charles Bronson, and before them, Johnny Weissmuller. Indeed, the muscle-bound character of Maciste that Steve Reeves often played originated in the 1913 Italian spectacle *Cabiria*.

Nor is the baring of chests for erotic purposes solely the province of second-string male movie stars. Charlton Heston, Kirk Douglas, Burt Lancaster, Yul Brynner – the list could go on endlessly – all have a beefcake side to their star personae. Obviously there are entire genres that celebrate male physiques, scantily robed, as sources of visual pleasure: biblical epics, ironically enough, as well as other forms of ancient and exotic epics; jungle films; sea-diving films; boxing films; Tarzan adventures; etc.

Nor are males simply ogled on screen for their bodily beauty. Some are renowned for their great facial good looks, for which the action is slowed down so that the audience may take a gander, often in 'glamor' close-ups. One thinks of John Gilbert and Rudolph Valentino in the twenties; of the young Gary Cooper, John Wayne, Henry Fonda and Laurence Olivier in the thirties; of Gregory Peck in the forties; Montgomery Clift, Marlon Brando, and James Mason in the fifties; Peter O'Toole in the sixties; and so on.[35] Nor is it useful to suggest a constant correlation between male stars and effective activity. Leslie Howard in *Of Human Bondage* (1934) and *Gone with the Wind* (1939) seems to have succeeded most memorably as a matinee idol when he was staggeringly ineffectual.

If the dichotomy between male/active images versus female/passive images ill-suits the male half of the formula, it is also empirically misguided for the female half. Many of the great female stars were also great doers. Rosalind Russell in *His Girl Friday* (1940) and Katherine Hepburn in *Bringing Up Baby* hardly stop moving long enough to permit the kind of visual pleasure Mulvey asserts is the basis of the female image in Hollywood cinema. Moreover, it seems to me question-begging to say that audiences do not derive visual pleasure from these performances. Furthermore, if one complains here that my counterexamples are from comedies, and that certain kinds of comedies present special cases, let us argue about *The Perils of Pauline*. [This mention of *The Perils of Pauline* exemplifies Carroll's use, at times, of a compressed reference that he fails to explicate. *The Perils of Pauline* (1914) was a serial for Pathé, starring Pearl White (1889–1938). Two later films with the same title, one in 1948 starring Betty Hutton and one in 1967 starring Pamela Austin, were loosely based on White's life. The original *Perils of Pauline* was characteristic of the film serial of the early twentieth century in that it was an action movie that portrayed its heroine in a highly active role: Carroll presumably cites it as an example of a genre other than comedy in which a woman is a 'great doer' who provides visual pleasure for audiences. As Ben Singer puts it in *The Oxford History of World Cinema* (1997): 'In their stunt-filled adventures as "girl spies", "girl detectives", "girl reporters", etc., serial heroines [such as Pauline/Pearl White] demonstrated a kind of toughness, bravery, agility, and intelligence that excited audiences both for its novelty and for its feminist resonance. Serial queens defied the ideology of female passivity and domesticity, and instead displayed traditionally "masculine" attributes, competences, and interests.'[36]]

After hypothesizing that visual pleasure in film is rooted in presenting the woman as passive spectacle through the agencies of conventional stylization, Mulvey claims that this project contains the seed of its own destruction, for it will raise castration anxieties in male spectators. Whether erotic contemplation of the female form elicits castration anxiety from male viewers is, I suppose, a psychoanalytic claim, and, as such, not immediately a subject for criticism in this essay. However, as we have seen, Mulvey goes on to say that the ways in which Hollywood film deals with this purported problem is through cinematic structures that allow the male spectator two particular avenues of escape: fetishism and voyeurism.

One wonders about the degree to which it is appropriate to describe even male viewers as either fetishists or voyeurs. Indeed, Allen Weiss has remarked that real-world fetishists or voyeurs would have little time for movies, preferring to lavish their attentions on actual boots and furs, on the one hand, and living apartment dwellers on the other.[37] Fetishism and voyeurism are literally perversions – involving regression and fixation at an earlier psychosexual stage – in the Freudian system, whereas deriving visual pleasure from movies would not, I take it, be considered a perversion, *ceteris paribus* [other things being equal or unchanged], by practising psychoanalysts. Mulvey can only be speaking of fetishism and voyeurism metaphorically.[38] But it is not clear, from the perspective of film theory, that these metaphors are particularly apt.

In general, the idea of voyeurism as a model for all film viewing does not suit the data. Voyeurs require unwary victims for their intrusive gaze. Films are made to be seen and film actors willingly put themselves on display, and the viewers know this. The fanzine industry could not exist otherwise. Mulvey claims that the conventions of Hollywood film give the spectators an illusion of looking in on a *private* world.[39] But what can be the operative force of *private* here? In what sense is the world of *The Longest Day* (1962) private rather than public? Surely the invasion of Normandy was public and it is represented as public in *The Longest Day*? Rather one suspects that the use of the concept of private in this context will turn out, if it can be intelligibly specified at all, to be a question-begging dodge that makes it plausible to regard such events as the re-enactment of the battle of Waterloo as a private event.

Also, Mulvey includes under the rubric of *voyeurism* the sadistic assertion of control and the punishment of the guilty. This will allow her to accommodate a lot more filmic material under the category of voyeurism than one might have originally thought that the concept could bear. But is Lee Marvin's punishment of Gloria Grahame in *The Big Heat* (1953) voyeurism? [In *The Big Heat*, Lee Marvin plays Vince Stone, a gangster, and Gloria Grahame plays Debby Marsh, his girlfriend.] If one answers yes to this, mustn't one also admit that the notion of voyeurism has been expanded quite monumentally?[40] □

This is a curious example in several respects. It provides a further instance of Carroll's use of a compressed reference that elides the work of explication and elaboration. By 'Lee Marvin's punishment of Gloria Grahame', he presumably means Vince's hurling of hot coffee into Debby's face, in a scene that has become notorious; but 'punishment', with its judicial and rational implications, is an odd term to apply to such an action, and might well invite psychoanalytical interpretation. Moreover, Carroll seems to slip from the idea of voyeurism as an aspect of *viewing* a film to an idea of voyeurism as *a possible aspect of the behaviour of a character in a film*; by means of his rhetorical question, he appears to affirm that it would expand the concept of voyeurism too far to suggest that *Vince's* action is voyeuristic because it is a sadistic assertion of control. It could be argued, however, that the coupling of voyeurism and sadism is perfectly legitimate in relation to Vince and violence, given that the throwing of the coffee is a direct assault on a woman's status as an object of the male gaze; as she herself says near the end of the film: 'Vince shouldn't have ruined my looks.' The good *looks* that have made her the target of male *looks* have given her a sense of identity – prior to the assault, she is often shown admiring herself in mirrors – and this is lost once her face is damaged. But any adequate analysis of this aspect of *The Big Heat* would have to consider not only the voyeurism and sadism of the *character* of Vince, but also the way in which the voyeurism of the *audience* is engaged, and Carroll does not address this. After the scalding, the film teases the audience, who cannot help but want, half-fearfully, to *look* at Debby's ruined *looks* beneath the bandages – a desire that is finally gratified when she tears them off in her last confrontation with Vince. The spectator *watches* the sadistic assertion of control through the hurling of the coffee (though the moment of impact itself is not shown, thus sharpening voyeuristic desire) and then *watches* the way in which its aftermath is primarily registered in terms of the reduced *visibility* of the woman – her face is no longer an object of contemplation or a potential source of attraction, and she is thus brought more strongly under the rule of the patriarchal gaze, ashamed to show her scarred face to male eyes.[41]

Carroll makes the same charge against Mulvey's use of the concept of fetishism that he has made against her use of the concept of voyeurism – that it is extended too far:

■ Extrapolating from the example of von Sternberg, any case of elaborate scenography is to be counted as a fetishization mobilized in order to deflect anxieties about castration. So the elaborate scenography of a solo song and dance number by a female star functions as a containing fetish for castration anxieties. But, then, what are we to make of the use of elaborate scenography in solo song and dance numbers by male stars? If they are fetishizations, what anxiety are they containing? Or, might not the elaborate scenography have some other function? And if it has some other function with respect to male stars, isn't that function something that should be considered as a candidate in a rival explanation of the function of elaborate scenography in the case of female stars?

In any case, is it plausible to suppose that elaborate composition generally has the function of containing castration anxiety? The multiple seduction jamboree in *Rules of the Game* (1939; original French title *La Règle du Jeu*), initiated by the playing of *Danse Macabre*, is one of the most elaborately composed sequences in film history. It is not about castration anxiety; it is positively priapic. Nor is it clear what textually motivated castration anxiety could underlie the immensely intricate scenography in the nightclub scene of *Play Time* (1967), directed by Jacques Tati (1908–82). That is, there is elaborate scenography in scenes where it seems castration anxiety is not a plausible concern. Why should it function differently in other scenes? If the response is that castration anxiety is always an issue, the hypothesis appears uninformative.[42]

Grounding the contrast between fetishistic and voyeuristic strategies of visual pleasure in the contrast between von Sternberg and Hitchcock initially has a strong intuitive appeal because those filmmakers are, pre-theoretically, thought to be describable in these terms – indeed, they come pretty close to describing themselves and their interests that way. However, it is important to recall that when commentators speak this way, or even when Hitchcock himself speaks this way, the notions of voyeurism at issue are nontechnical.

Moreover, the important question is even if in some sense these two directors could be interpreted as representing a contrast between cinematic fetishism and voyeurism, does that opposition portend a systematic dichotomy that maps onto all Hollywood cinema?[43] Put bluntly, isn't there a great deal of visual pleasure in Hollywood cinema that doesn't fit into the categories of fetishism and voyeurism, even if those concepts are expanded, metaphorically and otherwise, in the way that Mulvey suggests? Among the things I have in mind here are not only the kind of counterexamples already advanced – male objects of erotic contemplation, female protagonists who are active and triumphant agents, spectacular scenes of the Normandy invasion that are difficult to connect to castration anxieties – but innumerable films that neither have elaborate scenography nor involve male characters as voyeurs, nor subject women characters to male subjugation in a demonstration of sadistic control. One film to start to think about here might be Arthur Penn's *The Miracle Worker* (1962) for which Patty Duke (Astin) received an Academy Award. (After all, a film that receives an Academy Award can't be considered outside the Hollywood system.)[44]

Of course, the real problem that needs to be addressed is Mulvey's apparent compulsion to postulate a general theory of visual pleasure for Hollywood cinema. Why would anyone suppose that a unified theory is available, and why would one suppose that it would be founded upon sexual difference, since in the Hollywood cinema there is pleasure – even visual pleasure – that is remote from issues of sexual difference.

It is with respect to these concerns that I think that the limitations of psychoanalytic film criticism become most apparent. For it is that commitment that drives feminist film critics toward generalizations like Mulvey's that are destined for easy refutation. If one accepts a general theory like psychoanalysis, then one is unavoidably tempted to try to apply its categorical framework to the data of a field like film, come what may, irrespective of the fit of the categories to the data. Partial or glancing correlation of the categorical distinctions to the data will be taken as confirmatory, and all the anomalous data will be regarded as at best topics for further research or ignored altogether as theoretically insignificant. Psychoanalytic-feminists tend to force their 'system' on cinema, and to regard often slim correspondences between films and the system as such that one can make vaulting generalizations about how the Hollywood cinema 'really' functions. The overarching propensity to fruitless generalization is virtually inherent in the attempt to apply the purported success of general psychoanalytic hypotheses and distinctions, based on clinical practice, to the local case of film. This makes theoretical conjectures like Mulvey's immediately problematic by even a cursory consideration of film history. One pressing advantage, theoretically, of the image approach is that it provides a way to avoid the tendency of psychoanalytic film feminism to commit itself to unsupportable generalizations in its attempt to read all film history through the categories of psychoanalysis[45] … …

The investigation of the image of women in film begins with the rather commonsensical notion that the recurring images of women in popular media may have some influence on how people think of women in real life. How one is to cash in the notion of 'some influence' here, however, will be tricky. In fact, it amounts to finding a theoretical foundation for the image of women in film model. Moreover, there may be more than one way in which such influence is exerted. What I would like to do now is to sketch one answer that specifies one dimension of influence that recurring images of women may have on spectators, especially male spectators, in order to give the model some theoretical grounding. However, though I elucidate one strut upon which the model may rest, it is not my intention to deny that there may be others as well.

Recent work on the emotions in the philosophy of mind has proposed that we learn to identify our emotional states in terms of paradigm scenarios, which, in turn, also shape our emotions. Ronald de Sousa claims:

> [M]y hypothesis is this: We are made familiar with the vocabulary of emotion by association with *paradigm scenarios*. These are drawn first from our daily life as small children and later reinforced by the stories, art and culture to which we are exposed. Later still, in literate cultures, they are supplemented and refined by literature. Paradigm scenarios involve two aspects: first a situation type providing the characteristic *objects* of the specific emotion type, and second, a set of characteristic or 'normal' *responses* to the situation, where normality is first a biological matter and then very quickly becomes a cultural one.[46]

Many of the relevant paradigm scenarios are quite primitive, like fear, and some are genetically preprogrammed, though we continue to accumulate paradigm scenarios throughout life and the emotions that they define become more refined and more culturally dependent. Learning to use emotion terms is a matter of acquiring paradigm scenarios for certain situations; i.e., matching emotion terms to situations is guided by fitting paradigm scenarios to the situations that confront us. Paradigm scenarios, it might be said, perform the kind of cognitive role attributed to the formal object of the emotion in preceding theories of mind.[47] However, instead of being conceived of in terms of criteria, paradigm scenarios have a dramatic structure. Like formal objects of given emotions, paradigm scenarios define the type of emotional state one is in. They also direct our attention in the situation in such a way that certain elements in it become salient.

Paradigm scenarios enable us to 'gestalt' situations [to grasp them as a whole in terms of pre-established patterns], ... 'to attend differentially to certain features of an actual situation, to inquire into the presence of further features of the scenario, and to make inferences that the scenario suggests'.[48] Given a situation, an enculturated individual attempts, generally intuitively, to fit a paradigm scenario from her repertoire to it. This does not mean that the individual can fully articulate the content of the scenario, but that, in a broad sense, she can recognize that it fits the situation before her. This recognition enables her to batten on certain features of the situation, to explore the situation for further correlations to the scenario, and to make the inferences and responses the scenario suggests. Among one's repertory of love-scenarios, for example, one might have, so to speak, a 'West Side Story' scenario which enables one to organize one's thoughts and feelings about the man one has just met. Furthermore, more than one of our scenarios may fit a given situation. Whether one reacts to a situation of public recrimination with anger, humility or fortitude depends on the choice of the most appropriate paradigm scenario.[49]

... I shall presume that the notion of paradigm scenarios has something to tell us about a component of emotional states in order to suggest how recurring images of women in film may have some influence on spectators, which influence is of relevance to feminists.

Clearly, if we accept the notion of paradigm scenarios, we are committed to the notion that the paradigm scenario we apply to a situation shapes the emotional state we are in. Some paradigm scenarios – for example, those pertaining to the relation of an infant to a caretaker – may be such that recognition of them is genetically endowed. But most paradigm scenarios will be acquired, and even those that start out rather primitively, like rage, may be refined over time by the acquisition of further and more complex paradigm scenarios. There will be many sources from which we derive these paradigm scenarios: observation and memory; stories told us on our caretaker's knee; stories told us by friends and school teachers; gossip, as well, is a rich source of such scenarios; and, of course, so are newspaper articles, self-help books, TV shows, novels, plays, films and so on.

These scenarios may influence our emotional behaviour. Male emotional responses to women, for example, will be shaped by the paradigm scenarios that they bring to those relations. Such paradigm scenarios may be derived from films, or, more likely, films may reflect, refine, and reinforce paradigm scenarios already abroad in the culture. One way to construe the study of the image of women in film is as an attempt to isolate widely disseminated paradigm scenarios that contribute to the shaping of emotional responses to women.[50]

The recent film *Fatal Attraction* (1987), for example, provides a paradigm scenario for situations in which a married man is confronted by a woman who refuses to consider their affair as easily terminable as he does. Armed with the *Fatal Attraction* scenario, which isn't so different from the *Crimes and Misdemeanors* (1989) scenario, a man might 'gestalt' a roughly matching, real life situation, focusing on it in such a way that its object, correlating to Alex (Glenn Close), is, as Dan (Michael Douglas) says, 'unreasonable', and 'crazy', and, as the film goes on to indicate, pathologically implacable. One might use the scenario to extrapolate other elements of the scenario to the real case; one might leap inductively from Alex's protests that her behavior is justified (you wouldn't accept my calls at the office so I called you at home), which are associated in the film with madness, to the suspicion that a real-life, ex-lover's claims to fair treatment are really insane. Like Dan, one guided by the *Fatal Attraction* scenario may assess his situation as one of paralysing terror, persecution and helplessness that only the death of the ex-lover can alleviate … …

Fatal Attraction provides a vivid exemplar for emotional attention that reinforces pre-existing paradigm scenarios. However, even if *Fatal Attraction* is not original, studying the image of the woman Alex that it portrays is relevant to feminists because it illuminates one pattern of emotional attention toward women that is available to men, which pattern of emotional attention, if made operational in specific cases, can be oppressive to women, by, for example, reducing claims to fair treatment to the status of persecutory, irrational demands.

That a paradigm scenario like *Fatal Attraction* is available in the culture does not imply that every man or even any man mobilizes it. But it does at least present a potential source or resource for sexist behavior. That such a potential even exists provides a reason for feminists to be interested in it. One aspect of the study of the image of women in film is to identify negative, recurring images of women that may have some influence on the emotional response of men to women. Theoretically, this influence can be understood in terms of the negative, recurring images of women in film as supplying para digm scenarios that may shape the emotional responses of real men to real women.

Recurring, negative images of women in film may warp the emotions of those who deploy them as paradigm scenarios in several different ways. They may distort the way women are attended to emotionally by presenting wildly fallacious images such as the 'spider woman' of *film noir*. Or, the problem may be that the range of images of women available is too impoverished: if the repertoire of images of women is limited in certain cases, for instance, to contraries like mother or whore, then real women who are not perceived via the mother scenario may find themselves abused under the whore scenario. The identification of the range of ways in which negative images of women in film can function cognitively to shape emotional response is a theoretical question that depends on further exploring the variety of logical/functional types of different images of women in film. That is a project that has hardly begun. Nevertheless, it seems a project worth pursuing ... ...

[T]he study of the image of women in film might be viewed as the search for paradigm scenarios that are available in our culture and which, by being available, may come to shape emotional responses to women. This aspect of the project should be of special interest to feminists with regard to negative imagery since it may illuminate some of the sources or resources that mobilize sexist emotions. Obviously, the theoretical potentials of the image of women in film model need to be developed. What I have tried to establish is the contention that there is at least a theoretical foundation here upon which to build.

... [I]n my concluding remarks I shall attempt to sketch some of the advantages of [the image of women] approach, especially in comparison to some of the disadvantages of the psychoanalytic model discussed earlier.

First, the image of women model seems better suited than the psychoanalytic model for accommodating the rich data that film history has bequeathed us. It allows that there will be lots of images of women and lots of images of men and that these may play a role as paradigm scenarios in lots of emotional reactions of all kinds. One need not attempt to limit the ambit of emotional responses to fetishism or voyeurism.

Of course, the image of women model may take particular interest in negative images of women in film, for obvious strategic purposes, but it can also handle the case of positive images as well. Whereas Rosalind Russell's character in *His Girl Friday* may be an inexplicable anomaly in the psychoanalytic system, she can be comprehended in the image approach. For this model allows that there can be positive images of women in film which may play a role in positive emotional responses to real women.[51] It is hard to see how there can be anything of genuine value in Hollywood film in Mulvey's construction. The image approach can identify the good, while acknowledging and isolating the evil.

The image of women in film model is less likely to lead to unsupportable generalizations. What it looks for are recurring images of women in film. It has no commitments about how women always appear in film.[52] Rather it targets images that recur with marked frequency. Moreover, it makes no claims about how all viewers or all male viewers respond to those images. It tracks images of women that reappear in film with some significant degree of probability and, where the images are negative, it can elucidate how they may play a constitutive role in the shaping of oppressive emotional responses to women. It is not committed to the kinds of specific causal laws that Mulvey must accept as underlying her account. It can[,] nevertheless, acknowledge causal efficacy to some paradigm scenarios – indeed, it can acknowledge causal efficacy to paradigm scenarios of all sorts, thereby accommodating the richness of the data.[53] □

This extract from Carroll's essay not only makes telling criticisms of Mulvey, and, more generally, of the use of psychoanalysis in film studies; it also demonstrates, with its invocation of logic, empiricism, and a concept – 'paradigm scenarios' – drawn from cognitive science, a different vocabulary, a different way of thinking about film from those that had come to dominate in the 1970s and 80s. Of course, work of this kind needs to be read no less critically than that of Mulvey or of other psychoanalytically-inclined critics. Carroll presents himself as the voice of reason, logic and empirical inquiry cutting through the pretensions of psychoanalysis; but he himself draws on rhetoric rather than reasoned argument to provide spurious reinforcement for his case. For example, when he attributes to Mulvey an 'apparent compulsion to postulate a general theory of visual pleasure for Hollywood cinema', 'compulsion' itself sounds like a pejorative use of a term with vaguely psychoanalytic connotations; why not simply say 'concern to postulate' or 'interest in postulating'? When he claims that 'generalizations like Mulvey's ... are destined for easy refutation', it is clearly the case that refutation is not so easy – or why is he working so hard to refute them? When he asserts that the attempt to apply psychoanalytic ideas to film brings with it an 'over-arching propensity to fruitless generalization', it can hardly be said that Mulvey's generalizations have been 'fruitless' – on the contrary, they have been highly fertile, productive, in herself and many other critics, of insightful interpretations of specific films, even if the general premises have been flawed. And is his presumption that the notion of paradigm scenarios 'has something to tell us about a component of emotional states' all that different from Mulvey's presumption that psychoanalysis has something to tell us about the way in which film works on the specta-tor? One might also raise a question about that unexamined metaphor of the 'scenario' – a metaphor whose primary associations, in the twentieth century, are cinematic, and which Carroll perhaps applies too easily to film. Though his claims for the 'paradigm scenarios' concept are largely couched in partial and tentative terms, he nonetheless employs it as an interpretative model – just as psychoanalytic critics do with the concepts of Freud and Lacan – and it proves, like psychoanalytic concepts, to be fruitful in some ways.

But if Carroll's work, and other work like it, needs to be viewed crit-ically, it undoubtedly helped to bring a different and important set of approaches into film theory and criticism. In the 1990s and in the new century, psychoanalytic film theory has continued to be important, but it lacks the innovative force that it had in the 1970s, and too often tends to be accepted and used uncritically. In the 1990s, fresh challenges to film theory were to come from cognitive film theory, from postcolonial cinema and from analytical philosophy. The last chapter of this Critical History explores these challenges and considers the function of film theory at the present time.

CHAPTER SIX

New Cognitions, Future Projections: Cognitive Film Theory, Postcolonial Cinema, Analytical Philosophy and Film Theory

In the 1990s, film theory shared in the retreat from grand theory to be found across the humanities and human sciences. The most widely publicised idea of the decade was postmodernism, and this claimed that the era of grand narratives – and, by implication, grand theories – was over; that these were false and potentially oppressive, totalitarian. Christianity, Hegelian philosophy, Marxism and structuralism were all consigned to the dustbin of a history that had effectively come to an end – of course, things would still go on happening, but no large-scale systematic change would ever again occur. What were left were local, partial, provisional narratives and theories, aware of their own fragility, and thus able to provide specific insights without ever proving oppressive. This chimed in with the advocacy of 'piecemeal theorising' by thinkers who would not have allied themselves with postmodernism, such as the cognitive film theorist Noël Carroll,[1] whose attack on Laura Mulvey's ideas was considered in the previous chapter of this Critical History.

Nonetheless, other cognitive film theorists did attempt to develop a rather less piecemeal and more comprehensive theory. One of the most interesting of these is Torben Grodal, in his *Moving Pictures: A New Theory of Film Genres, Feelings, and Cognition* (1997). In this book, Grodal sees cognitive science – and not only that subdivision of cognitive science that concerns itself with film theory – as a set of concepts and methods that is opposed to psychoanalysis, behaviourist psychology, post-structuralism and deconstruction. It does, however, share some common ground with gestalt psychology, phenomenology and structural linguistics. These are Grodal's objections, from a cognitive standpoint, to psychoanalysis:

- [P]sychoanalytic theories describe desires and emotions in relation to cognitive functions within a romantic, dualist model incompatible with a theory that describes cognition and emotion as aspects of a fundamentally unified psychosomatic whole. According to psycho-analytic theory, man is torn between id and superego, between prin-ciples of pleasure and principles of reality. As a consequence of this, visual fictions are often described as if they were battlefields: some aspects of fictions are expressions of feelings, desires, or the body, and they confront the rational order, the law, the phallus, or the centred bourgeois or Cartesian subject. Emotions become alternative 'cogni-tions'. Reason, the reality principle, or the secondary processes demand that two plus two equals four; desire, emotions, or primary processes say that the sum might be any given number. The Cartesian subject tries to establish his priorities; the alternative subject enjoys living in an eternal flux.[2] ☐

It is not wholly accurate to call psychoanalysis a 'dualist' model, as Grodal does. In two major respects at least, psychoanalysis is a tripartite model in which the mind consists not only of two terms, the id and the superego, but also of a crucial third term, the ego, the conscious self, which mediates between the id, the pressure of instinctual forces, and the superego, the set of imperatives and interdictions that can be abstracted from the ideology of a given society. Grodal seems to have left out this third term, a lapse which in itself might invite some psychoanalytic inter-pretation – psychoanalysis has always been interested in what is omitted, deliberately or inadvertently, from any oral or written statement. This omission is compounded by the absence, from Grodal's invocation of the pleasure and reality principles, of a key third term, the death drive, the drive towards a state of inorganic quiescence that lies beyond both the pleasure and reality principles. But Grodal is correct to suggest that the psychoanalytic vision of human beings – or, in his gendered term, 'man' – is of creatures riven by conflicts, even though those conflicts cannot be fully conceptualised, as he erroneously implies, in a dualist way.

Against this vision of conflict, Grodal proposes what he calls an 'ecological/evolutionary' view of a kind that, allowing for variations bet-ween individual theorists, is central to cognitive film theory:

- The cognitive skills of humans have not been developed in opposition to their emotions and their bodies; on the contrary, they have been developed to carry out the preferences of the body-mind totality. The evolution of cognitive skills has pragmatic origins: it is easier to obtain food and avoid danger if we have precise cognitive maps of the world than it is if the world is just an eternal deconstructed flux. The emotional ties among humans have developed because such affective [emotional] bonding has had a positive ecological value. The cognitive processes, which Freud and others call 'secondary' processes, are, from the point of view of evolution, the primary ones, which we share with the rest of the animal kingdom because we want to perceive and represent the world in such a way that by actions we can implement our body-brain preferences in an optimal way.[3] □

This sense of a 'body-mind totality' is crucial to Grodal's cognitive approach, and places it in opposition not only to psychoanalysis but also to behaviourist psychology. Behaviourist psychology discounts the importance or sometimes even the existence of mental processes, and aims to explain even apparently highly conscious and complex human behaviour and its associated emotional components in terms of physiologically-based reaction to stimuli. To sum up this psychology in a brief, caricatural way, all human life can be understood as an extension of the dog that has learned to salivate when a bell is rung, because it associates the ringing of the bell with the provision of food. Cognitive science judges this approach to be inadequate to the phenomena it seeks to explain, and contends that in order '[t]o understand language, visual phenomena, or behaviour', it is necessary 'to understand the mechanisms and structures by which these activities are processed by the human mind-brain';[4] and for Grodal, 'the human mind-brain' includes the perceptual system – the senses of sight, hearing, smell, taste, touch – by which we receive stimuli and data from the external world and from our own bodies.

As well as differing sharply from psychoanalysis and behaviourist psychology, cognitive science also differs, even more sharply, from post-structuralism and deconstruction. Both post-structuralism and deconstruction are primarily concerned with hermeneutic concepts and practices – in other words, with ideas about the interpretation of texts and the ways in which such interpretation is conducted – and both reject the idea that interpretation can ever arrive at a fixed and definite meaning. In post-structuralism and deconstruction, the notion of 'text' may be extended to cover every apparent phenomenon and practice – a landscape or a football match is as much of a text as a manuscript or printed book – and the meaning of a text can never be finally and definitely ascertained. Without wishing to efface the complexity and variety of post-structuralist and deconstructive approaches, it may be said, schema tically, that they comprise three main, often overlapping, attitudes to meanings. Meanings may be fundamentally arbitrary, their apparent relationship to reality the product of accident sanctioned by social con sensus. Or, meanings may be covertly or explicitly oppressive, serving the interests of dominant groups whose activities reproduce the meanings that seem best suited to preserve their own power. Or – and this is par ticularly the deconstructive emphasis – meanings may be philosophical errors, insofar as they are regarded as endorsed by, arising from or cor responding to immutable metaphysical essences. Cognitive science, how ever, takes a constructive and functionalist approach. It concurs with post-structuralism and deconstruction in acknowledging that meanings are constructed and are not metaphysical essences that can be grasped through intuition or through a particular interpretative procedure; but it sees such constructions as the product of social negotiations between human beings with brains and bodies who are trying to function effec tively in a world of which they are a part – trying to know, to gain accu rate cognition of, the world and themselves. The fact that they may not gain accurate cognition – that their interpretations of the meanings of the world and of themselves may be wrong – does not entail that such cognition is arbitrary, oppressive or impossible; rather, the possibility of error entails the possibility of accuracy. If it is possible to get the mean ing wrong, it is also possible to come to know that it is wrong and to find ways in which a correct meaning might be found.

While cognitive science differs from psychoanalysis, behaviourist psychology, post-structuralism and deconstruction, it does have links with gestalt psychology, phenomenology and structural linguistics. Gestalt psychology developed in the early part of the twentieth century in Germany and influenced some of the earlier film theories that this Critical History has considered, such as those of Münsterberg and Arnheim. '*Gestalt*' means 'whole', and gestalt psychology concerns itself with the way in which the human mind seems able to perceive and grasp wholes. As Grodal observes, '[t]erms like "gestalt" are closely related to cognitive terms like "pattern" and more loosely related to cognitive terms like "schema"'.[5] Cognitive science can also be linked with phen omenology, the analysis of the modes in which human beings apprehend the phenomena of the world, including – and this is significant for film theory – aesthetic objects.

A third link is between cognitive science and structural linguistics:

■ [M]any aspects of cognitive science are genetically closely related [that is, related in their origins and growth] to structural linguistics (and to theories of information from Shannon/Weaver onwards), and freely share terms like 'code', just as the symbiosis of computer science and structural linguistics has made terms like 'syntax' household words in cognitive science. The cognitive study of stories and scripts, as carried out by Mandler[6] and Schank/Abelson[7] has roots in the structural studies of narratives from Propp onwards. Structural and semiotic text-analysis (Jakobson, Barthes, Todorov, Greimas, [and others]) also has strong roots in Russian formalism, so that claims made by some critics for a formalist approach totally different from structuralism and semiotics do not seem warranted.[8] □

Grodal goes on, however, to stress major differences between cognitive science and structuralism; for example, structuralism concerns itself with the supposedly fixed and objective structures that underlie phenomena and practices, not with 'the mental principles and the processes in the human mind that generate the structures'. It should be said, however, that this is not altogether true of certain structuralist theorists, such as Jean Piaget. Grodal goes on to contend that '[t]he concept of language as a fixed social system, and the idea of the fixed relation between signifier and signified, is not a good basis for understanding the functioning and processing of information in the individual mind'. As it happens, cognitive science concurs again here with post-structuralism and deconstruction, which also challenged the idea of fixity that was crucial to structuralism, although they did not share the cognitive concern with the functioning and processing of information in the individual mind, and indeed questioned the notions of 'information' and 'the individual mind'. But structuralism, post-structuralism and deconstruction, whatever their differences from each other, all shared a belief in language as the primary or only model and metaphor for all kinds of human activity (even if they disliked the word 'human'). Grodal acknowledges that this belief is appropriate to the analysis of some cognitive structures, such as narrative ones, which resemble language; but he contends that it 'is detrimental to understanding, for instance, the way in which vision works according to non-linguistic principles and the types of mental phenomena processed by non-linguistic means and often by non-arbitrary, innate mechanisms … [M]any visual phenomena are structured and processed by means of mechanisms quite different from linguistic structures.'[9]

In contrast to the refusal of the idea of the whole that characterises post-structuralism, deconstruction and postmodernism, Grodal aims 'to show the way in which cognitions and emotions in the experience of viewing visual fiction are part of a holistic framework' that 'has its origin in the way that fictions are experienced by the viewer'. His 'holistic framework' is one that takes 'the relations between body, mind, and world as an interacting whole'. It is within this framework that it becomes possible to understand the way in which visual fiction sets off 'a simulation of body-mind states'. Grodal proposes a middle way between realism, which assumes that fiction is an unproblematic representation of (possible) reality, and formalism, which focuses on a visual fiction, or any other text, as an organisation of formal features with no necessary reference to the real world. His middle way is based on the belief that 'aspects of the human mind have been formatted by evolution';[10] that is, evolutionary development has produced frameworks in the human mind that are the result of human attempts to know the world but that also affect the way in which the world is understood. These 'hardwired' frameworks can be distinguished from the frameworks produced by specific cultures and environments; while the latter are cultural and therefore changeable, the former have been wired in by evolution and cannot be altered, except perhaps by a fundamental evolutionary shift.

Grodal's use of metaphor can be slightly confusing. The notion of 'formatting' could summon up the associated metaphor of the mind as a floppy disk, which, it might be presumed, is relatively easy to re-format. But the 'hardwired' metaphor suggests a state of affairs that evolution has brought about and that is much less easy to change. When Grodal goes on to talk of 'innate' mental models, he resorts to a rather older metaphor. These ambiguities and shifts in Grodal's use of metaphor raise the question of whether his technical terms function to promote scientific precision or to endow his argument with an aura of quasi-scientific authority. But his overall point is clear: these mental models are pretty permanent, and it is visual fiction, such as film, that makes them especially visible, 'because audiovisual media are the most sophisticated yet invented by man for simulating and manipulating the many different aspects of the ways in which we perceive, feel, think, act, memorize, associate, and socialize'.[11]

The idea of simulation is important in Grodal's cognitive film theory. Film can simulate reality, and in order to do so it employs 'the same cognitive and affective mechanisms that we use in our real-life experiences and in our mental representations of them. Higher mental life relies on the ability to execute hypothetical, fictitious imaginations.'[12] Grodal takes the view that the human mind cannot access the world directly; it operates, rather, by making evaluations, based on knowledge, understanding and emotion, of the degree of reality – or, as Grodal terms it, the 'reality-status' – of a particular configuration of images. We are constantly making judgements as to whether an apparent phenomenon is reality, fantasy, or dream, fact or fiction, credible or unbelievable. Such evaluations are complex acts involving a range of procedures, and in visual and other fiction they can be rendered uncertain by a variety of techniques. For example, the 'reality-status' of the shot of the burning motorbike part way through the film *Easy Rider* (1969) is difficult to evaluate on a first viewing, without a knowledge of the rest of the film: is it a dream, a vision, a warning, a symbol, a glimpse of the future?[13] Dream sequences or flashbacks in a film may be fairly clearly signalled as such – for instance, by switching into black-and-white and/or slow motion and/or silence – but they may also be presented without obvious signposting and initially cause disorientation in the viewer. The creation of uncertainty about the 'reality-status' of a set of film images contributes to a film's aesthetic effect.

A film works by activating a range of psychosomatic dimensions in which mind and body work together – perception, cognition, memory, emotion, and what Grodal calls 'enaction', the carrying out of acts in response to situations and stimuli. In watching a film, one cannot enter the screen world to participate in its action, and one does not usually carry out, in the off-screen world, the acts suggested by one's response to the situations and stimuli that the screen presents – though exceptions can occur, as with the audiences who rioted at screenings of *The Blackboard Jungle* (1955) and *Rock Around the Clock* (1956). Nonetheless, one's mind and body may prepare for and/or imagine such acts, as when one tenses one's muscles, for fight or flight, in response to a situation represented on the screen that, if it occurred in real life, could demand the enaction of such responses. A film also activates two different mental processes: the associative, in which one phenomenon is linked to another by some likeness; and the sequential, in which one phenomenon follows another. Usually, mental flow moves 'downstream' – that is, from perception to enaction, or at least, to preparation for enaction. An analogous 'downstream' flow is to be found in what Grodal calls 'canonical narratives'. Grodal's use of the term 'canonical' is a specialised one; it should be kept distinct from the more common use of the term 'canonical' to denote those texts that form part of a 'canon', a collection of established, highly valued texts (as when it is said that

Shakespeare is part of the canon of English Literature, or that *Citizen Kane* is part of the canon of twentieth-century film). 'Canonical narratives', in Grodal's sense, may be part of a canon in the more usual sense, but they need not be. Their distinguishing features are that they follow the downstream flow, from perception to enaction, that has already been mentioned, and that they are linear in form. Their linear form is not due to abstract logic, but to 'real-world constraints on the sequencing of events and ... the "downstream" relations between motives, cognitions, and acts'.[14] If this flow is disrupted, for example by the activation of associative mental forms or by representing a consequence before a cause, different aesthetic effects and different emotional tones will be produced.

Given that the conscious capacity of human beings is limited, any audiovisual experience will comprise a mental hierarchy in which some phenomena – often those that arouse a strong desire for an enactive response, a desire to do something – will be the focus of attention. Other phenomena will not disappear, but will form 'a non-conscious associative network enriching the experience', or 'a macro-frame, a set of propositions determining the nature'[15] of the focus to which one is attending. The experience may involve what Grodal terms proximal, 'subjective' experience, and distal, 'objective' experience. In proximal experience, phenomena 'are experienced as located in the body-mind' and may be described in terms such as 'causes pleasure to mouth, skin, causes pain to mouth, skin, causes inner feelings, releases cognitive and hormonal response'. In distal experience, phenomena 'are experienced as located in the exterior world' and may be described in terms such as 'a given item is sweet, soft, sharp, appealing, green'.[16] Grodal sees subjective experience in film as linked, not to a freer play of the mind and feelings, but, paradoxically, to a greater constraint on voluntary acts. 'Subjective camera' entails strict limitations on the placing of the camera, since the camera has to be positioned where the eyes of the protagonist, in any given scene, are supposed to be. Subjective representations may constrict our vision, for instance by showing a scene that is too bright or too dark, or by portraying an object from an unusual, 'sub-optimal' angle so that its identity is not immediately apparent. Such constraints may contribute to a distinct subjective tone; subject to the same limitations that a character would experience, we come closer to experiencing them ourselves. The experience of time produced by a visual fiction is also an element of subjective tone. With film, different experiences of time may be produced by changing perceptual sequences, so that, for example, they go faster or slower, and by changing the sequences of 'act schemata' (the ideas that one has of how a given class of acts occurs), by leaving out elements that one would normally expect to be present, or by inserting elements that one would not usually expect to find. Experiences of time may also be related to the temporal connotations of that which is represented, as with 'eternity' or 'the summer'.

Since fiction films tackle human concerns, the film viewer will identify with and empathically simulate the cognitive, motivational-emotional and enactive processes of the protagonists. But films can inhibit such processes of identification and empathy, or even partly reverse them, by using what Grodal calls 'frames and filters',[17] like 'realism', 'fiction', 'comedy' and the conventions of a given genre. Despite such inhibiting devices, 'general and holistic models of humans' nonetheless remain 'central to our cognitive-emotional experience of visual fictions'. On the basis of such models, 'we experience the general formation of the protagonist's body in space, and the importance of "hedonic tone" (pleasure or pain) as motivators of the body-mind configuration'. We judge whether a given being is 'human' according to the degree to which it shows 'flexibility, empathy and emotions, consciousness, and intentional, goal-directed behaviour'. Grodal affirms that these functions 'are based on innate brain-circuitry', and provide 'basic models for the way in which we orient ourselves in the physical and social world'.[18] The presence of such functions produces an effect of familiarity; their absence produces an effect of unfamiliarity.

Our experience of behaviours and scenarios is significantly linked with whether they relate to 'non-conscious, autonomic types of reactions … or to conscious, voluntary, goal-directed, telic behaviours'. Autonomic processes include laughter, crying, orgasm and shivering, and are based on non-voluntary mechanisms that the autonomic nervous system supports. Telic behaviours are those forms of behaviour directed towards a certain end, the attainment of which will reduce emotional, intellectual and physical activation. Songs and certain kinds of emotional behaviour are linked with autonomic reactions. Canonical narratives are mostly linked with telic, end-orientated behaviours. Some forms of behaviour, like dancing, include both telic and autonomic features, and Grodal terms these behaviours 'paratelic'.[19] He applies the same term to functions that aim to increase rather than reduce the level of activation. Gathering these notions together, Grodal sketches a typology of genres:

- The central genres will often be strongly determined by their relation to a mental function: lyrical genres to autonomic or paratelic forms, canonical narratives to telic forms, horror fictions to autonomic responses, and so on. Genres of visual fiction will further be determined by whether the fiction cues an unmediated simulation of the fiction from the point of view of a protagonist, whether some emotional filters mediate the relation to the protagonists (as in metafictions [fictions that explore and perhaps explicitly comment on the nature of fiction]), or whether some other mechanisms take place, like comic reactions in comic fictions, or dissociation of holistic experiences as in schizoid fictions.

... [E]ight genre-types are central prototypes: associative lyricism; canonical narratives of action; obsessional fictions of paratelic cognition and enaction; melodramas of the passive position; fictions of horror; schizoid fictions; comic fictions; and metafictions ... [M]any viewers of visual fiction have emotional impact as an important parameter when they choose the film they wish to see. Producers of visual fiction therefore tend to produce visual fictions which rely on optimizing their emotional impact. This does not mean that we have an innate genre system, only that we have innate emotional functions and schemata which may or may not be used as a basis for creating an overall emotional tone by those producing visual fiction. My typology is meant as a guideline for understanding some of the parameters determining the prototypical emotional effect of dominant genre-patterns, and for understanding the way in which changes of certain parameters (for example, a change from a telic to a paratelic pattern) will influence the experience of emotional tone, and the reason for this. The prototypical patterns can be mixed in many ways; for example, the cueing of comic reactions or the production of metaframes can also be applied to any other genre.[20] □

It can be seen that Grodal offers a formidable and comprehensive theory that marshals a range of terms and concepts rather different from those of psychoanalytic film theory and that, in its emphasis on 'innate brain-circuitry', sets itself against the post-structuralist emphasis on the endlessly mobile, always reconstructible subject. How does his theory work in practice? Here is an extract from his discussion on 'Crime and Horror Fiction' that is interesting in its own right, in the way in which it continues the argument with psychoanalysis, and in the different interpretations it provides of films that have become classic points of reference in film theory and criticism, especially of a psychoanalytic kind – Hitchcock's *Rear Window* (discussed in chapter three of this Critical

History by Claude Chabrol and in chapter four by Laura Mulvey – see pp. 109–13, 162–3 above), and Welles's *Touch of Evil* (discussed in chapter four by Stephen Heath – see pp. 145–52 above):

■ In some respects the detective functions as a concrete representation of the viewer in his capacity as distant onlooker, so that crime fiction might appear to be a kind of metafiction, and clearly mysteries have some affinity with metafiction. Our experience of what happens has often to pass the perceptual-cognitive 'frame' of the detective, so that our direct empathic identification is with the detective, not with the other agents. But, contrary to metafiction, the 'frame' is the primary narrative agent, and the distanciation is experienced in a personified mode, as traits characterizing the detective as a subject-actant in the narrative, not as an exterior frame filtering the narrated. ['Actant', a term in narrative theory, means that which performs a certain narrative function such as 'discovering the truth'. It may be a fictional human character but it can also be non-human or inanimate. In a detective story or thriller, the 'actant' that performs the function of 'discovering the truth' may well be embodied, for the most part, in the central character, the detective; but the detective may be assisted by other characters, by non-human creatures and by inanimate objects ('clues'), and these thus also function as actants that perform the truth-discovery function.] Therefore many crime fictions are characterized by the importance given to the cognitive and emotional makeup of the hero-detective, while the 'frame' aspects are experienced as the grandiose 'personality' of the detective, from Holmes via Marlowe to Columbo and Inspector Morse.

The distanciation characteristic of several types of crime fiction has been treated extensively by directors and critics in connection with a Freudian theory of voyeurism. The 'detective', like Jeff in *Rear Window*, or Peter and Jeffrey in thrillers like *Dressed to Kill* (1980) or *Blue Velvet* (1986), is a [P]eeping Tom finding satisfaction in looking at other people's emotional behaviour or naked bodies from a safe distance. The word 'private eye' is imbued with voyeurist associations. Now, these three films and many similar ones are heavily influenced by Freudian psychology, so the connection between voyeurism and detectives is a consciously built-in feature. It could be said that these and similar films have two main types of message: the weaker one states that there are such people as 'voyeurs' in the world, and they might even satisfy their desires by becoming detectives. Even films like *Dirty Harry* (1971) describe the detective as a voyeur, but add 'so what?' The stronger message states that the detective is just a representative of the viewer (see Douchet ...[21]) or 'modern man' (both of whom have become voyeurs). This latter message often comes with a moral undertone: voyeurism is a perversion, and is somehow connected with the perversity of modern life,[22] in which seeing is preferred to relating, caring, and doing. The logical ultimate position consequent to this point of view would be to ban visual representations in order to let people live in an 'unmediated world', and to ban all types of restrictions on visual access to phenomena in real life, making voyeurism pointless.

I shall now argue against the moralistic associations often linked to the very broad use of 'voyeurism' in fiction production and fiction criticism. One of the classic examples of crime fiction which plays on the relations between distanciation and full identification is Hitchcock's *Rear Window*. The 'Freudian' director links the distanciation of detection with voyeurism quite explicitly. The 'detective', Jeff, is almost completely immobilized as a result of a broken leg, and his detection is therefore mostly visual: like another [P]eeping Tom, he watches what is going on in the flats opposite, using binoculars and a telephoto lens. His point of observation imposes some restraints on his access to this world, which is only visible through certain 'window' peepholes, while many 'scenes' are masked by the walls. We may assume that Hitchcock intends to convey the Freudian message that Jeff is temporarily 'impotent', and that he is therefore more interested in his 'voyeurism' than in interacting with his lovely girlfriend.

But even for the viewer who does not wholly grasp Hitchcock's Freudian-voyeurist overtones the film makes good sense. It could be argued that many aspects of 'voyeurist' features derive from the fact that visual fiction makes the processes of vision intersubjective. In an age before film and television, people also looked at each other: dress codes, ranging from the dramatic Islamic veiling of the female face to a minimal veiling of the genitals in other cultures, demonstrate a certain cross-cultural interest in looking at the human body and in regulating those acts of viewing. An understanding of other people's behaviour and motives mostly implies an ongoing, 'passive-cognitive' social curiosity by which we process the behaviour of our fellow human beings. Most of what Jeff sees is not strange: the unusual is that the persons looked at do not look back and, furthermore, that Jeff needs special equipment like binoculars and a telephoto lens to establish visual contact. The scenes he sees are mostly quite ordinary everyday events: a young girl dancing or working out in her bikini; a 'Miss Lonely Heart[s]' having trouble finding a boyfriend, whose acts indicate at one point that she is going to commit suicide; a newlywed couple (probably) making love behind the blinds; a composer trying to compose a tune. Jeff further observes an elderly married couple, and notes that the wife is ill. The couple interacts in a non-spectacular way until the wife disappears, and, using this fact and the husband's seemingly perfectly ordinary behaviour, Jeff enjoys some guesswork which leads him to the conclusion that the husband has murdered his wife. Except for the murder, which is inferred rather than shown, the phenomena viewed are the trivia of everyday life. To observe these phenomena is, except for the binoculars and the one-sidedness of the activity, not 'voyeurism' in any strict sense (which would imply the observation of sexual intercourse, as in *Blue Velvet*).

Instead of seeing the 'voyeurist' elements in *Rear Window* as a realist description of 'the activity of the viewer or modern man' it might be more relevant to describe these elements from a functionalist point of view, as frames which create defamiliarization and tensity by the system of high-order motivation. ['Tensity' means the emotional mood that is linked with the arousal of telic, enactive response – that is, it is the mood associated with the desire to act in order to achieve a goal that will reduce emotional, intellectual and physical excitation. 'High-order motivation' means providing a strong causal framework for a particular representation; thus the 'reason' for, the motivation of, the close, covert observation of the activities of others in *Rear Window* is not, in Grodal's perspective, to gratify a voyeuristic instinct – it is to discover whether a murder has been committed; the viewer shares the investigator's desire to reduce the curiosity that has been aroused by finding out, gaining cognition of, exactly what is going on.] These high-order systems of motivation are connected with the prominence given to the cognitive and emotional attitude of the detective. In *Raiders of the Lost Ark* (1981), the viewer often shares the hero's reactions quite spontaneously: when we see a huge stone rolling towards Indy, we do not need reaction-shots to establish the hero's reaction, and, if such shots are produced, they are purely for the sake of emphasis. But, in many types of crime fiction, it is the 'reaction' of the detective which constitutes the object, the seen. When Jeff and the viewer see the villain Thorwald packing or carrying a suitcase, it is as a trivial scene which is only imbued with meaning and evokes emotions by the reactions of Jeff/detective, via the non verbal communication of excitement reflected in facial expressions and the attention shown, and via the schemata expressed verbally, which link the trivial with the non-trivial: murder and its motives. Familiar, trivial phenomena have been made unfamiliar, demanding a new, special explanation. Large parts of the film are actually series of reaction-shots. From this point of view, the 'voyeurist' perspectives are rhetorical devices, used to create salience and emphasis in the viewer's perception of the seen.

The intense interest aroused by the indexing of phenomena by means of camera-work and the facial expressions of the 'detectives' presupposes that we actively construct our emotions and interests in accordance with the mental states of the detective; we are 'on a guided tour' (although we are assisted by a competence constructed from our knowledge of many schemata drawn from crime fiction). Noël Carroll[, in *Mystifying Movies*,] has given an account of the potential for controlling viewer-attention in the popular narrative film by means of indexing, scaling, and bracketing. This is especially important in many types of crime fiction which deal with the creation of attention to clues and arouse an interest in establishing information about the not yet seen and not yet known. To make the information-processing salient we need the motivational support of the detective's expressions of tense cognitive involvement.

Audiovisual communication makes perceptual, cognitive, and motivational processes intersubjectively transparent by the way in which we can follow the visual and acoustic attention of other people, and this transparency seems to create *malaise* in the critics who propagate the voyeurist theory of modern society. Antonioni's *Blow-Up* (1966) and *The Conversation* (1974) directed by Francis Ford Coppola (born 1939) represent two film reactions in which peeping and eavesdropping are condemned, and in which these activities are linked with modern equipment for chemical-electronic recording and recreation of reality. These films express a constructivist nightmare: all the schemata are in the mind of the beholder; the data collected with the camera or tape-recorder do not create a firm basis from which anything can be inferred about the exterior world, but we just project the files of our inner hard disk onto the exterior world. The problems of the perceptual-cognitive processing of data assume an intersubjective, spectacular form by the use of camera, magnifying devices, tape-recorders, or filters, but ... human perception relies on sophisticated systems of selective attention, filtering, scaling, top-down hypotheses, and other devices. [A 'top-down hypothesis' is one that starts from culturally acquired skills, procedures and information (the 'top') in order to interpret a specific situation (the 'bottom'), whether real or fictional.[23]] The use of technical devices to represent these processes in an intersubjective form makes the mental processing visible; the gadgets are real, but they are also an extension of the way normal perception and cognition work, and are therefore mental models of perception and cognition. The exterior form, however, brings about a defamiliarization which isolates the mental processes from modality synthesis and from their normal integration with emotions.

The way in which normal experience integrates different perceptual modalities and emotions into a complex totality is beautifully and negatively demonstrated in the final scene in *Blow-Up*. The hero-photographer watches a tennis game performed by mime actors. There is no visible ball, there are no rackets, the 'players' make no sound; but, nevertheless, they seem tensely occupied with their game, just as the spectators follow the trajectory of the imaginary ball with their eyes. Shortly afterwards, the imaginary ball is 'shot' out of the tennis court and ends near the hero, who is asked to throw it back into the court. He accepts and throws it back, thus accepting the game, and now we only see his eyes, not the game, but, at the same time, the sound of the racket and the ball hitting the ground is heard. A tennis game consists of a set of schemata, rules, and movements, some visual and acoustic perceptions, and some emotional reactions linked to watching or playing tennis. Antonioni produces a defamiliarization by breaking the game experience up into smaller modules, so that one modality, such as vision, is realized although in an incomplete form (lack of ball and rackets), just as the attentional and motor schemata are activated whereas the sound is absent. Later, the visual presentation is absent, whereas the acoustic representation of the ball is present in combination with a representation of the visual attention and emotional reaction of a spectator. Antonioni's intention is to point to a deeper meaning, whereas, from our perspective, the scene is an experiment which creates an emotional impact by breaking up a holistic experience. The attentional bracketing of normal holistic experiences is central to the construction of affects in crime fiction, but, whereas a metafictional crime film like *Blow-Up* draws attention directly to the procedures of bracketing, normal crime fictions motivate the procedures within the diegetic world.

Thrillers and Hard-Boiled Crime Fiction

Classic detective fiction is often able to enforce a strict distanciation between the embedded series of vices and crimes and the embedding series of detection (fictions like *Rear Window* keep the distance until the very last episodes, in which the watchers, in turn, become the watched, and are even physically attacked). In hard-boiled American crime fictions this distanciation is weakened, sometimes to the point of a total breakdown of distanciation so that the two levels merge. The hard-boiled crime fictions are therefore closer to a clear-cut canonical narrative (unless, as '*noir*-hardboiled' fictions, they take up melodramatic features). The decrease in distanciation goes with a toning-down of the hermeneutic-intellectual level and a greater emphasis on physical action. The tendency to merge the levels of detection and crime is very obvious in, for instance, *The Maltese Falcon* (1941). The detective Sam Spade falls in love with his client, who also turns out to be the main villain and killer. Spade is motivated in his effort of detection by the wish to avenge the death of his partner Lew Archer, and is himself a suspect because he has had an affair with Archer's wife. There is a distance to the embedded series: a group of fortune-hunters have for years pursued the quest for a falcon, and Spade does not really share their goal or their fascination with the metal bird. But Spade's distance is more personal, less professional, than Sherlock Holmes's; his distance is often motivated by 'the cynicism of urban life', rather than being the intellectual distance of Dupin and Holmes, for whom crimes are mental puzzles. The same is true of Marlowe in *The Big Sleep*, for instance; Marlowe starts out as the professional, distant observer, but finally falls in love with one of the women from the embedded series, just as his in-fights with the criminals make a physical distance to the level of detection impossible.

In *The Maltese Falcon*, as in many *noir* crime dramas, the heroine is an ambiguous *femme fatale* who is both love-object and criminal. This reinforces the oscillation between enforcing and destroying the separation of the two series. The attraction towards the woman merges the two series, whereas the repulsion enforces the distance between the two levels. Not only do the love story and the revenge drama diminish the distance between the two series, but the emphasis on physical confrontation also diminishes the aloofness of detection; the life and physical well-being of Spade and other tough detectives are at stake ...

Touch of Evil is another example of the way in which the distance between embedding and embedded series breaks down in the tough crime thriller. The hero, Vargas, starts out as a 'detective' who is morally engaged in the enforcement of justice, but not personally interested in the crimes committed. During part of the film the viewer follows the way in which his wife Susan is threatened with sexual harassment and exposed to what looks like rape, whereas Vargas, who knows nothing of this development, carries out a classic detective job. At last, when he discovers this information, the detective throws off the social role of distanciation and behaves, in his own words, 'as a husband', not as a 'cop'.

Touch of Evil demonstrates the way in which tense situations tend to become saturated horror stories because of the overwhelming power of the 'evil' compared to that of the weak protagonist. Or, to put it another way, if the narrative descriptions tend to focus extensively on the crimes from the point of view of their possible victims, the distanciation and control will evaporate. The very title expresses an implicitly passive position, Subject: Evil, Act: Touch, Object: X. The focus of attention has shifted from mind-control to body-object. In the film the object is (not surprisingly) an innocent, blonde, all-American girl, Susan, trapped in a desert motel and later in a sleazy hotel, whereas the evil forces are dark Mexican males who supposedly enjoy a tacit acceptance of their acts by the overweight and crooked 'cop', Quinlan.

Several features of the horror scene link it to Hitchcock's *Psycho* (1960), which was released two years later. However, the two scenes evoke different emotional responses. The scene in the Welles film plays prominently on the viewer's shadow-construction of tense expectations that now Vargas will smell a rat and arrive as the 'hero on a white horse' to save a damsel in distress, expectations thus dividing between the two parallel sequences (Vargas actively detecting, wife threatened by evil sexuality) and in that way diminishing the horror element. Hitchcock's damsel is totally at the mercy of the evil 'touch', and thrill has become horror.

Vargas is in personal control the whole time, and when he discovers what has happened to his wife while he has been involved in detection[,] he explodes in a new series of acts that finally puts him in total control of the situation. So, although the distance between embedding and embedded series closes in, the two continue to be distinct sets of events. This is even more obvious if we look at the relation between *mise-en-scène* and narrative. The background to the detection is often an unfamiliar, night-time world, a run-down border town where the dark oil-derricks and steel constructions, the night clubs, and the hoodlum-ridden streets are frightening, but are, at the same time, fascinating symbols of heteronomy and the surrendering of free will. ['Heteronomy' means 'subject[ion] to an external law' (*OED*), subjection to otherness, in contrast to 'autonomy', the freedom to decide for oneself.] This is especially expressed by means of the symbolic use of a mechanical piano to indicate an ambivalent fascination for evil forces. The scenery is photographed from odd, often low, angles, with a climax in the subjective shot which shows how the wife wakes up from her drugged condition and sees the weird and bloody head of a murdered man turned upside-down above her. In relation to the embedded series, the *mise-en-scène* strengthens the experience of saturated heteronomy [that is, the experience of being subject to an external law, to otherness, without being able to imagine how one might act to discharge effectively the emotional, instinctive and motor responses that such subjection arouses]. However, in the detection series, the background only functions as a means of increasing the level of arousal. In the final scenes, Vargas shadows the crooked 'cop' physically and by means of a radio transmitter to another, bugged 'cop', who accompanies Quinlan. Vargas is in control, despite temporary transmitter fall-out and the brief moment in which he is held at gunpoint by Quinlan. The uncanny, dark oil-rigs and bridge pillars serve as backdrops.

In many 'thriller' narratives, the cognitive and enactive distance and control diminish further, so that the subject-actant moves toward a position similar to that of the object in horror fiction. The 'agent' turns into 'patient' in a kind of 'embedding in reverse'. In a Hitchcock thriller like *Notorious* (1946), the narrative structure in some respects has an embedding/embedded structure like *Touch of Evil*, with 'Cary Grant' as a subject-actant but emotionally linked to 'Ingrid Bergman' as an 'agent' turned 'patient'; the viewers are predominantly subjected to saturated feelings by witnessing the way in which the evil forces gain the upper hand, although the viewers also activate optional tensity by expecting the hero to take action. In many typical Hitchcock thrillers, however, like *North by Northwest* (1959), the subject-actant is a 'patient' for prolonged stretches of time, without knowledge or ability to act, sometimes even moved to the verge of entrapment in mentally dissociated interpretations of an opaque world, bereft of cognitive and enactive control, like the intoxicated or persecuted Thornhill.[24] □

The readings of specific films and the wider comments on particular genres that Grodal offers in the above extract demonstrate the capacity of cognitive film theory to produce fascinating interpretations and analyses. Clearly the capacity of a theory to generate fascinating analyses is one criterion by which it might be judged. But it is a pragmatic criterion: as earlier chapters showed, *auteur* theory and psychoanalytic theory can also generate fascinating analyses, whether they are right or wrong. A further criterion for the evaluation of a comprehensive film theory could be the range of films for which a theory could account: it is notable that the above analysis adheres to what might be seen as canonical texts of Hollywood cinema, and it might be asked how far it could apply to films that have another provenance, that come from what is still, for the West, elsewhere – African films, for example. There can be no doubt that the cinema of postcolonial Africa constitutes a major body of work; but how is it to be understood? Here the idea of an all-embracing theory runs up against the charge that it may be imposing inappropriate frames of reference on cultural practices and representations that emerge from a situation of otherness – and the idea of 'otherness' itself, very popular in postcolonial cultural theory, might also be seen to exemplify an inappropriate frame of reference. The problem is vividly addressed in the following extract from Oliver Bartlet's prize-winning book *Les cinémas d'Afrique noire* (1996), translated as *African Cinemas: Decolonizing the Gaze* (2000). Bartlet's tone is polemical and his explicit concern is criticism more than theory, especially in a French-speaking context; but his comments clearly have implications for any theory that claims to be more than 'piecemeal' and that has 'universal' aspirations:

■ **The Western Diktat**

When Hollywood took over the colonial stereotypes of Africa, they went into the making of some forty Tarzan films over a seventy-year period. Today, Hollywood is more likely to offer liberation films in which Blacks are upstaged by white liberals. For example, *Cry Freedom* (1987), directed by Richard Attenborough (born 1923), shifts the focus from black leader Steve Biko to a white journalist, Donald Woods, wrestling with his conscience. Françoise Pfaff has shown how such a strategy is directed at achieving commercial success, but is not a demystification of African realities.[25] If Western cinema is not grappling with that particular agenda, the cinema cultures of Black Africa certainly are attending to it, but they lack an audience.

Even what are generally regarded as the most thoughtful newspapers sometimes publish some amazing value judgements on African film. Abderrahmane Sissako (born 1961) was angered when *Libération* discussed his film *Octobre* (1992) in terms of its director's 'charm'.[26] And in the *Cahiers du Cinéma*, Charles Tesson, writing about *Yeelen* (*Brightness*, 1987), directed by Souleymane Cissé (born 1940), summed up 'what gives African cinema its charm and irreducible otherness: it is a cinema of origins, naïve and primitive'.[27] This is almost beyond belief. 'Authenticity', 'ingenuousness', 'naturalness', 'naïvety' – the clichés rain down from sloppy journalists in a hurry, who can't be bothered to take more trouble over their writing.

The reception in France of *Le cri du coeur* (1994) by the Burkinabè director Idrissa Ouedraogo (born 1954) was highly revealing in this context. Ouedraogo, a filmmaker with a fine reputation for the quality of his 'African tales' (*Yaaba* (*Grandmother*, 1989), *Tilai* (*A Question of Honor*, 1990), *Samba Traoré* (1993; the title of the film is its protagonist's name)), ventured to Lyons to film the relationship between an immigrant child (Saïd Diarra) and a hard-bitten drifter (Richard Bohringer), who none the less opens up to him. The director has acknowledged that his film may have certain faults – it 'may perhaps be too demonstrative'[28] – but he is saddened that it has been judged against his earlier work. The critics were disappointed by a camera 'which did not manage to recover its African grace',[29] and advised him to 'have a serious rethink and take up again a path he has made his own'.[30] This African ought to make 'African films', and not 'leave the landscapes and villages of his homeland', since he so 'enchant[ed] us in his previous films'.[31] The film, which was released in only two Parisian cinemas, had total audience figures of just 1,180 in its first week.

Do French directors get told to make 'French' films? 'People say our cinema doesn't develop because we're always doing the same thing', says the Guinean Mohamed Camara [born 1945; director of *Denko* (1992)], 'but when I do something different they tell me it's not African enough!'.[32] The relationship to artistic creation in the countries of the South is still terribly marked by a neo-colonialist attitude in which artists are required to show 'authenticity'. This attitude takes the form of a stunning ignorance of the existence of contemporary art in those countries, and the rejection of any autonomous expression which does not correspond to Western 'exotic' expectations ... ... When you seek to confine the Other to his or her difference, there is nothing special to say about him or her which can be coherent. It is in order to sidestep this demand for cultural difference, which slips surreptitiously into film criticism, that young directors living in Europe reject the term 'African filmmaker' with such vigour. 'I thought I was becoming a filmmaker', said the Guinean David Achkar (1960–98) …

> And the colour of my skin made me an African filmmaker from the very outset … So a particular kind of criticism keeps me in a particular sort of academicism, a style, a tone, a way of filming. I would advise the critics concerned to go back to the cinema and see that Ousmane Sembène [the Senegalese film director, born 1923] has never made a village film … We are up against a great deal of ignorance. Which critics go to the Fespaco? [The Festival Panafricain du Cinéma et de la Télévision de Ouagadougou, a major pan-African film festival held every two years in Burkina Faso][33]

Towards a Subjective Criticism

On the other hand, when an African ventures to evoke magic as the cultural expression of an ancient knowledge which is able to cast light upon the present – a magic in which he himself declares that he does not believe[34] – Western critics see this as a 'majestic mystery, inducing contemplation'.[35] Souleymane Cissé rails against this perception of *Yeelen*: 'It is a profoundly political work in which you have to get beyond the surface of the image'.[36] *Yeelen*, the first African film to receive the Jury's Special Prize at the Cannes Film Festival (1987), has at times been regarded as inaccessible and at others praised to the skies as a masterpiece of African cinema. None of this has led, however, to a real understanding of the film: 'Everyone told me "It's very fine", and that was the end of it because no one had understood'.[37] The critics, fascinated by the film's symbolic power, mostly liked it, as did the general public, though it remained difficult of access. It would have been logical and positive for them to have attempted to understand it. However, as Nixon K. Kariithi shows in his critique of the errors committed by Western critics in their attempts to explain the film, it was not so much the – ultimately understandable – lack of knowledge of African traditions that was the problem as the incapacity to read a foreign film without applying their own interpretative grids.[38]

It is the very process of criticism that is at issue here: it is tempting to apply an analytical method to a film rather than to give free rein to one's subjectivity by asserting a personal opinion which translates the emotion one felt when viewing it. Sheila Petty observes that if you apply a feminist or psychoanalytic grid to reading *Hyenas/Ramatou* (1992; directed by Djibril Diop Mambéty, born 1945), you find you are confronted with problems of interpretation which can hide the real meaning of the film.[39] Only personal subjectivity can attempt to perceive the deep cause of the film, its real 'need to exist', not its objective genesis. Filmmakers draw that 'need to exist' from their culture, experience and deep knowledge of their own situation. This is where the emotional power of a work and its topicality meet. Critics must allow space for improvisation!

Here again, however, the road to hell is paved with good intentions. A widely shared tendency is to apply a universal reading, to the detriment of the culture one is trying to explain. 'At what point does the universality of a theme reveal itself to be the product of a cultural misunderstanding?' asks Stéphane Malandrin.[40] In 1992, Mohamed Camara made *Denko*, his first short. In order to break the curse on him, a mother sleeps with her blind son in order to restore his sight. Camara was praised for his astute reversal of Sophocles' *Oedipus Rex*. 'It begins as a dialogue of the deaf', says Malandrin. 'The listener takes over the speaker's words to hear what he already knows. The person telling the story in a sense loses paternity of the images he invents, because the person hearing asserts that he already knows them'. It is this misunderstanding which makes it impossible to grasp the spirit of a work, to take what the filmmaker attempted to put into it, not what you think you recognize in it. It would be better to allow oneself willingly to lose one's bearings, to let oneself be carried along by emotion, to replace a deductive approach by an intuitive perception of the film, and let oneself learn what the Other is teaching that is new. Respect for a different cinema requires this detour if we are to avoid liking it for what it is not – and if we are not to prevent it from existing as what it is.[41] □

Bartlet's challenging account identifies a series of interpretative problems that can be tackled both in terms of criticism and theoretically. In terms of criticism, it is clearly a matter of engaging more closely with African films – and with films from other areas of world cinema. But theoretical issues are also inevitably involved. As Bartlet points out, paraphrasing Nixon K. Kariithi, the incapacity to read a foreign film may be a problem of the implicit and/or explicit theoretical perspectives that a critic applies. In viewing a film that comes from a culture other than his or her own (or indeed any film), it may well be provisionally useful for a critic, as Bartlet suggests, to try to throw off the rigid interpretative grids provided by feminism, psychoanalysis, cognitive theory or whatever, to accept a degree of disorientation, and to give freer rein to a subjective response, an intuitive perception, that might incorporate more aspects of the film. But it is questionable how far such grids can be dispensed with: reliance on a subjective response may circle back into an unthinking reaction to stereotypes (of 'authenticity', for example). Better that criticism and theory work together, criticism engaging with the particularities (including subjective responses) for which theory must account, theory providing general explanations that can be checked against specifics. It is not a matter, as Bartlet implies, of rejecting 'universality'; the idea of 'universality' may indeed result in cultural misunderstanding when different cultural forms and practices are interpreted according to a supposedly universal norm; but the very concept of 'cultural misunderstanding' depends upon a universal concept of correct understanding, and examples of 'cultural misunderstanding' can only be recognised as such in the perspective that such a concept provides. 'Piecemeal theory' may seem to be a way of avoiding or lessening the danger of applying an oppressive and inappropriate interpretative grid; but such theory may also bring its blind spots, and the danger is best met by making one's theoretical perspectives, one's interpretative assumptions, explicit in general terms so that they can be checked and criticised in the fullest possible way.

It is in this process of checking and criticism that analytical philosophy may play a role. From a facile postmodernist or postcolonialist perspective, it could be argued that such philosophy is 'Western' and thus, perhaps, inherently inadequate to produce a theory that could account for, say, African film. But analytic philosophy could also be employed to show the weaknesses of the assumptions that Bartlet castigates in the above extract and to explore what a proper understanding of films from different cultures might involve. In 'The Film Theory that Never Was: A Nervous Manifesto' (1996), Gregory Currie outlines his sense of the role of analytical philosophy in film theory and of the questions that it should address:

■ 'Analytical philosophy of film' is not a very satisfactory description … primarily because it suggests a commitment to the 'philosophy is conceptual analysis' equation which few of us now accept and to an Olympian perspective from which the philosopher hopes to see further than other beings. But it does suggest a basis of thought within the Anglo-American tradition, with its emphasis on clarity of expression and argument, on the role of logic, and on respect for science. In this sense, analytical philosophy is a thriving enterprise. But analytical philosophy of *film* is a cottage industry existing on the margins of academic philosophy as practised in English-speaking countries. Unlike the more familiar psychoanalytic approach to film, it does not have an established and overarching theoretical structure, and indeed some of its practitioners actively discourage the search for one.[42] Its only distinctive features might be these: (i) a dissatisfaction with the kind of philosophy appealed to in recent film theory; (ii) a commitment to the broadly analytical approach as defined above, as well as the integration, where appropriate, of philosophical ideas with results about the mind and other relevant phenomena from the most predictive research in psychology, cognitive science, and other empirical disciplines; (iii) a desire to approach particular films, film genres, and film styles with as light a theoretical baggage as possible, so that the films themselves should not disappear or become distorted under the burden of theory.[43] What I aim to do here is to offer an absurdly ambitious concept of what an analytical philosophy of film would look like if it took seriously the aim of constructing a systematic and globally connected theory ... I shall describe a connected set of questions, of roughly increasing specificity, which would jointly constitute a budget of central problems in relation to film, from the most general questions about the nature of the medium to the most specific ones about the interpretation of individual films. Any set of answers to these questions, or to some substantial subset of them, where the answers derive from some roughly coherent set of theories, would then constitute a philosophy of film.

So I say that practitioners of philosophy of film should take seriously the search for grand theory. The grand theory in question need not be arrived at all at once, and the best way to get it might not be for many or any of us to spend our time looking for a synthesis; it might just grow naturally. But still, other things being equal, a theory that is strongly integrated across the domain of film and strongly linked to successful work in other areas will be better – more simple, coherent, and therefore more credible – than a bunch of disparate theories isolated from other branches of knowledge. And since simplicity and coherence are epistemic virtues that admit of degrees, achieving the aim is not crucial; a partially realized grand theory could be preferable to a disparate collection of partially realized small theories.

What is the budget of questions that we should be aiming to answer? The questions will resolve themselves into rough groupings. One group will concern film's *nature*: what distinguishes film from other media? What are film's near relatives and what its distant cousins? What is the minimal set of features a work must have to be a film? (The answer to that last question might be 'none'.) Another group will concern the *modes* of filmic representation: the kinds of contents which film is capable of conveying, or is most apt to convey. A third concerns the appropriate or standard kinds of *engagement* with film: how is the viewer drawn into the diegesis? How does the viewer construct/understand the narrative presented? A fourth concerns the *individuation* of filmic elements and their connections: scene, shot, point of view, montage, etc. A fifth group concerns film *production*: is there a distinctive filmic process, and how do we weigh the important elements within that process? How does the filmic process bear on the understanding and appraisal of the outcome, the finished film? Next will be the questions about film *kinds*: what are filmic genres, and how does grouping by genre compare with grouping by authorship? Then there will be questions about film *style*: what elements of film, if any, can be designated as stylistic elements? What stylistic features, if any, are invariant across filmic kinds identified in terms of genre, authorship, or other non-stylistic features? Finally there will be questions about *individual* films – questions which, ideally, would be informed by the answers given to earlier questions in our list. So when we try to understand and appreciate a particular film we shall want to bear in mind our decisions about the nature of film and filmic representation, together with general principles concerning the viewer's response. But we shall also and more specifically need to understand the particular elements of *this* film and their connection in the light of our theory of individuation, to understand how far the facts about *this* particular filmic process affect the nature and value of the outcome, and to locate *this* film in its appropriate kind or kinds and to identify *its* stylistic features.

On this view, film theory aims at a body of knowledge organized along an axis of increasing specificity, where everything is (potentially) relevant to everything else and everything (actually) comes together in the analysis of particular films. Whatever we call it, it will be at least in part a philosophical activity, for various reasons. First, some of its questions – concerning essence, representation, individuation, kind, style, and the relations between process and result – are themselves ineluctably philosophical; deciding what content these notions have requires philosophical reflection. But it will be philosophical also in the sense that any large-scale theoretical undertaking is, because it will depend for its success on a sensitivity to the logical and conceptual connections between different components.

Of course different and conflicting theories can be constructed along these lines; how are we to choose between them? Internal coherence will be one consideration, but it cannot be the only one. Another will be simply: coherence with the rest of our knowledge. We ought not to say anything about film which we cannot, ultimately, integrate with our beliefs about other things. And we certainly should not insulate our beliefs about film from our other beliefs by convincing ourselves that film is *sui generis* [in a class of its own]. What we say about film genres ought to cohere with what we say about genres in other artistic and representational forms; similarly for film style, and the other issues announced above. That is not to say that there is nothing distinctively filmic about film genre or film style. Rather, the claim is that applying a notion like genre or style to film in a special way needs justification in terms of the special features of the filmic medium or by reference to some other consideration available within the theory itself. That way we avoid the accusation that we are re-shaping general notions in an ad hoc way to fit a special purpose. But the most important constraint on a theory of the kind I have described will be that it lead to interesting and enlightening analyses of particular films. 'Contemporary interpretation-centred criticism ... has become boring', says David Bordwell, and I am inclined to agree with him.[44] We must never forget that what we are doing as theorists would have no application or even any meaning without there being a body of particular films, many bad and some good, which give point to the questions we ask. Unless we can, in answering these questions, help to make the best of these individual works that can be made of them, we might as well be doing something else.[45]

But this 'bottom up' constraint on theory – that theory be interpretively fecund – offers no universal methodology for film studies, for there is no theory-neutral conception of what is to count as an illuminating interpretation. I suspect that we are never going to get a universally applicable standard for appraising theories of film, or any other art for that matter.[46] But that does not mean that every theory of film will be self-validating, for it will be possible for a theory of film to generate interpretations which are, by its own lights, dull and pedestrian.

The constraint of interpretive fecundity will affect the ways we have of satisfying the constraint of coherence. We can always achieve coherence in a top-down fashion, rejecting hypotheses lower down if they conflict with higher-level hypotheses already accepted. But fecundity requires us to regard our theoretical system as reticulated [constructed or arranged like a net], with clashes between components resolvable in any direction; a critical judgement of a particular film cannot, if it is to be taken seriously, depend on a theoretical notion for which no defence can be given, but high-level theory may have to give way if it leads to dull or highly counter-intuitive criticism. Indeed there is an argument for saying that items lower down ought to be given more weight than items higher up. This is a consequence of the demand for *respect for common sense*. G. E. Moore said that we ought never to put more faith in a high-level philosophical theory than we put in a common-sense judgement like 'I have two hands'. Consequently, in his view, we ought never to believe any philosophy which has as its conclusion the non-existence of material things. In film theory we are not likely to be met with such a stark contrast between arid theory and rock-bottom intuitive conviction. But we ought to start from the assumption that our judgements about particular films are more likely to be reliable than our theories of medium, style, genre, and the rest. Consequently, a theoretical principle would have to have a lot going for it in other areas if it is to force us to abandon an intuitively illuminating interpretation of a particular work.[47]

It is not just that our judgements about particular films are fashioned in response to the direct experience of the particularity and detail of those works, whereas our general conceptions of medium, style, and the rest are rather remote from direct experience. There is another reason that judgements about particular works should count more heavily than judgements about theoretical concepts. It is that, in the case of judgements about particular works, our judgements themselves are partly *constitutive* of the phenomenon, but our judgements about concepts like genre are not. Genre is a theoretical-explanatory notion, and our views about genre can be quite radically wrong, as can our views about quarks and gluons. But at least some of our views about particular works do not seem to be so fallible. Thus, as has frequently been observed, it makes questionable sense to suppose that everyone could find a film frightening, funny, moving, or dull, and yet the work itself should not actually be frightening, funny, moving, or dull. It is possible for an individual to be wrong about these things, as would be the case where that individual's response was a perverse or otherwise radically atypical one. But this point can be made: to the extent that I take seriously my judgement about this particular work – that it is funny – then to that extent I must see my judgement as constitutive of its being funny, and not see my judgement as a guess, even an informed one, about some quality the work has quite independent of my response to it. But if I take some stand on the notion of genre, thinking of genres in, say, an Aristotelian way, then that really is just a hypothesis on my part, and it is a hypothesis which is only as good and reliable as the methods of theory-formation by which I arrived at it. I cannot cite the simple fact of my holding that view of genre as supportive of the view.

[T]his approach to film [is] open to criticism from outside, struggling for inner coherence, giving strong weight to intuitive judgement and searching for comprehensiveness.[48] □

Currie's 'manifesto' for film theory need not be so nervous; it is valid in many respects. But, appearing more than a century after the Lumière Bros showed their first flickering films in Paris, it must give us pause. It seems that, after a hundred years of film theory, a century of building cinemas of the mind, we arrive, not at a definitive theory, but at a kind of prescriptive meta-theory, a theory of what theory should be, what aspects of film it should aim to cover and explain. This could seem to cast the whole enterprise of film theory into doubt, insofar as it aims at a comprehensive and conclusive explanation of the phenomenon it takes as its object. Might it not be better to fall back into the project of piecemeal theory, as advocated by Noël Carroll, or to take the view, associated with the American pragmatic philosopher Richard Rorty, that even grand theory can be no more than a part of our ongoing cultural conversation, rather than a quest for truth? The answer is no: the project of grand theory – though we might seek for some other adjective to 'grand', with its connotations of pomp and pretension – remains the most effective way of producing insights and concepts adequate to the problems it addresses. Such insights and concepts may be wrong; but they can be revealed as wrong only by an alternative theory that addresses or recon-

stitutes the same problems. Even postmodernism, the dominant opponent of grand theory in the 1990s, was effective, for a time, because it
offered a grand theory of the end of grand theory: in the global culture
of the twenty-first century there is a peculiarly powerful, and sometimes
painful, awareness of worldwide interconnections that postmodernism,
already on the wane, will not be able adequately to understand.

To talk of the 'effectiveness' of a theory may seem to invoke, once
again, a pragmatic criterion: a theory, whether of film or anything else, is
OK for a time, because it works insofar as it seems to account for what
it aims to explain and to provide plausible and insightful interpretations
of relevant data; it will then – due to changed historical circumstances,
perhaps – be discarded, and replaced by another theory. But the more
fundamental criterion for evaluating a theory that has been invoked
above is 'adequacy': a theory must be adequate to what it seeks to explain.
The danger of circularity is obvious here – a theory may construct what
it seeks to explain in such a way as conveniently to validate its premises
and perspectives. But even a theory that proceeds in this way will still be
open to the pressure of anomalies. If these anomalies – elements that the
theory cannot account for – reach a certain critical mass, the theory will
either change or be displaced. This happens most distinctively in the paradigm shifts of scientific theory; but, as the Introduction to this Critical
History pointed out, philosophical theories – or theories of film – are not
so decisively superseded. This does not mean, however, that no progress
has been made; in many ways, we do understand much more about film
at the start of the twenty-first century than we did in the middle of the
twentieth. But we do not yet have explanations adequate to some of its
fundamental features. It may be said that such explanations are unlikely
to be found, insofar as they merge into traditional, perhaps perennial,
philosophical problems. But explanations that aim to account for as
many relevant features as possible, and to do so more adequately than
previous or rival explanations, are likely to be richer and stronger than
those which merely reiterate the insolubility of adequate explanations.

The project of grand theory in film is worth reviving. Its central
problem should be the one that runs through this Critical History – the
problem of the relationship of film to reality. To formulate the problem
in such a way may seem to evade the issue of whether it is appropriate to
speak of a relationship between film and reality, rather than, as in some
semiotic and post-structuralist perspectives, of different kinds of representations or signifying systems. There should, however, be no question
today, in the aftermath of semiotic and post-structuralist challenges, of

exploring the problem without recognising that such categories as 'representation' and 'reality' are, to use a favourite post-structuralist term,
'problematic'. But the post-structuralist challenge has, arguably, proved
inadequate to the phenomena it seeks to understand.

It could also be argued that the problem of film and reality can hardly
be considered in isolation from the broader question of the relationship
between representation and reality; that this question arises in relation to
all forms of representation, in the visual arts, in theatre, in electronic
media. Certainly, more general explorations of this question are valuable
– and this Critical History has provided a range of examples of the way
in which film theory may be enriched by comparisons with other forms
of representation. But the particular form of representation that is moving pictures, the moving image, seems to have a specificity of its own
that merits independent investigation – even if such investigation can be
powerfully informed by findings from the exploration of other forms of
representation.

To talk of the moving image raises another issue: for in the twenty-
first century, we are vividly aware that we have other modes of the moving image that can have a much greater impact than film – above all, television. Should not film theory now be subsumed within a larger project
of moving image theory, in which television might be the dominant
object of investigation? Undoubtedly there is a strong argument for this:
but it remains the case that film provides the prototypical example of
the moving image, even if only as a result of a concatenation of socio-
technological circumstances (for it is not inconceivable that TV might
have been invented before film). Thus, the theories that have been
devised to understand film have much to teach about other modes of the
moving image – above all with regard to the question of the relationship
between moving image and reality in an era in which 'reality TV' has
achieved an unprecedented power.

It might be argued, however, that 'the moving image' itself is now
a slightly archaic category (we have *museums* of the moving image).
Enormous though the change from the still to the moving image was, it
could be regarded as the technological actualisation of a tendency inherent in the still image from the start: from the cave paintings of Altamira
to the sculptures of the Parthenon frieze to the canvases of Tintoretto to
the photographs of Eadweard Muybridge, all still images aspire to the
condition of motion. As the Introduction to this Critical History observed, a greater change is now upon us: the huge transition from an analogue to a digital culture: from a culture based on the notion that still

and moving images issue from, and refer to, their likenesses in reality to a culture in which images can apparently be reconstructed and even created without reference to a real world: a world of simulacra, of copies without originals. This is the world adumbrated by the postmodernist thinker Jean Baudrillard, but it is not merely a matter of theory; it is the way we live now, the conceptual net and empirical texture of our everyday lives. It could be argued that theoretical efforts should be addressed to this change, above all; and that film theory, whatever its intrinsic interest, can play only a minor part in this greater project.

The importance of understanding the change from analogue to digital culture cannot seriously be doubted; but film theory could contribute considerably towards a definition of digital culture. This Critical History began by linking cinema with one of the oldest philosophical movies, that of Plato's cave; in conclusion, it can be suggested that cinema may be linked with the newest philosophical question – though one, of course, that has many traditional precedents – of the relationship between analogue and simulacrum. Moving between two and three dimensions, between fiction and fact, between imagination and observation, between memory and desire, between illusion and reality, cinema flickers on the interface of the real and the simulated: in this, it may not only be a prototype of the moving image, but also of the strangeness of digital culture itself.

In making its contribution to the comprehension of digital culture, film theory should deepen, not discard, its attempt to understand the relationship between film and reality. Such an understanding requires fresh thought, checked and refined by the increasing richness and sophistication of moving-image archives[49] and by the technological tools, such as DVD, that make precise analysis of film possible in a way that comes close to the established – though always tentative – procedures for the analysis of the written or printed text and the still image. It also requires, however, a rereading and revaluation of the film theories produced in, but not consigned to, the past: the theories considered in this Critical History, which are the bases on which to build future cinemas of the mind.

NOTES

INTRODUCTION

1 Several fascinating studies might be undertaken of the representation of the cinema in film itself, on TV, in fiction, in poetry, in painting, and in other media. For an account of literary representations of cinema, see Nicolas Tredell, *Panoramic Sleights: Figures of Cinema in Literature* (forthcoming).

2 See Antony Easthope, 'Introduction', in Easthope, ed., *Contemporary Film Theory*, Longman Critical Readers series (London and New York: Longman, 1993): 'In the area of film theory the break with the naturalist fallacy was made in the 1970s' (p. 1); 'arguably, what defines classic film theory was its belief that cinema copies the world we perceive' (p. 2); classic film theory, whether formalist or realist, rests on the assumption 'that cinema, based as it is in photography, must be judged as in part a mechanical reproduction, whether feeble or convincing ... Classic film theory is superseded when this assumption gets overthrown' (p. 5); 'Supersession of the naturalist fallacy is the foundation on which contemporary film theory is constructed' (p. 18). Although the selection was published in 1993, when cognitive film theory was well advanced, it contains no examples of this theory, consigning mention of it to an endnote (pp. 21–2, note 29) and to a section of the Bibliography (p. 211).

3 See Easthope (1993), p. 1: 'Every version of contemporary theory has begun by breaking with the naturalist attitude. Naturalism in this sense is the assumption, stretching back to Plato's belief that the real world was a copy of a world of ideal forms, that texts try to imitate reality and may be judged in terms of how well or badly they succeed in reproducing it.' It seems that Plato, too, was in the grip of the naturalist fallacy that contemporary film theory has confidently 'superseded'.

4 See Nicolas Tredell, *Notes towards a Definition of Digital Culture* (forthcoming).

CHAPTER ONE

1 Georges Méliès, 'Cinematographic Views', in Richard Abel, ed., *French Film Theory and Criticism: A History/Anthology. Volume I: 1907–1929* (Princeton, NJ: Princeton University Press, 1988), p. 36.

2 Abel (1988), p. 37.

3 Abel (1988), p. 38.

4 Abel (1988), p. 48.

5 Rémy de Gourmont, 'Épilogues: Cinématograph', in Abel (1988), p. 38.

6 Adolphe Brisson, 'Theatre Column: *L'Assassinat du Duc de Guise*', in Abel (1988), p. 50.

7 Abel (1988), pp. 50–1.

8 Abel (1988), p. 51.

9 Ricciotto Canudo, 'The Birth of a Sixth Art', trans. Ben Gibson, Don Ranvaud, Sergio Sokora, Deborah Young, in Abel (1988), p. 58. Abel has 'Agriculture' rather than 'Architecture', but the context makes 'Architecture' the more likely reading.

10 See Henri Agel, *Esthétique du Cinéma*, Que Sais-Je? series (Paris: Presses Universitaires de France, 1962), p. 8.

11 Abel (1988), p. 59.

12 Abel (1988), pp. 59–60.

13 [*Abel's note:*] Canudo's concept of the *Festival* seems to come out of ancient Greek culture rather than out of the European Medieval period or Renaissance. It is a mark of Canudo's contradictory interests or his ambition to synthesize widely divergent ways of thinking that, on the same page, he can bring together ancient Greek culture and Italian Futurism or a classical literary tradition and a potential new art form, the cinema.

14 Abel (1988), p. 60.

15 Abel (1988), p. 61.

16 Abel (1988), pp. 61–2, 64–5.

17 Hugo Münsterberg, *The Film: A Psychological Study: The Silent Photoplay in 1916*, with a new foreword by Richard Griffith (New York: Dover Publications Inc., 1970), p. 16.

18 Münsterberg (1970), pp. 60, 61
19 Münsterberg (1970), p. 58.
20 Münsterberg (1970), p. 62.
21 Münsterberg (1970), p. 64.
22 Münsterberg (1970), p. 88.
23 Münsterberg (1970), p. 87.
24 Münsterberg (1970), p. 88.
25 Münsterberg (1970), p. 89.
26 Münsterberg (1970), p. 86.
27 Münsterberg (1970), p. 89.
28 Münsterberg (1970), p. 90.
29 Rudolf Arnheim, *Film als Kunst* [*Film as Art*] (Berlin: Ernst Rowohlt Verlag, 1932); trans. L. M. Sieveking and Ian F. D. Morrow, with 'Preface' by Paul Rotha, as *Film* (London: Faber and Faber, 1933). Parts of *Film* are included in *Film as Art* (London: Faber and Faber, 1958), edited, re-translated and amended by Arnheim himself. References in these notes are to the 1933 Faber edition. This quotation, p. 8.
30 Arnheim (1933), pp. 68–9.
31 Arnheim (1933), p. 20.
32 Arnheim (1933), p. 35.
33 Arnheim (1933), p. 69.
34 Arnheim (1933), pp. 69–70.
35 Arnheim (1933), pp. 75–6.
36 See Arnheim (1933), pp. 234–9, 'Should Sound Film Be Stereoscopic?'
37 Arnheim (1933), p. 134.
38 Arnheim (1933), p. 135.
39 Béla Balázs, *Theory of the Film* (*Character and Growth of a New Art*), trans. from the Hungarian by Edith Bone, International Theatre and Cinema series (London: Dennis Dobson, 1952). According to Balázs, pp. 39–45 of this book are from *Der Sichtbare Mensch* and pp. 195–8 from *Der Geist des Films*.
40 J. Dudley Andrew, *The Major Film Theories: An Introduction* (London, Oxford, New York: Oxford University Press, 1976), p. 85.
41 The most notable inconsistency is between the distinctive characteristics of film listed on p. 31 and p. 155. See note 56 below.
42 In his Introduction to Balázs (1952), Herbert Marshall says that *Theory of the Film* 'sums up all the work, thought and experience [Balázs] put into his previous pioneering works, which have since become classics' (p. 11).
43 Balázs (1952), p. 17.
44 Balázs (1952), p. 17.
45 Balázs (1952), p. 18.
46 Balázs (1952), p. 18.
47 Balázs (1952), pp. 19–20.
48 Balázs (1952), p. 21.
49 See Marshall in Balázs (1952), p. 11: 'The European generalisation about England still seems to hold good; that we are empiricists in art and despise theory. Certainly this appears to be so in relation to theatre and cinema, for the publication of original works in French, German and Russian is extremely large compared to the number of similar books published here.' Written in 1952, Marshall's remarks are anticipations of the much more general move towards theory that would manifest itself in UK film studies in the journal *Screen* in the 1970s and in UK literary studies from the 1980s onwards.
50 Balázs (1952), p. 21.
51 Balázs (1952), p. 23.
52 Balázs (1952), p. 24.
53 Balázs (1952), p. 24.
54 Balázs (1952), p. 30.
55 [*Editor's note:*] The practice of promenade theatre, in which members of the audience can walk around and sit in different places during the performance, can be seen as an attempt to provide theatre audiences with the variability of distance and angle that characterise film.
56 Balázs (1952), pp. 30–1. At the start of Part II of *Theory of the Film*, Balázs offers another summary of 'the new methods of expression provided by the film', which runs as follows:

'[T]he division of scenes into shots, i.e. pictures of detail;
the change of angle and set-up within the same scene;
the "identification" between spectator and camera;
the close-up;
montage (editing, cutting).' (p. 155)

In this summary, the '[v]arying distance' mentioned in the first summary (Balázs (1952), p. 31) has become 'the close-up', and the other formal features – division, change of angle and set-up, and montage – have been joined by a feature that belongs to another category, that of the psychology of the film viewer: 'the "identification" between spectator and camera'.

57 Balázs (1952), p. 30.
58 Balázs (1952), p. 35.
59 Balázs (1952), p. 36.
60 Balázs (1952), p. 48.
61 Balázs (1952), p. 31.
62 Balázs (1952), p. 55, has 'issues' rather than 'tissues', but 'tissues' seems more appropriate to the metaphor of 'cell-life'.
63 Balázs (1952), pp. 54–5.
64 Balázs (1952), p. 55.
65 Balázs (1952), p. 55.
66 See Sigmund Freud, 'The Uncanny' (1919), in *The Standard Edition of the Complete Psychological Works of Sigmund Freud, Volume XVII* [17] (*1917–1919*), trans. under General Editorship of James Strachey, in collaboration with Anna Freud, assisted by Alix Strachey and Alan Tyson (London: The Hogarth Press and the Institute of Psycho-Analysis, 1955), pp. 217–52.
67 See Jean-Paul Sartre, *La Nausée* (Paris: Gallimard, 1938; Folio, 1985), especially the famous description of the chestnut-tree root, pp. 178–90; English translation by Robert Baldick, *Nausea* (Harmondsworth: Penguin, 1965), pp. 183–93.
68 Balázs (1952), p. 56.
69 Balázs (1952), p. 56.
70 Balázs (1952), p. 56.
71 Balázs (1952), p. 60.
72 Balázs (1952), p. 62.
73 Balázs (1952), p. 62.
74 Balázs (1952), p. 62.
75 Balázs (1952), p. 63.
76 Balázs (1952), p. 64.
77 Balázs (1952), p. 65.
78 Balázs (1952), p. 74.
79 Balázs (1952), pp. 74–5.

80 Balázs (1952), p. 75.
81 Balázs (1952), p. 90.
82 Balázs (1952), p. 92.
83 Balázs (1952), pp. 91–2.
84 Balázs (1952), p. 118.
85 Balázs (1952), p. 119.
86 Balázs (1952), p. 122.
87 Balázs (1952), p. 125.
88 Balázs (1952), p. 126.
89 Balázs (1952), p. 127.
90 Balázs (1952), p. 128.
91 Balázs (1952), p. 143.
92 Balázs (1952), p. 144.
93 Balázs (1952), p. 146.
94 Balázs (1952), p. 196.
95 Balázs (1952), p. 197.
96 Balázs (1952), pp. 197–8.
97 Balázs (1952), pp. 194–5.
98 S. M. Eisenstein, 'Eisenstein on Eisenstein: The Director of Potemkin', in S. M. Eisenstein, *Selected Works: Volume I: Writings, 1922–34*, ed. and trans. Richard Taylor (London: BFI Publishing; Bloomington and Indianapolis: Indiana University Press, 1988), p. 74.
99 S. M. Eisenstein, 'At Last' (1934), in Eisenstein (1988), p. 296.
100 Walt Whitman, *Song of Myself*, part 50, lines 1324–5, in *Walt Whitman: The Complete Poems*, Francis Murphy, ed., Penguin English Poets series (Harmondsworth: Penguin, 1975), p. 123.
101 S. M. Eisenstein, 'Constanta (Whither "The Battleship Potemkin")' (1926), in Eisenstein (1988), p. 69.
102 S. M. Eisenstein, 'The Montage of Film Attractions' (1924), in Eisenstein (1988), p. 39.
103 Eisenstein (1988), p. 40.
104 Eisenstein (1988), pp. 40–1.
105 In Eisenstein (1988), p. 308, note 6, Richard Taylor observes that Eisenstein 'had studied the later works of Vladimir M. Bekhterev (1857–1927)', an exponent of 'reflexology'.
106 Eisenstein (1988), p. 75.
107 Eisenstein (1988), p. 81.
108 Eisenstein (1988), p. 133.
109 'Beyond the Shot' (1929), in Eisenstein (1988), p. 138.

110 Eisenstein (1988), p. 139.

111 Eisenstein (1988), p. 178.

112 Eisenstein (1988), p. 287.

113 'Through Theatre to Cinema', in Sergei Eisenstein, *Film Form; Essays in Film Theory and The Film Sense*, ed. and trans. Jay Leyda (Cleveland and New York: Meridian Books; The World Publishing Company, 1957), p. 10.

114 See Eisenstein (1988), p. 144: 'What then characterises montage and, consequently, its embryo, the shot? Collision. Conflict between two neighbouring fragments. Conflict. Collision.'; 'my view of montage as a *collision*, my view that the collision of two factors gives rise to an idea.'; and pp. 163–4: '*montage is ... an idea that* DERIVES *from the collision between two shots that are independent of one another.*'

115 'Help Yourself' (1932), in Eisenstein (1988), p. 236.

116 S. M. Eisenstein, 'Montage 1938' (1939), in *Selected Works: Volume II: Towards a Theory of Montage*, Michael Glenny and Richard Taylor, eds; trans. Michael Glenny (London: BFI Publishing, 1991), pp. 296–7.

117 Eisenstein (1988), p. 186.

118 Eisenstein (1988), p. 187.

119 Eisenstein (1988), p. 187.

120 Eisenstein (1988), p. 188.

121 Eisenstein (1988), p. 189.

122 Eisenstein (1988), p. 181.

123 Eisenstein (1988), p. 182.

124 Eisenstein (1988), p. 182.

125 Eisenstein (1988), p. 182.

126 Eisenstein (1988), p. 182.

127 Eisenstein (1988), p. 183.

128 Eisenstein (1988), p. 191.

129 Eisenstein (1988), p. 194.

130 Eisenstein (1988), p. 193.

131 Eisenstein (1988), p. 158.

132 Eisenstein (1988), p. 199.

133 T. S. Eliot, 'The Metaphysical Poets' (1921), in *Selected Essays*, 2nd edn. (London: Faber and Faber, 1934), p. 288.

134 'Hamlet' (1919), in Eliot (1934), p. 145.

135 See Eisenstein (1988), p. 199: 'In early times, the times of magic and religion, science was simultaneously an element of emotion and an element of collective knowledge. With the advent of dualism things became separated and we have, on the one hand, speculative philosophy, pure abstraction, and, on the other, the element of pure emotion.'

136 Eisenstein (1991), p. 330.

137 Eisenstein (1991), pp. 330–1.

138 Eisenstein (1991), p. 331.

139 Eisenstein (1991), p. 332.

140 Roger Scruton, 'Photography and Representation', in *The Aesthetic Understanding: Essays in the Philosophy of Art and Culture* (Manchester: Carcanet Press, 1983), p. 125.

141 Eisenstein, Vsevolod Pudovkin, Grigori Alexandrov, 'Statement on Sound' (1928), in Eisenstein (1988), p. 113.

142 Eisenstein (1988), p. 114.

143 See David Sterritt, *The Films of Jean-Luc Godard: Seeing the Invisible*, Cambridge Film Classics series (Cambridge: Cambridge University Press, 1999), pp. 26–7: '[I]n many of Godard's mature works, such as *Hail Mary* (1985; original French title *Je vous salue Marie*) and *Nouvelle Vague* [*New Wave*] (1990), meaning comes not only from the manifest content of images and sounds, but also from the evocative "space between" different elements of the film. This space seems deeper and wider in Godard's works than in most others, since he emphasizes the disjunctions and discontinuities built into cinema – cuts between shots, *contrasts between sound and picture*, and so forth – that conventional movies cover with devices stressing narrative flow instead of poetic allusiveness [*Editor's italics*].'

144 Eisenstein (1988), p. 236.

145 Eisenstein (1988), p. 235.

146 Eisenstein (1988), p. 229.

147 Eisenstein (1988), pp. 235–6. The sequence as written in the script is published in Sergei M. Eisenstein, *The Film Sense*, ed. and trans. Jay Leyda (London

and Boston: Faber and Faber, 1986), pp. 186–90.

148 Eisenstein (1988), p. 236.
149 Eisenstein (1991), p. 332.
150 Eisenstein (1991), p. 329.
151 Eisenstein (1991), p. 330.
152 Eisenstein (1991), p. 337.

CHAPTER TWO

1 André Bazin, *Qu'est-ce que le cinéma: Ontologie et langage* [*What is Cinema? Ontology and Language*] (Paris: Les Éditions du Cerf, 1958), p. 9. (Editor's translation.)

2 André Bazin, 'The Ontology of the Photographic Image', in *What is Cinema?*, essays selected and trans. Hugh Gray (Berkeley, Los Angeles, London: University of California Press, 1967), p. 9.

3 Charles Lebrun was 'a French painter and art theorist, the dominant painter of Louis XIV's reign'. Ian Chilvers, ed., *The Concise Oxford Dictionary of Art and Artists* (Oxford and New York: Oxford University Press, 1990), p. 258.

4 Bazin (1967), p. 10.
5 Bazin (1967), p. 11.
6 Bazin (1967), p. 12.
7 Bazin (1967), pp. 13–14.
8 Bazin (1967), pp. 14–15.

9 [*Editor's note:*] See André Malraux, *Esquisse d'une psychologie du cinéma* (Paris: Gallimard, 1946), collected in Denis Marion, ed., *André Malraux*, Cinéma d'aujourd'hui series no. 65 (Paris: Éditions Seghers, 1970), pp. 82–9. Bazin is alluding to the first section of Malraux's essay, 'Birth of a New Means of Expression', which is incorporated almost word for word into André Malraux, *Les voix du silence* (Paris: Pléiade, 1951), pp. 120–1; trans. Stuart Gilbert, *The Voices of Silence* (St Albans: Paladin, 1974), pp. 122–3.

10 Bazin (1967), pp. 24–8.
11 Bazin (1967), pp. 28–9.
12 Bazin (1967), p. 35.
13 Bazin (1967), p. 37.

14 [*Editor's note:*] 'Souvenirs 1938', in *Jean Renoir parle* (Lyon: Serdoc, 1962), p. 12.

15 In the original, this sentence reads: 'Elle suppose le respect de la continuité de l'espace dramatique et naturellement de sa durée' (Bazin, 1958), p. 142.

16 David A. Cook, *A History of Narrative Film*, 2nd edn. (New York and London: W. W. Norton, 1990), p. 916.

17 Bazin (1967), pp. 31–7, 38–40.

18 Siegfried Kracauer, *Theory of Film: The Redemption of Physical Reality*, with an introduction by Miriam Bratu Hansen (Princeton, NJ: Princeton University Press, 1997), p. xlix.

19 Kracauer (1997), p. xlix.

20 Kracauer (1997), p. xlix. Fredric Jameson, in *Signatures of the Visible* (New York: Routledge, 1992), pp. 196–7, observes: '[T]he fascination with leaves and their relationship to motion seems to have marked photography (and film) from their beginnings – "leaves [that] ripple and glitter in the rays of the sun" [a phrase used by Cook and Bonnelli, who, around 1860, developed a device known as a 'photobioscope' (Kracauer, 1997), p. 27]; the Lumière brothers' first highly praised shorts of "the ripple of leaves stirred by the wind" [(Kracauer, 1997), p. 31]; D. W. Griffith's 1947 denunciation of the degradation of Hollywood, its loss of interest in "the beauty of moving wind in the trees" [(Kracauer, 1997), p. 60]. Philosophically, when the crucial issue of movement appears within the ontological meditations of Sartre's *Nausea* it is in the form of wind moving in the leaves and moving them [(Sartre (1985), pp. 186–8; (1965), pp. 189–91)]. The massy foliage of *Eclipse* (1962; original title *L'Eclisse*) [directed by Michelangelo Antonioni (born 1912)] is nothing but an episode; in [Antonioni's] *Blow-Up*, however, the great trees of Maryon Park [the South London park in which crucial scenes in *Blow-Up* take place] are shaken with wind as though by a kind of permanent violence, day or

might never at rest, it is as though in this place above the city the god of wind reigned in perpetuity. So crucial is this sound that in the most remarkable moment of the film, as David Hemmings [who plays its photographer protagonist] grimly contemplates his ultimate motionless blow-up [photographic enlargement], the wind returns in the soundtrack as though to certify its authenticity.'

21 Kracauer (1997), p. 37.
22 Kracauer (1997), p. 39.
23 Kracauer (1997), p. 40.
24 Kracauer (1997), p. 41.
25 Kracauer (1997), p. 42.
26 Kracauer (1997), p. 44.
27 Kracauer (1997), p. 45.
28 Kracauer (1997), pp. 45–6.
29 Kracauer (1997), p. 46.
30 Kracauer (1997), p. 50.
31 Kracauer (1997), p. 52.
32 Kracauer (1997), p. 53.
33 Kracauer (1997), pp. 53–4.
34 Kracauer (1997), p. 54.
35 Kracauer (1997), p. 55.
36 Kracauer (1997), p. 56.
37 Kracauer (1997), pp. 56–7.
38 Kracauer (1997), p. 57.
39 Kracauer (1997), p. 58.
40 Kracauer (1997), p. 58.
41 Kracauer (1997), pp. 58–9.
42 Kracauer (1997), p. 60.
43 Kracauer (1997), p. 60.
44 Kracauer (1997), p. 60.
45 Kracauer (1997), p. 61.
46 Kracauer (1997), p. 61.
47 Kracauer (1997), p. 62.
48 Kracauer (1997), p. 63.
49 Kracauer (1997), p. 64.
50 Kracauer (1997), p. 64.
51 Kracauer (1997), p. 65.
52 Kracauer (1997), p. 65.
53 Kracauer (1997), p. 66.
54 Kracauer (1997), p. 66.
55 Kracauer (1997), p. 66. [*Kracauer's note:*] Cf. Parker Tyler, 'The Film Sense and the Painting Sense', *Art Digest* (15 February 1954), p. 12.
56 Kracauer (1997), p. 66.
57 Kracauer (1997), pp. 67–8.
58 Kracauer (1997), p. 68.
59 Kracauer (1997), p. 68.
60 Kracauer (1997), p. 310.
61 Kracauer (1997), p. 69.
62 Kracauer (1997), p. 71.
63 Kracauer (1997), p. 71.
64 Kracauer (1997), p. 72.
65 Kracauer (1997), p. 73.
66 Kracauer (1997), p. 79.
67 Kracauer (1997), p. 81.
68 Kracauer (1997), p. 80.
69 Kracauer (1997), p. 81.
70 Kracauer (1997), p. 82.
71 Kracauer (1997), p. 83.
72 Kracauer (1997), p. 84.
73 Kracauer (1997), p. 90. Kracauer gives the source as: Ebbe Neergaard, *Carl Dreyer: A Film Director's Work*, trans. from the Danish by Marianne Helweg, New Index series no. 1 (London: The British Film Institute, 1950), p. 27.
74 Kracauer (1997), p. 91.
75 Kracauer (1997), p. 91.
76 Kracauer (1997), p. 95.
77 Kracauer (1997), p. 97.
78 Kracauer (1997), p. 103.
79 Kracauer (1997), p. 106.
80 Kracauer (1997), p. 158.
81 Kracauer (1997), p. 159.
82 Kracauer (1997), p. 160.
83 Kracauer (1997), p. 163. [*Kracauer's note:*] Gabriel Marcel, 'Possibilités et limites de l'art cinématographique' ['Possibilities and limits of cinematic art'], *Revue internationale de filmologie* (July 1954), 5:18–19, p. 171. See also Kracauer (1997), p. 163. See also Horst Meyerhoff, *Tonfilm und Wirklichkeit: Grundlagen zur Psychologie des Films* [*Sound Film and Reality: The Basis of the Psychology of Film*] (Berlin: no publisher given, 1949), pp. 81–2.
84 Kracauer (1997), p. 163.
85 Kracauer (1997), p. 164. [*Kracauer's note:*] See Kracauer, 'National Types as Hollywood Presents Them', *The Public Opinion Quarterly* (Spring 1949), 13:1, p. 72.
86 Kracauer (1997), p. 164.

87 Kracauer (1997), p. 164.

88 Lucien Sève, 'Cinéma et méthode', *Revue internationale de filmologie* (Jul–Aug 1947), 1, pp. 45–6.

89 Kracauer (1997), pp. 164–5.

90 Kracauer (1997), p. 165.

91 Kracauer (1997), p. 165.

92 Kracauer (1997), p. 166.

93 Kracauer (1997), p. 168.

94 Kracauer (1997), p. 169.

95 Kracauer (1997), p. 171. On the same page, Kracauer quotes from a German audience survey that cites a woman teacher's observations on her position as a film spectator: 'One is, so to speak, like God who sees everything and one has the feeling that nothing eludes you and that one grasps all of it.' Kracauer gives his source as: Wilhelm Wolfgang, *Die Auftriebswirkung des Films* [*The Uplifting Effect of Films*], Inaugural-Dissertation, Leipzig (Bremen: no publisher given, 1940), p. 22.

96 Kracauer (1997), p. 211.

97 Kracauer (1997), pp. 211–12.

98 Kracauer (1997), p. 212.

99 Kracauer (1997), p. 213.

100 Kracauer (1997), p. 211.

101 Kracauer (1997), p. 213.

102 Kracauer (1997), p. 214.

103 Kracauer (1997), p. 218.

104 Kracauer (1997), p. 219.

105 Kracauer (1997), pp. 220–1.

106 Kracauer (1997), p. 221.

107 Kracauer (1997), p. 223.

108 Kracauer (1997), p. 230.

109 Kracauer (1997), p. 236.

110 Kracauer (1997), p. 237.

111 Kracauer (1997), p. 238.

112 Kracauer (1997), p. 239.

113 Kracauer (1997), p. 245.

114 Kracauer (1997), p. 255.

115 Kracauer (1997), p. 262.

116 Kracauer (1997), p. 266.

117 Kracauer (1997), p. 267.

118 Kracauer (1997), p. 272.

119 Kracauer (1997), p. 273.

120 Kracauer (1997), p. 300.

121 Kracauer (1997), p. 300.

122 Kracauer (1997), p. 301.

123 Kracauer (1997), p. 304.

124 Kracauer (1997), p. 305.

125 Kracauer (1997), p. 306.

126 Kracauer (1997), p. 306.

127 Kracauer (1997), p. 308.

128 Kracauer (1997), p. 309.

129 Eric Auerbach, *Mimesis: The Representation of Reality in Western Literature*, trans. Willard R. Trask (Princeton, NJ: Princeton University Press, 1968), p. 552.

130 Kracauer (1997), p. 310.

131 Roland Barthes, 'The Great Family of Man', in *Mythologies*, selected and trans. Annette Lavers (St Albans, Herts: Paladin, 1973), pp. 100–02.

CHAPTER THREE

1 Jim Hillier, 'Preface and Acknowledgements', in Hillier, ed., *Cahiers du Cinéma: The 1950s: Neo-Realism, Hollywood, New Wave* (Cambridge, MA: Harvard University Press, 1985), p. ix.

2 In *The American Cinema: Directors and Directions 1929–1968* (New York: Dutton, 1968), p. 25, Andrew Sarris observes: 'I first employed the term "*auteur* theory" in an article entitled "Notes on the Auteur Theory in 1962" (*Film Culture*, 27, Winter 1962–63).'

3 Hillier (1985), pp. 3, 1.

4 Jacques Rivette, 'The Genius of Howard Hawks' ('Génie de Howard Hawks') (1953), trans. Russell Campbell and Marvin Pister, adapted from a translation by Adrian Brine, in Hillier (1985), p. 126.

5 Hillier (1985), p. 127.

6 John Walker, ed., *Halliwell's Film and Video Guide 2001*, 16th edn. (London: HarperCollins Entertainment, 2000), p. 815.

7 Hillier (1985), pp. 126–31.

8 See Frank Kermode, *Forms of Attention*, The Wellek Library Lectures, 1984 (Chicago: University of Chicago Press, 1985).

9 Claude Chabrol, 'Serious Things' ('Les Choses Sérieuses') (1955), trans. Liz Heron, in Hillier (1985), p. 136.

10 [*Chabrol's note:*] In addition the couple with the dog represent the sterile marriage, in Stewart's mind; which explains why it is a dog and not a child. Ever since *Sabotage* (1936), Hitchcock is very wary of children's deaths, which a person of average sensitivity has some difficulty in tolerating.

11 Hillier (1985), pp. 136–9. [*Chabrol's note:*] The final sequence of *Rear Window* is characteristic of the cosmetic transformation of a scene into its opposite, at which Hitchcock is a past-master. Order is re-established, and two amusing notations turn into a 'happy ending'; in reality what is involved is purely and simply a terrible observation – people and things have stayed blindly the same.

12 Chris Baldick, *The Concise Oxford Dictionary of Literary Terms* (Oxford: Oxford University Press, 1991), p. 121.

13 Eric Rohmer, 'Ajax or the Cid' ('Ajax ou le Cid') (1956), trans. Liz Heron, in Hillier (1985), pp. 111–15.

14 André Bazin, 'On the [*De la*] *politique des auteurs*' (1957), trans. Peter Graham, in Hillier (1985), pp. 249–50. Hereafter referenced as Hillier (1985).

15 W. H. Barber, 'Beaumarchais', in Anthony Thorlby, ed., *The Penguin Companion to Literature: Europe* (London: Allen Lane, The Penguin Press, 1971), p. 92.

16 See Jean-Paul Sartre, 'M. François Mauriac et la liberté' (1939), in Sartre, *Situations, I: Essais Critiques* (Paris: Gallimard, 1947), p. 52: 'Dieu n'est pas un artiste; M. Mauriac non plus.' ('God is not an artist; neither is Mr Mauriac.')

17 [*Hillier's note:*] [See] Erich Rohmer, 'Une Fable du Xxe siècle [A Twentieth-century Fable]' (on *Confidential Report*), *Cahiers*, 61 (July 1956), pp. 37–40; [see] *Cahiers*' 'All-Time Best Films' (1958) in Appendix I in [Hillier (1985), pp. 287–8, where *Confidential Report* is ranked sixth in a list of twelve].

18 Cook (1990), p. 408.

19 Hillier (1985), p. 126.

20 [*Hillier's note:*] [See] André Bazin,

'Beauté d'un western' (on Mann's *The Man from Laramie* (1955)), *Cahiers*, 55 (January 1956), pp. 33–6, trans. in [Hillier (1985)] as 'Beauty of a Western' [pp. 165–8].

21 [*Hillier's note:*] [See] André Bazin, 'Évolution du Western', *Cahiers*, 54 (Christmas 1955), pp. 22–6, trans. in André Bazin, *What is Cinema?*, vol. 2, essays selected and trans. Hugh Gray (Berkeley, Los Angeles, London: University of California Press, 1971), pp. 149–57, as 'Evolution of the Western', reprinted in Bill Nicholls, ed., *Movies and Methods: An Anthology*, vol. 1 (Berkeley, Los Angeles, London: University of California Press, 1976), pp. 150–7.

22 Hillier (1985), pp. 250–4, 255–8.

23 Roland Barthes, 'The Death of the Author', in *Image–Music–Text*, ed. and trans. Stephen Heath (London: Fontana/Collins, 1977), pp. 142–8.

24 See Michael Scriven, *Sartre's Existential Biographies* (London: Macmillan, 1984).

CHAPTER FOUR

1 See Colin MacCabe, 'Class of '68: Elements of an Intellectual Autobiography 1967–81', in MacCabe, *Theoretical Essays: Film, Linguistics, Literature* (Manchester: Manchester University Press, 1985), p. 32, note 5: 'I am convinced that much of the hostility I encountered [at Cambridge] was because of my work in television and film.'

2 MacCabe (1985), p. 6.

3 'Stephen Heath', in Nicolas Tredell, *Conversations with Critics* (Manchester: Carcanet, 1994), p. 187.

4 *The Grapes of Wrath* (1939; a novel by John Steinbeck (1902–68); filmed 1940 by John Huston); *The Sound of Music* (1965; a very popular musical film, directed by Robert Wise (born 1914) and starring Julie Andrews); *L'Assommoir* (1877; a novel by Émile Zola (1840–1902); the title means both 'a club or bludgeon' and a 'dive', in the

sense of a disreputable drinking-place, and there are at least nine film adaptations, under various titles: seven French versions (1902, 1909, two in 1911, 1921, 1923, and, in 1956, as *Gervaise*, by René Clément); an American version (1909, by D. W. Griffith); and an English version (1917); *Toad of Toad Hall* (a play of 1930 by A. A. Milne (1882–1956), adapted from the novel *The Wind in the Willows* (1908) by Kenneth Grahame (1859–1932)).

5 Eisenstein (1986), pp. 36, 37. In the version in Eisenstein (1991), p. 310, an '*affidavit-exposition*' is rendered as an '*objective statement*', and the phrase that MacCabe quotes runs as follows: 'Cinematically speaking, they would all be *simple depictions shot from a single set-up.*'

6 Colin MacCabe, 'Realism and the Cinema: Notes on Some Brechtian Theses', in MacCabe (1985), pp. 37–40, 41–2, 44–5.

7 [*Editor's note:*] MacCabe gives the source for the Lacan quote as Moustafa Safouan, 'De la structure en psychanalyse'. This is in Oswald Ducrot, Tzvetan Todorov, Dan Sperber, Moustafa Safouan, François Wahl, eds, *Qu'est-ce que le structuralisme?* (Paris: Seuil, 1968), pp. 239–98. Safouan quotes Lacan on pp. 252–3 and references it as: Jacques Lacan, 'Psychanalyse et Médicine', in *Lettres de l'École Freudienne*, no. 1, p. 45. The translation is presumably MacCabe's own.

8 See 'John Ford's *Young Mr Lincoln* [a collective text by the Editors of *Cahiers du Cinéma*]', trans. Helen Lackner and Diana Matias, *Screen*, 13:3 (Autumn 1972), pp. 5–44, with an 'Afterword' by Peter Wollen, pp. 44–7.

9 Terry Hodgson, ed., *The Batsford Dictionary of Drama* (London: B. T. Batsford, 1988), p. 151.

10 MacCabe (1985), pp. 45–50.

11 See Louis Althusser, 'Ideology and Ideological State Apparatuses (Notes towards an Investigation)', in *Essays on Ideology*, no translator named (London

and New York: Verso, 1984), especially pp. 39–44.

12 MacCabe (1985), pp. 51–5.

13 Stephen Heath, 'On Screen, in Frame: Film and Ideology', in *Questions of Cinema*, Communications and Culture series (London: Macmillan, 1981), pp. 7–8.

14 [*Editor's note:*] Heath does not give a reference here, but he may be alluding to the discussion of *Touch of Evil* in André Bazin's *Orson Welles: A Critical View*, trans. Jonathan Rosenbaum (London: Elm Tree Books, 1978), pp. 123–30. On p. 124, Bazin says: 'The script of [*Touch of Evil*] opposes a corrupt old policeman convinced of a suspect's guilt and an honest young official who tries to overthrow him ... ... Considered hastily and superficially, the story seems to oppose the good, honest, democratic policeman and the crooked cop who is ready to sacrifice every principle and pull any trick to frame suspects.' This is Bazin's version of what Heath calls the 'narrative image' of *Touch of Evil*. Bazin goes on to argue that the opposition of the good Vargas and the bad Quinlan 'becomes turned around and inverted if one pays a little more attention to the script and the characters'. Bazin also acknowledges, however, that when he interviewed Welles, Welles himself rejected Bazin's account and affirmed that, morally, he absolutely condemned Quinlan, along with the 'bad' protagonists of his other films – Arkadin, Harry Lime, Macbeth and Charles Foster Kane – even if he could not 'help but admire them in his heart for their "human qualities"' (p. 129, first footnote).

15 Roland Barthes, *Le plaisir du texte* (Paris: Seuil, 1973), p. 76; trans. Richard Miller as *The Pleasure of the Text* (London: Cape, 1976), p. 47.

16 Stephen Heath, 'Film, System, Narrative' (1975), in Heath (1981), pp. 133–6.

17 Heath (1981), p. 136.

18 Roland Barthes, 'En sortant du cinéma', *Communications*, 23 (1975), p. 104.
19 The riddle that the sphinx poses to Oedipus is: 'What goes on four feet, on two feet, and three,/But the more feet it goes on the weaker it be?' Oedipus's solution is that it is a man, who crawls on all fours as an infant, walks upright on two feet as a man, and has a stick to support himself as an old man. *Brewer's Dictionary of Phrase and Fable*, Centenary Edition, revised by Ivor H. Evans (London: Book Club Associates, 1977), p. 1025.
20 Jean Collet, '*La soif du mal* [*Touch of Evil*]', *Études cinématographiques*, 24–25 (1963), p. 116.
21 Heath (1981), pp. 137–43. For Heath's extended analysis of *Touch of Evil*, see 'Film and System: Terms of Analysis. Part I', *Screen*, 16:1 (Spring 1975), pp. 7–77; 'Part II', *Screen*, 16:2 (Summer 1975), pp. 91–113.
22 Quoted Heath (1981), p. 131. From Christian Metz, *Psychoanalysis and Cinema: The Imaginary Signifier*, trans. Celia Britton, Annwyl Williams, Ben Brewster, Alfred Guzzetti, Language, Discourse, Society series (London and Basingstoke: Macmillan, 1982), p. 35.
23 Tredell (1994), p. 188.
24 Laura Mulvey, 'Visual Pleasure and Narrative Cinema', *Screen*, 16:3 (Autumn 1975), pp. 6–18. Reprinted in Mulvey, *Visual and Other Pleasures* (Basingstoke and London: Macmillan, 1989), pp. 14–26. Subsequent references to Mulvey (1989).
25 '"Magnificent Obsession": An Introduction to the Work of Five Photographers', in Mulvey (1989), p. 146.
26 Mulvey (1989), p. 14.
27 Mulvey (1989), p. 15.
28 Mulvey (1989), p. 16.
29 Mulvey (1989), p. 16.
30 Mulvey (1989), p. 16.
31 See 'Introduction', Easthope (1993), p. 15.
32 [*Editor's note:*] See Sigmund Freud, 'Infantile Sexuality' (1905), in *On Sex-uality. Three Essays on the Theory of Sexuality and Other Works*, trans. James Strachey, ed. and compiled Angela Richards, The Pelican Freud Library, vol. 7 (Harmondsworth: Penguin, 1977), pp. 109–10.
33 [*Editor's note:*] See Jacques Lacan, *Écrits: A Selection*, trans. Alan Sheridan (London: Tavistock, 1977), pp. 1–7.
34 Mulvey (1989), pp. 16–18.
35 Mulvey (1989), p. 18.
36 Mulvey (1989), pp. 16–19.
37 Mulvey (1989), p. 14.
38 Sigmund Freud, 'The Dissolution of the Oedipus Complex' (1924), in *The Standard Edition of the Complete Psychological Works of Sigmund Freud, Volume XIX* [19] (*1923–1925*) (London: The Hogarth Press and the Institute of Psycho-Analysis, 1961), pp. 177–8; also in *On Sexuality: Three Essays on the Theory of Sexuality and Other Works* (Harmondsworth: Penguin, 1977), p. 320. 'The female sex, too, develops an Oedipus complex, a super-ego and a latency period. May we also attribute a phallic organization and a castration complex to it? The answer is in the affirmative; but these things cannot be the same as they are in boys. Here the feminist demand for equal rights for the sexes does not take us far, for the morphological distinction [the distinction between the biological form of men and women] is bound to find expression in differences of psychical development. "Anatomy is Destiny", to vary a saying of Napoleon's.'
39 Mulvey (1989), p. 15.
40 Mulvey (1989), p. 19.
41 [*Editor's note:*] The *Ziegfeld Follies* were a series of musical shows named after the American producer Florenz Ziegfeld (1867–1932), and first suggested by his wife, the musical comedy actress Anna Held (1873–1918). The series began in 1907 and continued into the 1930s and 40s, with revivals in 1956–7. Putting women on visual display was an important aspect of their

appeal, as can be seen from the way in which they were billed in 1922: 'A National Institution Glorifying the American Girl.' See Peter Gammond, *The Oxford Companion to Popular Music* (Oxford: Oxford University Press, 1993), pp. 626–9.

42 [*Editor's note:*] Busby Berkeley (1895–1976) was a choreographer and director renowned for films such as those in the *Gold Diggers* series in which female dancers (chorus girls or chorines) were shown dancing in complex patterns. It should be noted, however, that male dancers and singers also feature as potential objects of the gaze – for example, Dick Powell in *Gold Diggers of 1933* (1933), and the mass dancers in the final sequences of *Gold Diggers of 1935* (1935).

43 See Baldick (1991), p. 57.

44 Baldick (1991), p. 57.

45 Mulvey (1989), p. 19.

46 [*Editor's note:*] Mulvey gives no reference for Sternberg's remark, but may be alluding to a passage in Josef von Sternberg, *Fun in a Chinese Laundry: An Autobiography* (New York: Macmillan, Collier Books, 1973), p. 325: 'Were I to instruct others how to use the camera, the first step would be either to project a film upside down or to show it so often that the actors and story become no longer noticeable, so that the values produced by the camera alone could not escape study.'

47 [*Editor's note:*] See François Truffaut, with the collaboration of Helen G. Scott, *Hitchcock*, first edn 1967, revised edn, Touchstone Books series (New York, London, et al: Simon and Schuster, 1985), p. 216. Truffaut asks Hitchcock: 'Would you say that Stewart [as L. B. Jefferies in *Rear Window*] was merely curious?' Hitchcock replies: 'He's a real Peeping Tom. In fact, Miss Lejeune, the critic of the London *Observer*, complained about that. She made some comment to the effect that *Rear Window* was a horrible film because the hero spent all of his time peeping out of the window. What's so horrible about that? Sure, he's a snooper, but aren't we all?' Truffaut responds: 'We're all voyeurs to some extent, if only when we see an intimate film. And James Stewart is exactly in the position of a spectator looking at a movie.' Hitchcock then says: 'I'll bet you that nine out of ten people, if they see a woman across the courtyard undressing for bed, or even a man puttering around in his room, will stay and look; no one turns away and says, "It's none of my business." They could pull down their blinds, but they never do; they stand there and look out.'

48 [*Editor's note:*] See Jean Douchet, 'Hitch and His Public', trans. Verena Conley. Originally published as 'Hitch et son public' in *Cahiers du Cinéma*, 113 (1960). Reprinted in Marshall Deutelbaum and Leland Poague, eds, *A Hitchcock Reader* (Ames, IA: Iowa State University Press, 1986), pp. 7–15.

49 [*Editor's note:*] Mulvey twice misspells this name as 'Jeffries', an error that goes uncorrected in Easthope (1993), p. 121, and in a number of other anthologies. In Freudian terms, this slip might be seen as symptomatic, as the correct spelling of Jefferies's surname is visually represented in the film in a striking way – not just in the cast list, but on the plaster cast that encases Jefferies's leg (symbolic of the phallus and/or castration) and that, early in the film, is shown to have his initials and surname inscribed upon it.

50 Mulvey (1989), pp. 19–20, 21–4.

51 Elise Lemire, 'Voyeurism and the Postwar Crisis of Masculinity in *Rear Window*', in John Belton, ed., *Alfred Hitchcock's 'Rear Window'*, Cambridge University Press Film Handbooks series (Cambridge: Cambridge University Press, 2000), p. 84.

52 Marian E. Keane, 'A Closer Look at Scopophilia: Mulvey, Hitchcock and *Vertigo*', in Deutelbaum and Poague (1986), p. 236.

53 Mulvey (1989), pp. 25–6.

CHAPTER FIVE

1 See Preface, Hegel's *Philosophy of Right*, trans. T. M. Knox (Oxford: Oxford University Press, 1967), p. 13: 'When philosophy paints its grey in grey, then has a shape of life grown old. By philosophy's grey in grey it cannot be rejuvenated but only understood. The owl of Minerva spreads its wings only with the falling of the dusk.'

2 Laura Mulvey, 'Afterthoughts on "Visual Pleasure and Narrative Cinema" inspired by King Vidor's *Duel in the Sun* (1946)', in Mulvey (1989), p. 29.

3 Mulvey (1989), pp. 29–30.

4 Sigmund Freud, 'Femininity' (1933 [in fact published 1932]), in *The Standard Edition of the Complete Psychological Works of Sigmund Freud, Volume XXII* [22] (*1932–1936*) (London: The Hogarth Press and the Institute of Psycho-Analysis, 1964), p. 131.

5 Mulvey (1989), p. 32.

6 Sigmund Freud, 'Creative Writers and Day-Dreaming' (1908), *Standard Edition, Volume IX* [9] (*1906–1908*) (London: The Hogarth Press and the Institute of Psycho-Analysis, 1959), pp. 143–53, especially pp. 149–150: 'One feature above all cannot fail to strike us about the creations of these [popular] story-writers: each of them has a hero who is the centre of interest, for whom the writer tries to win our sympathy by every possible means and whom he seems to place under the protection of a special Providence. If, at the end of one chapter of my story, I leave the hero unconscious and bleeding from severe wounds, I am sure to find him at the beginning of the next being carefully nursed and on the way to recovery; and if the first volume closes with the ship he is in going down in a storm at sea, I am certain, at the opening of the second volume, to read of his miraculous rescue ... without which the story could not proceed. The feeling of security with which I follow the hero through his perilous adventures is the same as the feeling with which a hero in real life throws himself into the water to save a drowning man or exposes himself to the enemy's fire in order to storm a battery. It is the true heroic feeling, which one of our best writers [Ludwig Anzengruber (1839–89), Austrian dramatist and novelist] has expressed in an inimitable phrase: "Nothing can happen to *me!*" ... It seems to me, however, that through this revealing characteristic of *invulnerability* [*Editor's italics*] we can immediately recognize His Majesty the Ego, the hero alike of every day-dream and of every story.'

7 Mulvey (1989), p. 33.

8 Mulvey (1989), p. 34.

9 Mulvey (1989), p. 34.

10 Mulvey (1989), pp. 34–5.

11 Mulvey (1989), p. 35.

12 Freud (1964), 'Femininity', p. 131. [*Editor's note:*] The version of the passage in Mulvey's essay differs from the version in the *Standard Edition* that she cites as her source. Here is Mulvey's version, with the words as they appear in the *Standard Edition* in italics and enclosed in square brackets: 'the development of femininity remains exposed to disturbances [*disturbance*] by the residual phenomena of the early masculine period. Regressions to [*the fixations of*] the pre-Oedipus phase [*phases*] very frequently occur; in the course of some women's lives there is a repeated alternation between periods in which femininity [*masculinity*] and [*or*] masculinity [*femininity*] gain [*gains*] the upper hand.' (Mulvey (1989), p. 30.)

13 Freud (1964), p. 131.

14 Sigmund Freud, 'Analysis Terminable and Interminable' (1937), *Standard Edition, Volume XXIII* [23] (*1937–1939*) (London: The Hogarth Press and the Institute of Psycho-Analysis, 1964), p. 251. [*Editor's note:*] As with the quotation referenced in note 12 above, the version on p. 37 of Mulvey's essay differs from the version

in the *Standard Edition* that she cites as her source. Here is Mulvey's version, with the words as they appear in the *Standard Edition* in italics and enclosed in square brackets: '(the phallic phase) ['the phallic phase' has no brackets in the original] ... then succumbs to the momentous process of repression [*whose outcome,*] as has so often been shown, that ['that' is not present in the original] determines the fortunes of women's [*a woman's*] femininity.' In the version given earlier in her essay, on p. 30, Mulvey does have 'a woman's femininity' in this last phrase.

15 Mulvey (1989), pp. 35–7.

16 Mulvey (1989), p. 30.

17 Steve Neale, 'Masculinity as Spectacle: Reflections on Men and Mainstream Cinema', *Screen*, 24:6 (Nov–Dec 1983), p. 4.

18 Neale (1983), p. 5.

19 Mulvey (1989), p. 20.

20 [*Neale's note:*] For further elaboration of these two related points, see Moustapha Safouan, 'Is the Oedipus complex universal?', *m/f*, 5/6 (1981), pp. 85–7.

21 Mulvey (1989), p 22.

22 Neale (1983), pp. 5–8, 9–12, 14–16.

23 Jackie Stacey, 'Desperately Seeking Difference: Jackie Stacey Considers Desire between Women in Narrative Cinema', *Screen*, 28:1 (Winter 1987), p. 48.

24 [*Stacey's note:*] For a discussion of films which might be included under this category, see Caroline Sheldon, 'Lesbians and Film; Some Thoughts', in Richard Dyer, ed., *Gays and Film* (New York: Zoetrope, revised edn, 1984).

25 Stacey (1987), p. 53.

26 [*Stacey's note:*] See, for example, Sigmund Freud, 'Some Psychical Consequences of the Anatomical Distinction between the Sexes' (1925) in *On Sexuality*, Pelican Freud Library, vol. 7 (Harmondsworth: Penguin, 1977), pp. 331–43.

27 [*Stacey's note:*] See Lacan (1977), pp. 1–7.

28 Stacey (1987), pp. 53, 54–61.

29 Stacey (1987), p. 51. The sources of the theories of Bellour and Doane to which she refers are: Raymond Bellour, 'Psychosis, Neurosis, Perversion', *Camera Obscura*, 3/4 (1979), p. 97; Mary Ann Doane, 'Film and the Masquerade: Theorizing the Female Spectator', *Screen*, 23:3/4 (Sept–Oct 1982), pp. 74–87.

30 Noël Carroll, *Theorizing the Moving Image*, Cambridge Studies in Film series (Cambridge: Cambridge University Press, 1996), p. 261. [*Carroll's note:*] It should also be noted that Mulvey herself has attempted to modify, or, perhaps more accurately, to supplement the theory that she put forward in 'Visual Pleasure and Narrative Cinema'. See, for example, her 'Afterthoughts on "Visual Pleasure and Narrative Cinema" inspired by King Vidor's *Duel in the Sun* (1946)' in [Mulvey (1989), pp. 29–38]. The latter essay, while not denying the analysis of male pleasure in the former essay, offers a supplemental account of female pleasure with respect to narrative film. Space does not allow for criticism of that supplemental account. However, it is interesting that its structure is analogous to the structure of her psychoanalysis of male pleasure insofar as Mulvey attempts to 'deduce' female pleasure at the movies from an earlier stage of psychosexual development whose masculine phase film narratives may, supposedly, reactivate.

31 [*Carroll's note:*] I stress that what is accepted without sufficient critical distance in this matter is the *scientific* viability of psychoanalysis. Feminist film critics, including Mulvey, are aware of and seek to cancel the patriarchal biases of psychoanalysis. But unless the elements of the theory show sexist prejudices, they tend to accept its pronouncements on matters such as psychosexual development and visual pleasure without recourse to weighing psychoanalytic hypotheses against those of competing theories or to considering the

often commented upon theoretical flaws and empirical difficulties of psycho-analysis.

32 [*Carroll's note:*] I have discussed the tendency in contemporary film theory to embrace theoretical frameworks without considering rival [views] at some length in my *Mystifying Movies: Fads and Fallacies in Contemporary Film Theory* (New York: Columbia University Press, 1988).

33 [*Carroll's note:*] Indeed, John Berger makes such a distinction – between the male as active and the female as passive – with respect to the iconography of easel painting without invoking psychoanalysis. See his *Ways of Seeing* (Harmondsworth: Penguin, 1972), especially chapter 2.

34 Mulvey (1989), p. 20.

35 [*Carroll's note:*] Other commentators have also questioned Mulvey's generalizations in this regard. See Kristin Thompson, 'Closure within a Dream? Point of view in *Laura* (1944)', in *Breaking the Glass Armor: Neoformalist Film Analysis* (Princeton, NJ: Princeton University Press, 1988), p. 185; and Miriam Hansen, 'Pleasure, Ambivalence, Identification: Valentino and Female Spectatorship', *Cinema Journal*, 25 (1986), pp. 6–32.

36 Ben Singer, 'Serials', in Geoffrey Nowell-Smith, ed., *The Oxford History of World Cinema* (Oxford: Oxford University Press, 1997), p. 109.

37 [*Carroll's note:*] Allen Weiss in the introduction to his unpublished doctoral dissertation on the films of Hollis Frampton (New York University, 1989).

38 [*Carroll's note:*] Mulvey may reject this interpretation of her essay. She may think that she is using these psychoanalytic terms literally. In the 'Summary' of her essa[y] [Mulvey (1989), p. 26], for example, she speaks of the neurotic needs of the male ego. But this seems tantamount to implying that the male ego is, at least, in our culture, inevitably and essentially neurotic. And I am not convinced that this is the way that clinical psychoanalysis would use this idea

of neurosis as a technical classification. Nor would the classification be of much scientific value if it applied so universally. Furthermore, Freud himself, in his study of Da Vinci, talks of sublimation as an alternative formation to perversions like fetishism. Why has sublimation dropped out of Mulvey's list of options for visual pleasure? [*Editor's note:* For Freud's discussion of Da Vinci, see Freud, 'Leonardo da Vinci and a Memory of his Childhood' (1910), in *The Standard Edition of the Complete Psychological Works of Sigmund Freud, Volume XI* [11] (*1910*) (London: The Hogarth Press and the Institute of Psycho-Analysis, 1957), pp. 63–137. Here, Freud explores the possible paths of the instinct for research that, in his view, originates with infantile sexual curiosity; and on p. 80 he identifies a path by which 'sexual repression comes about, but it does not succeed in relegating a component instinct of sexual desire to the unconscious. Instead, the libido evades the fate of repression by being sublimated from the very beginning into curiosity and by becoming attached to the powerful instinct for research as a reinforcement. Here, too, the research becomes to some extent compulsive and a substitute for sexual activity; but owing to the complete difference in the underlying psychical processes (sublimation instead of an irruption from the unconscious) the quality of neurosis is absent; there is no attachment to the original complexes of infantile sexual research, and the instinct can operate freely in the service of intellectual interest.']

39 Mulvey (1989), p. 17 ['conditions of screening and narrative conventions give the spectator an illusion of looking in on a private world'].

40 Carroll (1996), pp. 262, 264, 265–6.

41 For an interesting discussion of the scalding scene and its immediate aftermath, see Colin McArthur, *The Big Heat*, BFI Modern [Film] Classics series (London: BFI Publishing, 1972), pp.

69–72. For a comment on its resonance in popular culture, see pp. 32–3.

42 [*Carroll's note:*] Christian Metz, perhaps the leading psychoanalytic film theorist, appears to hold such a view. For arguments against this hypothesis, see the second chapter of my *Mystifying Movies*.

43 [*Carroll's note:*] Here one might object that Mulvey is not committed to regard the fetishism/voyeurism dichotomy as systematic; so I am attacking a straw position. But I think she is committed to the notion of a systematic dichotomy. For if the problem of castration anxiety with respect to the female form is general, and fetishism and voyeurism are the only responses, then where there is no castration anxiety, won't that have to be a function of strategies of voyeurism and fetishism? Perhaps Mulvey does not believe that there is always castration anxiety in response to the female form. But then we would have to know under what conditions castration anxiety will fail to take hold. Moreover, we will have to ask whether these conditions, once specified, won't undermine Mulvey's theory in other respects. Of course, another reason why one might deny that Mulvey's claims involve a systematic dichotomy between fetishistic and voyeuristic strategies is that she believes that there are other strategies for containing castration anxiety. But then the burden of proof is on her to produce these as yet unmentioned alternatives.

44 [*Carroll's note:*] This film was, of course, based upon a highly acclaimed Broadway production. So, it is a counterexample that should also be considered by theater critics who wish to apply the generalizations of feminist film critics to the study of their own artform. Likewise, TV critics, with the same ambition, should want to ponder the relevance of this example to the successful remake of the theater and film versions of *The Miracle Worker* for TV in 1979 by Paul Aaron where Patty Duke (Astin) plays the Anne Sullivan role.

45 [*Carroll's note:*] There is another line of argumentation in Mulvey's essay that I have not dealt with above. It involves a general theory of the way in which cinema engages spectators in identification and mobilizes what Lacanians call 'the imaginary'. The sort of general theory that Mulvey endorses concerning these issues is criticized at length in my *Mystifying Movies*.

46 [*Carroll's note:*] Ronald de Sousa, *The Rationality of Emotion* (Cambridge, MA: MIT Press, 1987), p. 182. The idea of scenarios is also employed by Robert Solomon, 'Emotion and Choice', in Amelia Rorty, ed., *Explaining Emotions* (Berkeley: University of California Press, 1980).

47 [*Carroll's note:*] E.g., Anthony Kenny's *Action, Emotion and Will*, Studies in Philosophical Psychology series (London: Routledge and Kegan Paul, 1963).

48 Ronald de Sousa, 'The Rationality of the Emotions', in Rorty (1980), p. 143.

49 [*Carroll's note:*] This example comes from Cheshire Calhoun's 'Subjectivity and Emotions', *The Philosophical Forum*, 20 (1989), p. 206.

50 [*Carroll's note:*] Of course, there could also be a research program dedicated to studying the image of men in film for the same purposes.

51 [*Carroll's note:*] Kristin Thompson, in conversation, has stressed that determining whether a paradigm scenario is positive or negative may crucially hinge on contextualizing it historically.

52 [*Carroll's note:*] Whereas psychoanalytic-feminism, given its avowal of the *general* laws of psychoanalysis, is tempted to say how woman must always appear as a result of deducing film theory from a deeper set of 'scientific' principles.

53 Carroll (1996), pp. 266–8, 269–71.

CHAPTER SIX

1 See Carroll (1988), pp. 232–4.

2 Torben Grodal, *Moving Pictures: A*

New Theory of Film Genres, Feelings, and Cognition (Oxford: Clarendon Press, 1997), p. 5.

3 Grodal (1997), pp. 5–6.

4 Grodal (1997), p. 13.

5 Grodal (1997), p. 13.

6 See Jean Matter Mandler, *Stories, Scripts and Scenes: Aspects of Schema Theory* (Hillsdale, NJ: Lawrence Erlbaum Associates, 1984).

7 See Roger C. Schank, *Tell Me a Story: A New Look at Real and Artificial Memory* (New York: Scribner, 1990); Schank and Robert P. Abelson, *Scripts, Plans, Goals and Understanding: An Inquiry into Human Knowledge Structures* (Hillside, NJ: Lawrence Erlbaum Associates, 1977).

8 Grodal (1997), p. 14.

9 Grodal (1997), p. 14.

10 Grodal (1997), p. 278.

11 Grodal (1997), p. 278.

12 Grodal (1997), pp. 278–9.

13 See Lee Hill, *Easy Rider*, BFI Modern [Film] Classics series (London: BFI Publishing, 1996), p. 54.

14 Grodal (1997), p. 279.

15 Grodal (1997), p. 280.

16 Grodal (1997), p. 131.

17 Grodal (1997), p. 280.

18 Grodal (1997), p. 281.

19 Grodal (1997), p. 281.

20 Grodal (1997), pp. 281–2.

21 [*Editor's note:*] See Deutelbaum and Poague (1986), pp. 7–15; and p. 247, note 48 above.

22 [*Grodal's note:*] Robert Stam and Roberta Pearson, in 'Hitchcock's *Rear Window*: Reflexivity and the Critique of Voyeurism', reprinted in Deutelbaum and Poague (1986), pp. 193–206, see the voyeurism in *Rear Window* as connected with film viewing in general, as well as with the McCarthy era and with male behaviour.

23 See Grodal (1997), p. 2.

24 Grodal (1997), pp. 239–45.

25 Françoise Pfaff, 'Hollywood's diehard jungle melodramas', in *L'Afrique et le centenaire du cinéma*, Fédération

Pan-africaine des Cinéastes (FEPACI) (Paris: Présence Africaine, 1995), pp. 194–9.

26 Michel Amarger, 'Les cinéastes africains et la presse se mettent à table', *Écrans d'Afrique*, 12 (1995), p. 39.

27 Charles Tesson, 'Genèse', *Cahiers du Cinéma*, 397 (June 1987). [*Editor's note:*] This and the following references, up to and including endnote 40, are Bartlet's, and he does not always give page nos.

28 'Entretien de Carlos Pardo avec Idrissa Ouedraogo', *Libération* (8–9 April 1995), p. 35.

29 Olivier de Bruyn, 'Hyène de vie', in *Les Inrockuptibles*, 4 (5–11 April 1995).

30 P.M., *Le Monde*, 6 April 1995.

31 C. Helffer, *Le Monde de l'Éducation* (May 1995).

32 Mohamed Camara, press conference, Fespaco, Ouagadougou, 1995.

33 Interview with David Achkar, Paris 1997, published in *Africultures*, 5 ('Jeunes créateurs africains') (Paris: L'Harmattan, 1998).

34 Souleymane Cissé, quoted in Ignacio Ramonet, '*Yeelen* ou la magie des contes', *Le Monde diplomatique* (December 1987).

35 Bernard Genin, 'Le voyage du fils', *Télérama*, no. 1977 (2 December 1987), p. 31.

36 From an interview with Souleymane Cissé by Philippe Elhem and Claude Waldmann, *Cinergie* (1987).

37 'Entretien de Marc Lalanne et Frédéric Strauss avec Souleymane Cissé', *Cahiers du Cinéma*, 492 (June 1995), p. 5.

38 Nixon K. Kariithi, 'Misreading Culture and Tradition: Western Critical Appreciation of African Films', in *L'Afrique et le centenaire du cinéma*, pp. 166–87.

39 Sheila Petty, 'Whose nation is it anyhow? The Politics of Reading African Cinema in the West', in *L'Afrique et le centenaire du cinéma*, pp. 188–93.

40 Stéphane Malandrin, 'Les cinémas africains en résistance', *Cahiers du Cinéma*, 492 (June 1995), p. 61.

41 Oliver Bartlet, *African Cinemas: Decolonizing the Gaze*, trans. Chris Turner (London and New York: Zed Books, 2000), pp. 210–13.

42 [*Currie's note:*] See David Bordwell and Noël Carroll, eds, *Post-Theory: Reconstructing Film Studies* (Madison: University of Wisconsin Press, 1996).

43 [*Currie's note:*] Exemplary of this approach is George Wilson's *Narration in Light* (Baltimore: Johns Hopkins University Press, 1986).

44 [*Currie's note:*] David Bordwell, *Making Meaning: Inference and Rhetoric in the Interpretation of Cinema* (Cambridge, MA: Harvard University Press, 1989), p. 261. Not that I agree with Bordwell's own theoretical recommendations; see Berys Gaut, 'Making Sense of Films: Neoformalism and its Limits', *Forum for Modern Language Studies*, 31 (1995), pp. 8–23, for criticism.

45 [*Currie's note:*] For the idea that the aim of criticism is to make the best of the work of art, see Ronald Dworkin, *Law's Empire* (London: Fontana, 1986).

46 [*Currie's note:*] See my 'Interpretation and Objectivity', *Mind*, 102 (1993), pp. 413–28.

47 [*Currie's note:*] What is to count as an intuitive judgement is ineluctably vague. But vague notions are not thereby incoherent notions. Indeed, since almost all our notions are vague, vagueness could not be a sign of incoherence. Vagueness is not even a drawback; for many purposes vague notions are more usable than precise ones, the boundaries of which one has constantly to track.

48 Gregory Currie, 'The Film Theory That Never Was: A Nervous Manifesto', in Richard Allen and Murray Smith, eds, *Film Theory and Philosophy* (Oxford: Clarendon Press, 1997), pp. 42–6.

49 See, for example, Jill Forbes, 'Film Theory and the New Historicism', in Christopher Flood and Nick Hewlett, eds, *Currents in Contemporary French Intellectual Life* (Basingstoke and London: Macmillan; New York: St Martin's Press, 2000). Discussing the Institut National de l'Audiovisuel (INA) in France, Forbes observes (p. 238): 'In making its archives accessible, INA has also introduced a sophisticated system of digital retrieval and cross referencing which, over time, will enable fulfilment of the creative potential of the material which it has in store, creating, thereby, the next theoretical frontier.'

SELECT BIBLIOGRAPHY

Early and Classical Film Theory

Abel, Richard, ed. *French Film Theory and Criticism: A History/Anthology. Volume I: 1907–1929.* Princeton, NJ: Princeton University Press, 1988.

Arnheim, Rudolf. *Film.* Trans. L. M. Sieveking and Ian F. D. Morrow. London: Faber and Faber, 1933. Adapted selections republished as *Film as Art.* London: Faber and Faber, 1958.

Balázs, Béla. *Theory of the Film (Character and Growth of a New Art).* Trans. Edith Bone. International Theatre and Cinema series. London: Dennis Dobson, 1952.

Bazin, André. *What is Cinema?* Selected and trans. Hugh Gray. 2 vols. Berkeley, Los Angeles and London: University of California Press, 1967 (vol. 1); 1971 (vol. 2).

Eisenstein, S(ergei) M(ikhailovich). *Film Form: Essays in Film Theory* and *The Film Sense.* Ed. and trans. Jay Leyda. Cleveland and New York: Meridian Books; The World Publishing Company, 1957.

—— *The Film Sense.* Ed. and trans. Jay Leyda. London and Boston: Faber and Faber, 1986.

—— *Selected Works: Volume I: Writings 1922–34.* Ed. and trans. Richard Taylor. London: BFI Publishing; Bloomington and Indianapolis: Indiana University Press, 1988.

—— *Selected Works: Volume II: Towards a Theory of Montage.* Eds Michael Glenny and Richard Taylor, trans. Michael Glenny. London: BFI Publishing, 1991.

Kracauer, Siegfried. *Theory of Film: The Redemption of Physical Reality.* With an introduction by Miriam Bratu Hansen. Princeton, NJ: Princeton University Press, 1997.

Münsterberg, Hugo. *The Film: A Psychological Study: The Silent Photoplay in 1916.* With a new foreword by Richard Griffith. New York: Dover Publications, 1970.

Semiotics, Psychoanalysis, Post-structuralism

Douchet, Jean. 'Hitch and His Public'. Trans. Verena Conley. Originally published as 'Hitch et son public' in *Cahiers du Cinéma*, 113 (1960). Reprinted in Deutelbaum and Poague (1986), pp. 7–15.

Heath, Stephen. *Questions of Cinema.* Communications and Culture series. London: Macmillan, 1981.

MacCabe, Colin. *Theoretical Essays: Film, Linguistics, Literature.* Manchester: Manchester University Press, 1985.

Metz, Christian. *Film Language: A Semiotics of the Cinema.* Trans. Michael Taylor. New York: Oxford University Press, 1974.

—— *Psychoanalysis and Cinema: The Imaginary Signifier.* Trans. Ben Brewster et al. London: Macmillan, 1982.

Gender

De Lauretis, Teresa. *Alice Doesn't: Feminism, Semiotics, Cinema.* London: Macmillan, 1984.

Doane, Mary Ann; Mellencamp, Patricia; Williams, Linda. *Re-Vision: Essays in Feminist Film Criticism.* Frederick, MD: American Film Institute, 1984.

Dyer, Richard. *Gays and Film.* London: BFI Publishing, 1987.

Keane, Marian E. 'A Closer Look at Scopophilia: Mulvey, Hitchcock and *Vertigo*'. In Deutelbaum and Poague (1986), pp. 231–48.

Lemire, Elise. 'Voyeurism and the Postwar Crisis of Masculinity in *Rear Window*'. In John Belton, ed., *Alfred Hitchcock's 'Rear Window'.* Cambridge University Press Film Handbooks series. Cambridge: Cambridge University Press, 2000, pp. 57–90.

Mulvey, Laura. *Visual and Other Pleasures.* Basingstoke and London: Macmillan, 1989.

Neale, Steve. 'Masculinity as Spectacle: Reflections on Men and Mainstream Cinema'. *Screen*, 24:6 (Nov–Dec 1983), pp. 2–16.

Stacey, Jackie. 'Desperately Seeking Difference: Jackie Stacey Considers Desire between Women in Narrative Cinema'. *Screen*, 28:1 (Winter 1987), pp. 48–61.

Cognitive and Analytical Film Theory

Allen, Richard and Smith, Murray, eds. *Film Theory and Philosophy.* Oxford: Clarendon Press, 1997.

Anderson, Joseph D. *The Reality of Illusion: An Ecological Approach to Cognitive Film Theory.* Carbondale and Edwardsville: Southern Illinois University Press, 1996.

Bordwell, David. *Making Meaning: Inference and Rhetoric in the Interpretation of Cinema.* Cambridge, MA: Harvard University Press, 1989.

Carroll, Noël. *Mystifying Movies: Fads and Fallacies in Contemporary Film Theory.* New York: Columbia University Press, 1988.

—— *Theorizing the Moving Image.* Cambridge Studies in Film series. Cambridge: Cambridge University Press, 1996.

Currie, Gregory. *Image and Mind: Film, Philosophy, and Cognitive Science.* New York: Cambridge University Press, 1995.

Grodal, Torben. *Moving Pictures: A New Theory of Film Genres, Feelings, and Cognition*. Oxford: Clarendon Press, 1997.

Scruton, Roger. *The Aesthetic Understanding: Essays in the Philosophy of Art and Culture*. Manchester: Carcanet Press, 1983.

African Cinema

Bakari, Ishaq Imruh and Cham, Mbye, eds. *African Experiences of Cinema*. London: BFI Publishing, 1996.

Bartlet, Oliver. *African Cinemas: Decolonizing the Gaze*. Trans. Chris Turner. London and New York: Zed Books, 2000.

Diawara, Manthia. *African Cinema: Politics and Culture*. Bloomington: Indiana University Press, 1992.

Ukadike, Nwachukwu Frank. *Black African Cinema*. Berkeley: University of California Press, 1994.

Anthologies

Bordwell, David and Carroll, Noël, eds. *Post-Theory: Reconstructing Film Studies*. Madison: University of Wisconsin Press, 1996.

Braudy, Leo and Cohen, Marshall, eds. *Film Theory and Criticism: Introductory Readings*. New York and Oxford: Oxford University Press, 1999.

Deutelbaum, Marshall and Poague, Leland, eds. *A Hitchcock Reader*. Ames, IA: Iowa State University Press, 1986.

Easthope, Antony, ed. *Contemporary Film Theory*. Longman Critical Readers series. London and New York: Longman, 1993.

Hillier, Jim, ed. *Cahiers du Cinéma: The 1950s: Neo-Realism, Hollywood, New Wave*. Cambridge, MA: Harvard University Press, 1985.

Kaplan, E. Ann. *Feminism and Film*. Oxford Readings in Feminism series. Oxford: Oxford University Press, 2000.

GLOSSARY OF CINEMATIC AND CRITICAL TERMS

Actant: A term in narrative theory which means the element in a story that performs a certain narrative function such as 'discovering the truth'. The concept of the actant is not the same as the concept of a character. It may be the case that a function such as 'discovering the truth' is fulfilled by a fictional human character, but the function may also be wholly or partly performed by a non-human creature or an inanimate object. In a detective story, for example, the actant that performs the function of 'discovering the truth' might well be embodied, for the most part, in the central character, the detective; but the detective may be assisted by other characters, by non-human creatures and by inanimate objects ('clues'), and these thus also function as actants that perform the truth-discovery function.

Behaviourism: A form of psychology that analyses human behaviour in terms of stimulus-response mechanisms and that discounts the importance, or even existence, of consciousness and will. It has proved a highly provocative approach, and can easily be caricatured as an attempt to see all human life in terms of the dog that salivates every time a bell rings because it has been conditioned to associate the ringing of a bell with the arrival of food. Behaviourism, however, is capable of rather more sophisticated formulations than this, and remains of interest to film theorists trying to understand the relationships between films and their spectators.

Blocking: The preparatory working out of the *mise-en-scène*, the visual composition of the scenes of a film. It involves planning and rehearsing the positions and movements of the actors, costume, sets, scenery, lighting and the position and set-up of cameras and other equipment.

Cognitive film theory: A sub-division or spin-off from cognitive science that explores the similarities and differences between the processing of information that takes place in viewing a film and the processing of information that occurs in the non-cinematic environment. A film can be regarded as a simulation of a (possible) real-life situation that engages the viewer's intellect, emotions and body, and that involves a complex negotiation between fiction and reality. Key cognitive film theorists include Joseph D. Anderson, David Bordwell, Edward Branigan and Noël Carroll in the USA; Murray Smith in the UK; Gregory Currie in

Australia; the Dutch film theorist Ed Tan; and the Danish film theorist Torben Grodal (an extract from Grodal's *Moving Pictures: A New Theory of Film Genres, Feelings, and Cognition* (1997) is included in chapter six of this Critical History). It is significant, and disturbing, that all of these theorists are male. Although there is no *a priori* reason why women should not become leading exponents of cognitive film theory, it is notable that such theory can, in some instances, take on a crass, stereotypically male, what-nonsense-you're-talking tone – see, for example, the extract from Noël Carroll's attack on Laura Mulvey in chapter five of this Critical History. While cognitive film theory is generally seen as opposed to psychoanalysis and to semiotics, a number of European film theorists have attempted to create an approach that combines cognitive film theory and semiotics in a 'cognitive semiotics' of film. These include Francesco Casetti, Christian Metz in his *The Impersonal Enunciation* (1995), Roger Odin, Michel Colin and Dominique Château. See Warren Buckland, *The Cognitive Semiotics of Film* (Cambridge University Press, 2000).

Cognitive science: A discipline that is concerned to explore and identify the ways in which the human mind comes to know – to cognise – the world through the senses, the mind and the emotions. It draws on biology, psychology and computer science in order to generate models of how human animals process information in order to survive and adapt in the environments in which they live. In contrast to psychoanalysis and post-structuralism, cognitive science tends to be holistic, to see the senses, the mind and the emotions as forming a psychosomatic whole rather than as riven by conflict and in thrall to desire and illusion. It also tends to be ecological, to explore the interaction between human beings, other living organisms, and their environment.

Deconstruction (sometimes called 'deconstructionism' or 'deconstructivism'): An approach to philosophical and cultural analysis primarily associated with the French thinker Jacques Derrida (born 1930). Deconstruction has three main targets: the idea of a fixed, single meaning, the idea of essence (for example, the view that there is an essential human nature), and the idea of presence (for instance, the idea that Shakespeare speaks to us in his sonnets). The characteristic deconstructive procedure is to examine a text very carefully in order to bring out the ways in which its ostensible or intended meaning is subverted by other meanings that can be discerned in that text, meanings that are often unnoticed, ignored, or relegated to subsidiary or marginal status. It aims to demonstrate that even the most apparently literal text is inevitably invaded by metaphors that destabilise it and lead it into contradiction. The same subversive processes undermine any appeal to essences and presences. A deconstructive approach to film would thus reject *auteur* theory – the idea that the presence of an author-director can be discerned through the marks of his style in a film – and reality theory – the view, associated with Bazin and Kracauer, that sees film first of all in terms of its relation to reality. Deconstruction would aim to show how any film calls into question its ostensible meanings, its reality-status and its essentialist propositions, and would attend to elements of the film that had hitherto been little discussed or explicitly set aside as unimportant.

Discourse: The kind of language employed in particular areas of cultural and social activity – for example, in medicine, law, and sexuality. Each discourse has its specialised vocabulary, structure and body of imagery. In the highly influential perspective of Michel Foucault (1926–84), discourses are never simply reflections of reality; rather, they serve to construct the reality that they purport to analyse, and to produce a knowledge of that 'reality' that furthers the interests of power and surveillance. For example, discourses of sexuality serve to produce particular categories of behaviour such as homosexuality, and to control sexuality (which does not necessarily mean repressing it). Foucault's ideas have been highly influential in the fields of feminism and of gay, gender and postcolonial studies, all areas in which discourses – about women, about homosexuality, about the 'native' and the 'Orient' – can be analysed in terms of the way in which they construct purported realities and serve the interests of power.

Embedded series, embedding series: Terms used by Torben Grodal in his *Moving Pictures*. An embedding series is a dominant narrative sequence within which another narrative sequence – an embedded series – is implied and made at least partly explicit. For example, in a detective thriller that centred around solving a murder, the embedding series would be the narrative sequence of the detective's quest to solve the murder, while the embedded series would be what the detective was trying to reconstruct and make explicit – the sequence of events that led up to the murder and the murderer's subsequent attempts to escape detection. Not all of the implicit details of an embedded series will necessarily be made explicit, however. There is a famous anecdote that Howard Hawks, while directing the film adaptation (1946) of Raymond Chandler's Philip

Marlowe novel *The Big Sleep* (1939), 'once cabled Chandler during the shoot to ask who was supposed to have killed General Sternwood's chauffeur during the original story. Chandler sent back a wire saying "NO IDEA".' (Tom Hiney, *Raymond Chandler: A Biography* (London: Vintage, 1998), p. 163) The murder of Sternwood's chauffeur was an event in the embedded series of *The Big Sleep*, but even the author of the original novel could not make it explicit.

Enaction, enactive: Terms employed by Torben Grodal in his *Moving Pictures* to indicate a physical and mental preparation for an active response to perceptual, associative and emotional stimuli. The viewer of a film does not usually translate this preparation into action, though this may happen sometimes – as with the audiences who rioted in response to the excitations provided by *The Blackboard Jungle* (1955), which used the song 'Rock Around the Clock' on its soundtrack, and the film *Rock Around the Clock* (1956) itself. Even so, the viewer cannot actually enter and act in the world represented on the screen. Nonetheless, as Grodal says, 'cognitive and "subliminal" motor stimulations of motor schemata exist as underlying, but suppressed and projected, patterns in the viewing situation … In moments of peak tension during an action-suspense fiction, this muscular pattern will surface as a barely suppressed muscular tension in the viewer aiming at release in physical action.' (Grodal (1997), p. 48)

Epistemology: The branch of philosophy concerned with the grounds and nature of knowledge and with the methods of arriving at knowledge. It addresses such questions as: What does it mean to say that we know something? What is the difference between knowledge and belief? Are there different kinds of knowledge – for example, the knowledge that we acquire through experience and the knowledge that we acquire through a supposedly scientific statement ('The earth goes round the sun')? In relation to film theory, epistemology can be applied in two main ways. It can be used to evaluate the claims to knowledge made by film theories themselves, so that, for example, a theory of film that draws heavily on psychoanalysis may be challenged (as it is, in this Critical History, by Noël Carroll) by questioning the status of psychoanalysis as a form of knowledge and pointing to its speculative, untestable nature. Epistemology can also be used to consider the kinds of knowledge that the viewer acquires from film – is it primarily knowledge of reality, for example, as Bazin and Kracauer might suggest, or knowledge of signifying practices, as a formalist or post-structuralist approach might emphasise? In what ways does the knowledge that the viewer might feel s/he is acquiring from a film relate to her knowledge that the film is an illusion? This is a fascinating field that merits further exploration.

Film noir: Literally meaning 'black film', the term was coined by French critics to refer to 1940s Hollywood films, most often thrillers, that took a dark view of human existence and were filmed in black-and-white in a way that made much use of shadow and contrast and the visual symbolism that these could provide – for example, the shadow of a Venetian blind falling across a face could be seen to resemble prison bars and to symbolise guilt and impending imprisonment. Such films often featured a male private detective who became involved, professionally and personally, with a *femme fatale*, a lethal, seductive woman who, if not resisted, would lead the lone male astray. Classic examples include the second version of *The Maltese Falcon* (1941), in which private eye Sam Spade (Humphrey Bogart) only just manages to resist the manipulative female crook Brigid O'Shaughnessy (Mary Astor) and send her to prison (though it should be noted that, in the first version of the film (1931; aka *Dangerous Female*), Bebe Daniels provides a more seductive, more proto-*noir* Brigid than Mary Astor); *Farewell My Lovely* (1944; aka *Murder My Sweet*), in which Philip Marlowe (Dick Powell) is, in his own words in the film, 'sapped twice, choked, beaten silly with a gun, shot in the arm [injected with a drug] until [he's] crazy as a couple of waltzing mice' (as quoted in *Halliwell's Film and Video Guide* 2001, p. 269) and nearly killed as he hunts for an elusive beauty; and *Double Indemnity* (1944), in which the seductive Phyllis Dietrichson (Barbara Stanwyck) entices insurance salesman Walter Neff (Fred MacMurray) into a plot to murder her husband and collect the insurance money. The latter part of the twentieth century saw attempts to remake *noir* films in colour (for instance, *Farewell My Lovely* (1975), directed by Dick Richards and with a rather elderly Robert Mitchum as Marlowe) and to update and revise them (for example, *Body Heat* (1981), written and directed by Lawrence Kasdan, which echoes some aspects of *Double Indemnity* but which lets the *femme fatale*, who must be punished in the classic *noir* film, get away with it). *Film noir*, as a generic category and in its specific examples, continues to fascinate viewers, critics and theorists and remains a key point of reference, debate and analysis in film theory, whether of a formalist, realist, *auteur*ist, semiotic, post-structuralist, psychoanalytic, feminist or cognitive kind.

Functionalism: The view that cultural practices are to be understood in terms of the functions that they serve in maintaining the existence of a society or a group within a society. In this perspective, even apparently non-functional practices – artistic or cinematic practices, for example – are seen as performing social functions, even if the way in which they do so is not obvious. Hollywood film can be seen, for example, as functioning to maintain the existence of the USA by reinforcing its dominant ideology (even when it may appear to challenge that ideology). When Eisenstein proposes an '*intellectual* cinema of unprecedented form and social functionalism' (see chapter one, p. 52, of this Critical History), he wants films that will function to contribute to the revolutionary transformation of society in a socialist direction. The coupling of 'form' with 'function' alludes to a highly influential idea in twentieth-century architecture, summed up in Louis Sullivan's maxim that 'form follows function' – that the functions that a building is to serve should determine its architectural design. A controversial idea within architecture itself, it is interesting to consider how it might be applied to film.

Gaze: A way of looking at other people that turns them into objects of sensuous and possibly sadistic contemplation. The term has been especially influential in the kind of feminist film criticism that derives from Laura Mulvey. In this perspective, woman, in a patriarchal order, is the object of the male gaze, and mainstream narrative film reinforces this order by displaying women as objects for that gaze. The idea of the gaze is closely connected with the idea of covert erotic observation – voyeurism – and with what Freud called *Schaulust* (usually translated as 'scopophilia'), the pleasure in looking that is a displaced form of the desire to look fully and frankly at the genitals.

Gestalt: A branch of psychological theory that argues that the human mind and senses work by perceiving patterned wholes rather than by assembling items of data. Gestalt psychology is interested, for example, in what it calls the 'Aha!' experience – the moment at which what has hitherto seemed a random assembly of data is perceived and understood as a patterned whole (as when, in watching a detective film, the viewer suddenly grasps the whole solution of the mystery). Gestalt psychology was influential in early film theory – in the work of Hugo Münsterberg and Rudolf Arnheim, for instance, which drew analogies between the patterning operations of the mind and the patterning techniques of cinema – but it proved difficult to reconcile with psychoanalysis, post-structuralism and deconstruction, all of which rejected the notion of the 'whole'. Recently, however, it has enjoyed some revival in cognitive film theory, for example in the work of Torben Grodal.

Hermeneutics: Derived from the ancient Greek word *hermeneus* (an interpreter), hermeneutics means the theory and practice of interpretation – of grasping and explicating the meaning of a text, a cultural practice, or indeed any phenomenon. When a critic provides an interpretation of a film, s/he is engaging in hermeneutics, even if s/he does not consciously use any specific hermeneutic theory. Originally the term was concerned with the correct interpretation of the Bible, and worked on the assumption that a correct interpretation was possible. Much literary and film criticism has worked on the same assumption and has sought to arrive at the correct interpretation of a poem or movie. Deconstruction and post-structuralism, however, challenge this assumption, arguing that meaning is always contradictory, self-subverting and shifting, and that therefore correct interpretation can never be arrived at; the interpreter can offer only a provisional and transient construction of the meaning of a text. Modern hermeneutics is divided between the view that correct interpretation remains more or less possible and the view that it is never possible. Any film theory, or indeed any film criticism, incorporates an implicit or explicit hermeneutics – a view of whether correct interpretation is possible and of how interpretation is conducted.

Imaginary/symbolic order: Concepts coined by the French psychoanalyst Jacques Lacan (1901–81) that have become very influential in semiotics, post-structuralism and certain kinds of feminism. The imaginary order is the pre-symbolic period in which the infant makes no distinction between itself and the body of the mother. The infant must renounce this imaginary unity in order to enter the symbolic order, the realm of language and culture in which the child takes up its position as a subject, an 'I'.

Law of the Father: In Jacques Lacan's revision of Freudian psychoanalysis, the Law of the Father severs the erotic unity of child and mother, forbids the child's desire for the mother, raises the spectre of castration, and enables the child to enter the symbolic order of language, culture and sexual difference – an order that entails a loss of primal ecstasy and the reinforcement of patriarchy. There is a debate within psychoanalysis and feminism as to whether the Law of the Father is to be understood as an inevitable and universal psychic mechanism or as a patri-archal construct. It is a term likely to occur in feminist-psychoanalytic film theory as a way of understanding the experience of the film viewer.

Metalanguage: A language in which we talk about language itself, or about the language of a particular field of intellectual inquiry – for example, a metalanguage of film theory would discuss the terms, struc-tures, imagery and other relevant features of the language in which theoretical propositions about film are presented.

Mise-en-scène: This literally means 'putting in the scene', and is a term that can be used of both film and theatre. It refers to all of the elements that contribute to the visual composition of a particular scene on the stage or shot in a film – the position of actors, their actions, their cos-tume, the set, the scenery. *Mise-en-scène* can be analysed as an aspect of the style of a particular *auteur*-director, as an element of montage or cut-ting, or as a component of film that is in tension with montage because it invites the director and viewer to linger on particular shots and scenes rather than to cut to other shots and scenes. Eisenstein proposed the term and concept *mise-en-cadre*, 'putting in the frame', as 'a leap from the *mise-en-scène*', 'a second-stage *mise-en-scène*, when the *mise-en-scène* of changing camera positions is superimposed upon the broken lines of the *mise-en-scène*'s displacement in space'. (Eisenstein (1991), p. 15) But this term does not seem to have caught on.

Pacing: The creation of a sense of tempo and rhythm in a film – so that it seems, for example, fast or slow, abrupt or fluid – by the frequency and manner of cutting. For instance, a long take, in which the camera dwells on a particular scene for some time, is likely to create a slower tempo than a succession of short takes that move from one scene to another. A jump cut, in which a middle section of a scene is eliminated by cutting the film or stopping the camera, produces an abrupt, jerky rhythm.

Perceptual salience: A term used by Torben Grodal in his *Moving Pictures*. It means the way in which certain elements of a film will become salient – that is, will stand out more than others – and will make a power-ful impact upon the perceiver. For Grodal, salience is 'the ability of a given fiction to evoke strong experiences and to attract close attention'. (Grodal (1997), p. 34)

Phenomenology: The philosophical exploration of the modes in which human beings apprehend phenomena, the things of this world. Originated in the earlier twentieth century by the German philosopher Edmund Husserl (1859–1938), it had a considerable influence on mid-twentieth-century European and North American thought, for example in the writings of Jean-Paul Sartre (1905–84) and Maurice Merleau-Ponty (1908–61), and in the literary criticism of Georges Poulet (1902–91) and J. Hillis Miller (born 1928) in his pre-deconstructive phase. In literary and film theory and criticism, a phenomenological approach can be author or *auteur*-centred, aiming to infer, from the totality of a writer or director's work, the primary ways in which he apprehends the phenomena of the world; or it can be reception-centred, concentrating on the ways in which readers or viewers apprehend literary works or films. Both André Bazin and Siegfried Kracauer can be seen as phenomenological to some extent in their approach, trying to account for the peculiar sense of presence that film can give the spectator. Phenomenology was displaced for a time by structuralism, post-structuralism and deconstruction; these three approaches tended to ignore the phenomenological dimension or regarded it as an illusion. But phenomenology remains of considerable interest, and has some links with cognitive film theory, although its vocabulary tends to be less (quasi-)scientific and more philosophical, experiential and existential.

Post-structuralism: This approach takes up the structuralist idea that cultural practices are to be seen in terms of structures and systems rather than in terms of human agency; but it rejects the structuralist quest to identify enduring, universal structures. Developing Saussure's notion that the relationship between signifier and signified is arbitrary, it sees meaning as unstable, constant only in that it is always mobile, subverting any attempt to identify a fixed, underlying system. In a post-structuralist perspective, the belief in fixed meaning is due partly to the desire to maintain the imaginary unity of self that the infant first achieves in the 'mirror stage' described by Lacan, and partly to the wish to ratify existing distributions of power by repressing the possibility of change. Post-structuralism often has a strong political edge, pointing out that what is held to be self-evident common sense is a fragile and questionable ideological production that serves to preserve existing power arrangements. A post-structuralist analysis of a cultural text, such as a film, would examine the ways in which its attempts to present particular meanings were undermined by moments of ambiguity. In many respects, post-structuralism is close to deconstruction.

Saturation: A term used by Torben Grodal in his *Moving Pictures* to indicate a state in which the input/output processing by the viewer of a visual fiction is blocked so that the translation of responses into potential action – into 'a motor attitude' – is suspended. The viewer is thus left saturated, or flooded, by sensations, emotions and images without being able to imagine how s/he might discharge them. Consider a film in which a character loved by the film's protagonist dies: there can be no remedy for this, and the viewer, through an empathic identification with the protagonist, is flooded with sensations, emotions and memories that cannot be translated, even in imagination, into action. It may be possible, however, to mitigate the saturation by some action such as taking revenge, in which case saturation would be succeeded by a mood of tensity, which is a state of arousal that aims at the eventual achievement of a goal that will reduce the arousal – as when, in *The Big Heat* (1953), the detective, Bannion, seeks those responsible for his wife's murder.

Semiotics: The 'science', or at least study, of signs, originally proposed by the linguist Ferdinand de Saussure (1857–1913). Semiotics analyses the way in which signs, understood in Saussure's term as combinations of signifiers and signifieds, construct meanings in particular cultural and historical situations. A seminal semiotic text is Roland Barthes's *Mythologies* (1957), which analyses a range of signs – on magazine covers and in advertising, for example – and examines the way in which they purvey myths in which socially constructed meanings are turned into supposedly 'natural' ones. For instance, a photograph, on the cover of *Paris-Match*, of a young black soldier saluting the French flag, conveys the notion that France's colonial subjects are 'naturally' loyal to the imperial power. Semiotics has been influential in a range of fields, such as feminism, cultural studies, literary studies, and film studies. In film studies, it has been used to analyse the way in which meaning is constructed through *mise-en-scène*, montage and narrative structure.

Signifier/signified: A definition and distinction developed by Ferdinand de Saussure that has been crucial to the development of semiotics and post-structuralism. In Saussure's view, the sign consists of a signifier – a sound or visual mark – and a signified – the mental concept with which a specific signifier has become associated in a particular language. The relationship between signifier and signified is arbitrary – that is, there is no necessary connection between a particular sound/visual mark and a particular mental concept, so that the same sound or visual mark can have different meanings in different languages, or even within the same language. The signified, the mental concept, should not be confused with the particular object to which a sign may refer; such an object is known as a referent.

Structuralism: An approach to the analysis of culture that aims to identify the underlying structures that shape and inform cultural practices. Its primary model is that of language: all cultural practices, like language, have a grammar, a syntax and a vocabulary that determine how meaning is produced. Structuralism is especially concerned with binary oppositions – good/bad, black/white, man/woman – and with their permutations through homologies – ways in which one structure parallels another – and variations. Structuralism tends towards the synchronic and the universal – towards seeing underlying structures as persisting beneath the apparent differences brought about by time and change, or by cultural variation – and it challenges the importance of human agency. 'Human beings' are seen more as products of structures than as producers of structures. Structuralism is thus sceptical of the idea of the author – or the *auteur* – as the origin and guiding presence of cultural texts. In a structuralist perspective, films are not primarily seen as the products of an *auteur*-director; the aim is to identify the implicit structures that give them meaning, structures that do not depend upon the particular interests of a director. Structuralism has come under attack from both post-structuralism and deconstruction, which claim that its idea of underlying structures is too fixed and rigid and fails to acknowledge the instability of the sign.

Tensity: A term used by Torben Grodal in his *Moving Pictures* to refer to the mood of the viewer of a visual fiction who desires the achievement of a particular goal in order to reduce his arousal. The viewer of a detective thriller, for example, will be aroused by the desire to solve the mystery and want the detective, eventually, to achieve the goal of finding the solution. Tensity can be contrasted with the mood of saturation, in which a particular goal – for example, the restoration of a dead person to life – seems impossible to achieve.

ACKNOWLEDGEMENTS

The editor and publisher wish to thank the following for their permission to reprint copyright material:

Richard Abel, ed., *French Film Theory and Criticism: A History/Anthology. Volume I: 1907–1929*. Copyright © 1988 by Princeton University Press. Reprinted by permission of Princeton University Press.

Béla Balázs, *Theory of the Film (Character and Growth of a New Art)*. Reprinted by permission of Dover Publications.

Sergei Eisenstein, *Selected Works: Volume I: Writings, 1922–34; Selected Works: Volume II: Towards a Theory of Montage*. Reprinted by permission of BFI Publishing.

André Bazin, *What is Cinema?* Reprinted by permission of University of California Press.

Siegfried Kracauer, *Theory of Film: The Redemption of Physical Reality*. Copyright © 1960 by Oxford University Press, Inc. Reprinted by permission of Oxford University Press, Inc.

Jim Hillier, ed., *Cahiers du Cinéma: The 1950s: Neo-Realism, Hollywood, New Wave*. Translation copyright © British Film Institute. Reprinted by permission of BFI Publishing.

Nicolas Tredell, *Conversations with Critics*. Reprinted by permission of Carcanet.

Colin MacCabe, *Theoretical Essays: Film, Linguistics, Literature*. Reprinted by permission of BFI Publishing.

Stephen Heath, *Questions of Cinema*. Reprinted by permission of Palgrave and Indiana University Press.

Laura Mulvey, *Visual and Other Pleasures*. Reprinted by permission of Palgrave.

Marian E. Keane, 'A Closer Look at Scopophilia: Mulvey, Hitchcock and *Vertigo*'. Reprinted by permission of Oxford University Press.

Steve Neale, 'Masculinity as Spectacle: Reflections on Men and Mainstream Cinema'. Reprinted by permission of the John Logie Baird Centre.

Jackie Stacey, 'Desperately Seeking Difference'. Reprinted by permission of the John Logie Baird Centre.

Noël Carroll, *Theorizing the Moving Image*. Reprinted by permission of Cambridge University Press and Noël Carroll.

Torben Grodal, *Moving Pictures: A New Theory of Film Genres, Feelings, and Cognition*. Copyright © 1997 by Torben Grodal. Reprinted by permission of Oxford University Press.

The editor's most heartfelt thanks go to his wife, Angela, with whom he has watched, enjoyed and discussed films for over twenty-five years. He is also very grateful to his good friend Hugh Humphreys, whose deep understanding and knowledge of film (and of much else) has made a crucial contribution to this Critical History. A rich source of further insight has been all the students, inside and outside the walls of Sussex University, who have allowed the editor to share their collective explorations of cinema. Duncan Heath's many suggestions made this a much better book.

Nicolas Tredell teaches film, theatre and cultural studies at Sussex University, and contributes to a wide range of British and American journals, such as the *London Review of Books*, the *Times Literary Supplement*, *PN Review*, *Victorian Poetry* and the *Review of Contemporary Fiction*. His many books include *The Critical Decade*, *Conversations with Critics* and *Fighting Fictions: The Novels of B. S. Johnson*. He is currently completing *Notes towards a Definition of Digital Culture* and a study of literary representations of cinema, *Panoramic Sleights*.

In case of difflculty in obtaining any Icon title through normal channels, books can be purchased through BOOKPOST.

Tel: +44 1624 836000
Fax: +44 1624 837033
E-mail: bookshop@enterprise.net
www.bookpost.co.uk

Please quote 'Ref: Faber' when placing your order.

If you require further assistance, please contact:
info@iconbooks.co.uk